S0-ADP-185

THE MEDIA IN THE 1984 AND 1988 PRESIDENTIAL CAMPAIGNS

Recent Titles in
Contributions to the Study of Mass Media and Communications

The News as Myth: Fact and Context in Journalism
Tom Koch

Cold War Rhetoric: Strategy, Metaphor, and Ideology
Martin J. Medhurst, Robert L. Ivie, Philip Wander, and Robert L. Scott

Foreign Policy and the Press: An Analysis of *The New York Times'* Coverage of U.S. Foreign Policy
Nicholas O. Berry

Sob Sister Journalism
Phyllis Leslie Abramson

The Course of Tolerance: Freedom of the Press in Nineteenth-Century America
Donna Lee Dickerson

The American Trojan Horse: U.S. Television Confronts Canadian Economic and Cultural Nationalism
Barry Berlin

Science as Symbol: Media Images in a Technological Age
Lee Wilkins and Philip Patterson, editors

The Rhetoric of Terrorism and Counterterrorism
Richard W. Leeman

Media Messages in American Presidential Elections
Diana Owen

The Joint Press Conference: The History, Impact, and Prospects of American Presidential Debates
David J. Lanoue and Peter R. Schrott

THE MEDIA IN THE 1984 AND 1988 PRESIDENTIAL CAMPAIGNS

Edited by
Guido H. Stempel III
and
John W. Windhauser

Contributions to the Study of
Mass Media and Communications, Number 21
Bernard K. Johnpoll, Series Editor

GREENWOOD PRESS
New York • Westport, Connecticut • London

Library of Congress Cataloging-in-Publication Data

The Media in the 1984 and 1988 presidential campaigns / edited by Guido H. Stempel III and John W. Windhauser.
p. cm.—(Contributions to the study of mass media and communications, ISSN 0732-4456 ; no. 21)
Includes bibliographical references.
ISBN 0-313-26527-5 (lib. bdg. : alk. paper)
1. Presidents—United States—Election—1984. 2. Presidents—United States—Election—1988. 3. United States—Politics and government—1981-1989. 4. Mass media—Political aspects—United States. I. Stempel, Guido Hermann. II. Windhauser, John W. (John William). III. Series.
E879.M43 1991
324.973'0927—dc20 90-2920

British Library Cataloguing in Publication Data is available.

Library of Congress Catalog Card Number: 90-2920
ISBN: 0-313-26527-5
ISSN: 0732-4456

First published in 1991

Greenwood Press, 88 Post Road West, Westport, CT 06881
An imprint of Greenwood Publishing Group, Inc.

Printed in the United States of America

The paper used in this book complies with the Permanent Paper Standard issued by the National Information Standards Organization (Z39.48-1984).

10 9 8 7 6 5 4 3 2 1

Contents

Tables

THE MEDIA IN THE 1984 AND 1988 PRESIDENTIAL CAMPAIGNS

1

Media Coverage of Presidential Campaigns as a Political Issue

Guido H. Stempel III

Criticism of the press for its political coverage is as old as the U.S. republic. Thomas Jefferson, in 1798 at the height of the conflict between the Federalists and the Republicans, wrote: "Were I to undertake to answer the calumnies of the newspapers, it would be more than all my own time and that of twenty aides could effect. For while I should be answering one, twenty new ones would be invented."[1]

Five years later, during his presidency, he wrote that "the abuses of freedom of the press have been carried to a length never before known or borne by any civilized nation."[2] That same year he wrote:

> The Federalists having failed in destroying the freedom of the press by their gag law, seem to have attacked it in the opposite form, that is by pushing its licentiousness and its lying to such a degree of prostitution as to deprive it of all credit. And the fact is that so abandoned are the tory presses in this particular that even the least informed of people have learnt that nothing in a newspaper is to be believed.[3]

In 1814, five years after he had left the White House, Jefferson had not changed his mind on the matter, as this comment shows: "I deplore with you, the putrid state into which our newspapers have passed, and the malignity, the vulgarity, and the mendacious spirit of those who write for them. As vehicles of information, and a curb on our functionaries, they have rendered themselves useless, by forfeiting all title to belief."[4]

Those who complain about the media today are less eloquent, but the basic complaint is still the same – the media are biased against us and for those on the other side. In recent years, much of the criticism has focused on the coverage of presidential election campaigns.

President Harry S. Truman started this tendency to be critical of the coverage. He was not the first president in this century to criticize the press, but he was the one who made coverage of presidential campaigns an issue. It happened in 1948 when Truman faced what appeared to be certain defeat at the hands of Thomas E. Dewey, the Republican nominee. Virtually every poll showed Dewey winning and winning handily. The widespread certainty that Dewey would win was reflected in a cutline that *Life* magazine ran under a picture of Dewey the week before the election. The cutline referred to him flatly as "the next president," as if it were already decided.

Truman did not concede the election. He set out in October on a coast-to-coast whistlestopping campaign. It featured two issues –what Truman called the "do-nothing 80th (Republican) Congress" and what he termed "the one-party press." When Election Day came, Truman won a clear-cut victory. The two issues had worked, and the lesson was not lost on other politicians. You could win votes by attacking the press.

Truman's one-party press charge began with a known fact – most newspapers in 1948 endorsed the Republican nominee for president, as they had done in many previous elections and have done in every election since, except in 1964. The exact record of the extent of this began in 1936 when *Editor & Publisher,* a trade magazine of the newspaper industry, began polling newspapers about endorsements. In that year, *Editor & Publisher* reported that 57 percent of the newspapers were supporting the Republican nominee, Alfred E. Landon, against the incumbent Democrat, Franklin D. Roosevelt. But Roosevelt won in a landslide.

By 1948 the margin had increased. Sixty-five percent of the newspapers responding to the *Editor & Publisher* poll endorsed Dewey, 15 percent endorsed Truman, 5 percent endorsed other candidates, and 5 percent did not endorse anyone. Thus more than four times as many newspapers endorsed Dewey as endorsed Truman. That Dewey was the editorial-page choice was fairly evident to the general public, but Truman's charge went beyond this. What Truman implied was that because most newspapers supported Dewey on the editorial page they also favored him in their news coverage.

That's a reasonable suggestion. How could reporters help but be influenced by their paper's editorial choice? Those in the newspaper business would point out that the editorial-page operation is clearly separated from the news operation on most papers. They would also point out that a reporter would consider it unprofessional to be swayed by the endorsement. But these points are not clearly understood by the general public, and it is evident that Truman's argument was effective.

Since Truman won, the argument became somewhat moot. If the press had been pro-Dewey on the front page as well as the editorial page, it certainly did not affect the outcome of the election. The matter rested there.

The issue, however, was revived in 1952. Once again, the charge came from the Democratic nominee, this time Adlai Stevenson. Once again the Republican nominee, Dwight Eisenhower, had the support of the vast majority of the newspapers. Stevenson, undoubtedly with Truman's 1948 charges in mind, charged that the press was biased, and he clearly indicated it was the news columns he was talking about.

The issue did not fade as quickly as it had in 1948. For one thing, Stevenson and his staff continued to talk about press coverage after the election was over, and Stevenson had lost, which made it a different matter. When Sigma Delta Chi, the professional fraternity for journalists, had its annual convention in late November 1952, the question was raised about examining the Stevenson charges by studying newspaper coverage of the campaign. The Sigma Delta Chi delegates concluded that it was not feasible to attempt such a study after the election was over.

The controversy, however, did spawn the first studies of press coverage of a presidential campaign. There were four studies of the 1952 campaign. Two were of the newspapers of a particular state, and only one was national. That one was done by Nathan Blumberg and became a book, *The One Party Press?*[5] The most significant part of the book title was the question mark. It signified that Blumberg had not found clear-cut evidence of bias in his study of the front pages of thirty-five newspapers. He concluded that only six of the thirty-five papers showed evidence of partiality in the news columns.

Interest in the issue was sustained enough that in 1955 the Committee on Ethics and News Objectivity of Sigma Delta Chi and the Council on Communication Research of the Association for Education in Journalism put together a proposal for a study of the 1956 campaign. The proposal was submitted to seventy-six editors and publishers for their reaction. Their response was nearly 2 to 1 against it, and the proposal was dropped.

The rejection of the proposal obviously dampened enthusiasm for any study of coverage, and only one was completed in 1956.[6] The issue did not go away, however. The Democrats once again complained about a one-party press, as well they might in a year when the Republican candidate was endorsed by 81 percent of the newspapers that endorsed a candidate.

The issue reached a climax in the 1960 campaign. Not only were the complaints louder, but they came from both sides. When Sigma Delta Chi met that December, Pierre Salinger, Kennedy's press secretary, was there to proclaim that the press, which had supported Richard Nixon by better than 3 to 1 on the editorial page, had been unfair in its coverage of John Kennedy. Herb Klein, later to he director of communications in the Nixon White House, was there to proclaim that the reporters, who personally favored Kennedy by better than 3 to 1, had been unfair in their coverage of Nixon.

More studies were made of the coverage of the 1960 campaign than had been made in the previous two campaigns and more than have been made of any campaign since. Those studies did not confirm the concerns of either Salinger or Klein.[7]

The issue has remained with us, and we have had studies every campaign since. Yet after thirty-seven years and more than fifty studies, we still do not have a definitive answer to the basic question. The preponderance of evidence has been that media coverage by and large has been reasonably equal in quantity for both parties and that it has been reasonably fair. But just as Blumberg in the first study found that some papers were not fair in their coverage, so other studies have found instances of what appears to be unfair coverage.

One reason that we do not have a definitive answer is that there have been limiting factors in the studies that have been made. There has been little consistency from study to study about which newspapers are studied and what methods are used. The senior author of this study analyzed coverage by fifteen newspapers labeled the "Prestige Press" for the 1960,1964, and 1968 campaigns. With another author, he analyzed the same group's coverage in 1980.[8] No other researcher has studied the coverage by the same group of newspapers in more than two campaigns, and only a few have studied coverage in more than a single campaign.[9]

Most studies have looked at small groups of newspapers – perhaps the newspapers of a state or region or perhaps a small purposively selected group. Findings from such studies cannot be readily generalized to the press as a whole.

Another limitation is the period covered. Tradition has it that a presidential campaign begins on Labor Day. In recent campaigns, the Democratic candidate has been in Detroit to make a kickoff speech on that date. It would seem essential that a study cover the period from Labor Day to election eve, but many have not. Many have included only the last month or so of the campaign. Our own studies have demonstrated very clearly that coverage is not the same in October as it is in September.

Another limitation has been the matter of which media were included. No study before 1968 included television news, even though television news clearly was a significant factor in political coverage at least by 1956. Given that researchers finally did get around to television news in 1968, there has been relatively little study of it since. Only two studies before this on have included both newspapers and television and thereby permitted comparison between those two major media.[10]

Even more neglected has been the news magazine. Despite the obvious significance of news magazines' political coverage and the frequency with which they have been studied in other regards, there has been only one study of their coverage of a presidential campaign.[11]

The studies that have been made thus add up to a patchwork quilt of media coverage of the past nine presidential campaigns. Some campaigns have been studied more than others, and it has not been the importance of the campaign or the closeness of the campaign that has determined the extent of the study. Rather, it has been sheer chance. The focus has been mainly on newspapers and on larger newspapers, with other media only occasionally being considered.

A final limitation has been the very nature of the problem. One-party press implies bias, but what is meant by bias? If both the Democratic and Republican candidates receive the same amount of coverage, most people would conclude that there was no bias. But if the Democratic candidate gets more coverage than the Republican candidate, is that bias, or is it possibly a reflection of the fact that the Democratic candidate made more news? It is difficult to reach agreement on how such a situation should be interpreted. If one adds to this proposition the information that the paper endorsed the Republican candidate, will that change the answer?

Some studies unfortunately have accepted minor amounts of imbalance in coverage as bias, without taking into account the nature of the events in the particular campaign. Bias tends to suggest a pattern of constant favoritism, but some studies have not asked whether such a pattern exists. Some studies, in other words, have been too quick to accept bias as the conclusion.

If one candidate gets substantially better coverage than the other, that well may be a significant factor in the campaign, regardless of what the reason may be. This too argues for looking more deeply into what has happened in the coverage.

The 1984 Campaign

The one-party press seemed a latent issue for the 1984 presidential campaign at the time we started this study. There was no reason to doubt that President Reagan would get a majority of the newspaper endorsements. As it turned out, he got a greater proportion of the editorial support than he had in 1980. The *Editor & Publisher* poll reported that 58 percent of the papers responding endorsed Reagan, whereas only 9 percent endorsed Walter Mondale, and 33 percent did not endorse anyone. Reagan thus had six times as many newspapers supporting him editorially as Mondale did. That could have inspired some criticism from the Democrats but did not do so to any appreciable extent.

Another reason for anticipating possible criticism of coverage was the state of the relationship between the president and the press. Reagan had had fewer press conferences than any modern-day president during a first term, and there were other indications of strained relations. It seemed conceivable that the White House might take exception to coverage under these conditions.

As it turned out, criticism of coverage was not extensive. There was one major bone of contention on each side, but neither situation led to wider charges about coverage, and neither lasted beyond the period of the campaign.

The first case was the coverage of Geraldine Ferraro's finances. It was the feeling of some observers that she was in fact subjected to a good deal more scrutiny than either Reagan or his running mate, George Bush. There were questions that could have been asked about Reagan's and Bush's finances, particularly Bush's, but they certainly did not get asked to the extent that questions were asked about Ferraro's finances.

The other situation was the coverage given Reagan's unsureness during the first debate and the subsequent discussion of his age. There was some feeling on the part of the Republicans that the particular incident had been blown out of proportion.

The fact that the discussion of these points did not continue beyond November and that there were not broader complaints after the campaign may well have been due to the one-sidedness of the election. It has tended to be the closer elections that have drawn complaints about coverage. The 1960 election, which drew the most complaints, was the closest presidential election of this century.

In 1988 there was criticism of press coverage, and the issue was still very much alive two years later. The criticism was a spinoff of complaints that the candidates were not talking about issues. The counterattack began at the second presidential debate when George Bush was asked about the apparent dearth of discussion of issues. He replied that his staff had issued a number of position papers spelling out where he stood on the major issues. Roger Ailes, Bush's media advisor, later placed the number of position papers at 105.[12] The absence of coverage of issues by the media then was a result of the media ignoring these position papers.

This study was undertaken to provide a more comprehensive answer to the long-standing questions about press coverage of presidential campaigns. It is a study of the 1984 and 1988 campaigns, but the results have a bearing on the matter of coverage of presidential campaigns in general. It also serves as a test of the Republican charges about coverage of the 1988 campaign because issue coverage is a major focus of the study.

We have collected more data on more media than was the case in any previous study of presidential campaign coverage. We have included newspapers, network television news, and news magazines. In including all three media, we make comparisons among them possible, something that has seldom been done before. The study covers the period from Labor Day to election eve in both 1984 and 1988. This is the traditional period of the campaign, as recognized by the parties themselves. It totals sixty-four days for both years.

We analyzed seventeen newspapers. Fourteen are the Prestige Press papers that we have studied in four previous campaigns.[13] We selected them originally in 1960 because they had been singled out in a national poll of editors as the best newspapers in the country. To this group, consisting mostly of newspapers east of the Mississippi River, we added three major papers from the region west of the

Mississipipi River in the interest of geographical balance. These seventeen newspapers are not representative of American journalism. Rather, as elite newspapers, they are representative of the best in American journalism, and what they do in covering presidential campaigns is therefore significant.

The fourteen Prestige Press papers are the Atlanta *Constitution*, the Baltimore *Sun*, the Chicago *Tribune*, the *Christian Science Monitor*, the Des Moines *Register*, the Kansas City *Star*, the Los Angeles *Times*, the Louisville *Courier-Journal*, the Miami *Herald*, the Milwaukee *Journal*, the New York *Times*, the St. Louis *Post-Dispatch*, the *Wall Street Journal* and the Washington *Post*. The three papers added to the prestige group are the Dallas *Morning News*, the Portland *Oregonian*, and the San Francisco *Chronicle*.

The television programs included are the early evening newscasts for ABC, CBS, and NBC. Although this obviously is not all of the television news there is, it is the best of coverage of that medium. All newscasts within the campaign period were included, and all campaign stories within those newscasts were analyzed.

The news magazines included are *Newsweek, Time* and *U.S. News and World Report*. They are the only general news magazines of national circulation in the country. The ten issues published during the campaign period were included, and all campaign stories were analyzed.

In analyzing these media, we did make two fundamental distinctions. First, we distinguished between news stories and opinion pieces. We have reported here primarily on news coverage, not opinion items, although two chapters will deal with newspaper editorials. Second, we distinguished between campaign coverage and other news coverage of the candidates. President Reagan, for example, continued to get coverage for certain routine duties of the office of president during the 1984 campaign. George Bush likewise got coverage in both 1984 and 1988 related to duties of the office of vice president. Michael Dukakis received coverage in 1988 related to his duties as governor of Massachusetts. The two Democratic vice presidential nominees, Senator Lloyd Bentsen in 1988 and Congresswoman Geraldine Ferraro in 1984, and Dan Quayle, a senator while campaigning for vice president in 1988, all got coverage related to their work in Congress. Such coverage was not campaign coverage, and we have not included it in our figures for campaign coverage.

We identified items about the campaign and then classified each one as to which candidate it was primarily about and what the direction of the story was. A story was thus classified in the 1984 campaign as dealing with Reagan, Bush, Republicans in general, Mondale, Ferraro, Democrats in general, or equally to two or more of these items. In the 1988 campaign, a story was classified as dealing with Bush, Quayle, Republicans in general, Dukakis, Bentsen, Democrats in general, of equally to two or more of these items. It was then classified as being favorable, unfavorable, or neutral with regard to its referrant.

"*Favorable*" was defined as a positive reference with regard to strength, morality, or activity. "*Unfavorable*" was defined as a negative reference with regard to strength, morality, or activity. "*Neutral*" was defined either as no favorability in either direction or an equal amount of favorable and unfavorable reference.

Thus we know not only how much coverage George Bush received in the Des Moines *Register* but also how much of that coverage was favorable, unfavorable, or neutral. We also know whether the coverage of the Republican campaign in 1988 emphasized the vice presidential candidate, Dan Quayle, as much as it emphasized Bush. We also are able to make comparisons between coverage in 1984 and 1988. This is more useful than it might ordinarily be because the 1984 campaign had an incumbent whereas the 1988 campaign did not. This was the first time in twenty years that there was no incumbent on the ballot.

For newspapers, we classified the headlines into five categories of size – streamers or banners, spread heads, two-column heads, major one-column heads, and minor one-column heads. *Streamers* are heads that go across the entire page. *Spread heads* are more than two-columns wide but less than a streamer. *Two-column heads* are heads that are only two columns wide. *Major one-column heads* are at least one inch deep, and *minor one-column heads* are less than an inch deep.

Finally, we determined the major issue of each story, using a system of thirteen subject-matter categories. Those categories were:

• **Politics and government**: All activities of government and political parties

• **War and Diplomacy:** References to war, diplomacy and foreign relations, defense activities, and military use of space

• **Economic Activity:** Stories dealing with prices, money, inflation, transportation, travel, agribusiness, labor and wages, and natural resources

• **Crime**: References to both adult and juvenile crime of all kinds

- **Public Moral Problems:** References to human relations problems such as alcohol, divorce, sex, drugs, race relations and personal or ethical standards
- **Public Health and Welfare:** References to public health, public welfare, public safety, pollution, child welfare, and social problems
- **Accidents and Disasters:** Stories about both human accidents and disasters, such as auto accidents, and natural ones, such as floods
- **Science and Invention:** Stories about all nonmilitary aspects of science and technology, including nondefense space and nondefense nuclear science
- **Education and Classic Arts**: Stories about education, arts, culture, religion, and philosophy
- **Recreation and Media:** Stories about leisure time activity, including amusements, recreation, and media
- **Human Interest:** Stories about the emotional aspects of life, such as senior citizens, animals, children, and people in general
- **Strength of Candidate:** Reference to candidates' qualifications, virtues, abilities, and experience and to chance of winning and endorsements
- **Horserace**: Reference to who is leading, especially poll stories

An additional aspect of the study was an effort to determine how aware the public is of editorial endorsements and what the public thinks about coverage. To do this, we made telephone surveys in Chicago and Louisville in the latter part of October and early November of 1984. These data enable us to compare what the public thinks about the coverage with how the coverage actually was.

In the remainder of this book, we will report findings in these indicated areas for newspapers, network television newscasts, and news magazines.

Chapter 2 – Newspaper Coverage of the 1984 and 1988 Campaigns
Chapter 3 – Network Television Coverage of the 1984 and 1988 Campaigns
Chapter 4 – How the News Magazines Covered the 1984 and 1988 Campaigns
Chapter 5 – The Editorial Pages of Leading Newspapers in 1984
Chapter 6 – The Editorial Pages of Leading Newspapers in 1988
Chapter 7 – Public Attitudes about Coverage and Public Awareness of Editorial Endorsements in the 1984 Campaign
Chapter 8 – The Total Picture: Press, Politicians, and the Public

Notes

1. Thomas Jefferson to Samuel Smith, August 22, 1798, in Leonard W. Levy, ed. *Freedom of the Press from Zenger to Jefferson* (Indianapolis: Bobbs-Merrill, 1966), p. 354.
2. Thomas Jefferson to Monsieur Pictet, in Levy, *Freedom of the Press,* p. 360.
3. Thomas Jefferson to Thomas McKean, in Levy, *Freedom of the Press,* p. 364.
4. Thomas Jefferson to Walter Jones, January 2, 1814, in Levy, *Freedom of the Press*, p. 373.
5. Nathan Blumberg, *One Party Press?* (Lincoln University of Nebraska Press, 1954). The other three studies were Sidney Kobre, "How Florida Dailies Handled the 1963 Presidential Campaign," *Journalism Quarterly*, 30:163-169 (Spring 1953); Charles E. Higbie, "Wisconsin Dailies in the 1952 Campaign: Space vs. Display," *Journalism Quarterly*, 31:56-60 (Winter 1954); and Malcolm W. Klein and Nathan Macoby, "Newspaper Objectivity in the 1952 Campaign," *Journalism Quarterly*, 31:285-295 (Summer 1954).
6. James W. Markham and Guido H. Stempel III, *Pennsylvania Daily Press Coverage of the 1956 Election Campaign* (University Park: Pennsylvania State University School of Journalism, 1957).
7. For description of the thirteen studies in 1960, see Charles E. Higbie, "1960 Election Studies Show Broad Approach, New Methods," *Journalism Quarterly*, 38:164-170 (Spring 1961).
8. Guido H. Stempel III, "The Prestige Press Covers the 1960 Presidential Campaign," *Journalism Quarterly*, 38:157-163 (Spring 1961); Guido H. Stempel III, "The Prestige Press in Two Presidential Elections," *Journalism Quarterly,* 42:15-21 (Spring 1965); Guido H. Stempel III, "The Prestige Press Meets the Third-Party Challenge," *Journalism Quarterly*, 46:699-706 (Winter 1969); Guido H. Stempel III and John W. Windhauser, "The Prestige Press Revisited: Coverage of the 1980 Presidential Campaign," *Journalism Quarterly*, 61:49-55 (Spring 1984).
9. See James Glen Stovall, "Foreign Policy Issue Coverage in the 1980 Presidential Campaign," *Journalism Quarterly,* 59:531-40 (Autumn 1982), and James Glen Stovall, "Coverage of the 1984 Presidential Campaign," *Journalism Quarterly*, 65:443-449 (Summer 1988).
10. Dru Evarts and Guido H. Stempel III, "Coverage of the 1972 Campaign by TV, News Magazines and Major Newspapers," *Jour-*

nalism Quarterly, 51:645-648, 676 (Winter 1974); C. Richard Hofstetter, *Bias in the News* (Columbus: Ohio State University Press, 1976).

11. Evarts and Stempel, "Coverage of the 1972 Campaign"

12. Roger Ailes, keynote address, Communication Week, Ohio University, April 24, 1989.

13. Anon., "Nation's Editors Pick 15 'Superior Papers,'" *Editor & Publisher*, April 12, 1960, p. 14.

2

Newspaper Coverage of the 1984 and 1988 Campaigns

Guido H. Stempel III and John W. Windhauser

We studied the coverage of the 1984 and 1988 presidential campaigns by seventeen major newspapers. Fourteen were newspapers whose coverage we had studied in four previous presidential campaigns.[1] We termed this group of newspapers the "Prestige Press" in the first study, which was of the 1960 presidential campaign. The name stuck and has been used by other researchers in studies of other aspects of coverage by this distinguished group of American newspapers. The group actually was selected in a poll of editors by the magazine *Practical English*, which asked the editors to list the newspapers that were "most superior for news coverage, integrity and public service."

The fifteen papers that the editors selected on that basis were the Atlanta *Constitution*, the Baltimore *Sun*, the Chicago *Daily News*, the Chicago *Tribune*, the *Christian Science Monitor*, the Des Moines *Register*, the Kansas City *Star*, the Los Angeles *Times*, the Louisville *Courier-Journal*, the Miami *Herald*, the Milwaukee *Journal*, the New York *Times*, the St. Louis *Post-Dispatch*, the *Wall Street Journal* and the Washington *Post*. The Chicago *Daily News* no longer exists, but the other fourteen papers were studied for both years. Because most of these papers are in the eastern half of the country, we added three prominent papers from the western half of the country – the Dallas *Morning News*, the Portland *Oregonian*, and the San Francisco *Chronicle*.

Our study began both years with coverage of the traditional Labor Day campaign kickoffs and ended with the issues of the newspaper published the day before the election. That was a total of sixty-four days for both 1984 and 1988.

Our four previous studies of coverage by the Prestige Press found their coverage of the presidential campaigns to be very balanced. We also have found very little relationship between a newspaper's choice of candidate in its editorial endorsement and its coverage. We therefore hypothesized:

1. The number of stories favoring each of the presidential candidates will be approximately equal in each of these newspapers and for the group overall.

2. The allocation of headlines to the candidates will be comparable for each candidate for each of these newspapers and for the group as a whole.

We sought to expand our previous studies by looking at two more aspects of coverage – coverage of issues and the relative share of coverage for the presidential and vice presidential candidates. We hypothesized:

3. The emphasis of coverage will not be on issues but on the candidates, their strengths and weaknesses and how the race is going.

4. The great majority of coverage will focus on the presidential candidates, not the vice presidential candidates.

Method

Our basic unit was the story. We coded all news stories dealing with the presidential and vice presidential campaigns both years. Editorials, columns, letters, and other forms of opinions were not included. The number of stories ranged from 132 in the Kansas City *Star* to 731 in the Washington *Post* in 1984 and from 192 in the *Wall Street Journal* to 695 in the *Post* in 1988. For each story, we determined which candidate the story was about, the direction of the story, the major issue in the story, the type of headline, and the direction of the headline. The following sections describe the categories we used for each of those determinations.

Candidate

In 1984 each story was classified as being either about Republican presidential candidate Ronald Reagan, Republican vice presidential candidate George Bush, Republican candidates in general, Democratic presidential candidate Walter Mondale, Democratic vice presidential candidate Geraldine Ferraro, or Democratic candidates in general or as not being about any one candidate primarily. In 1988 the categories were Republican presidential candidate George Bush, Republican vice presidential candidate Dan Quayle, Republican candidates in general, Democratic presidential candidate Michael Dukakis, Democratic vice presidential candidate Lloyd Bentsen, Democratic candidates in general, and no one candidate.

Direction

Each story was classified as being favorable, unfavorable, or neutral with reference to the candidate it was about. To arrive at the direction for the story, we classified each paragraph. The direction of the story was then the direction of the majority of the paragraphs. If there was no majority direction, the story was classified as neutral.

Issues

The issue categories were Politics and Government; War, Defense and Diplomacy; Economic Activity; Crime; Public Moral Problems; Public Health and Welfare; Accidents and Disasters; Science and Invention; Education and Classic Arts; Recreation and Media; Human Interest; Strength of Candidate; and Horserace. Detailed definitions of these categories, which are also used in Chapters 3 and 4, are in Chapter 1.

Headlines were classified as being streamers, spread heads, two-column heads, major one-column heads, or minor one-column heads. Definitions of these categories are in Chapter 1. Direction in headlines was coded according to the categories used for direction of stories.

Results

As we found in our earlier studies, coverage was, for the most part, favorable to the candidates, as Tables 1 and 2 indicate. Favorable stories outnumbered unfavorable stories about the candidates by better than 2 to 1. All seventeen newspapers had more favorable than unfavorable stories about Mondale in 1984, and only the Louisville *Courier-Journal* had more unfavorable stories about Reagan. Although the two vice presidential candidates in 1984 had more favorable than unfavorable coverage, they were not treated as favorably as the presidential candidates. The *Wall Street Journal* also had more unfavorable than favorable stories about Ferraro, whereas the Miami *Herald*, the Portland *Oregonian*, and the St. Louis *Post-*

Table 1: Number of Favorable, Unfavorable and Neutral Stories about Each Candidate in the 17 Newspapers in 1984

	Mondale			*Ferraro*			*Democrats*			*Reagan*			*Bush*			*Republicans*			
	+	-	0	+	-	0	+	-	0	+	-	0	+	-	0	+	-	0	*N
Atlanta *Constitution*	63	8	8	13	11	4	5	1	0	42	29	14	2	0	1	0	1	0	51
Baltimore *Sun*	74	22	8	24	10	1	7	3	1	72	47	11	9	6	0	6	3	0	22
Chicago *Tribune*	81	21	4	32	5	4	4	0	0	99	19	7	11	2	1	5	1	2	69
Christian Science Monitor	31	13	14	4	3	4	2	1	0	37	9	16	5	1	1	2	0	0	34
Dallas *Morning News*	39	19	14	9	5	7	11	3	3	56	51	5	3	9	7	9	3	1	60
Des Moines *Register*	36	18	7	14	8	5	1	0	0	58	30	6	5	5	4	5	2	0	35
Kansas City *Star*	31	6	5	7	1	3	2	0	1	25	6	4	4	1	0	2	0	0	34
Los Angeles *Times*	98	20	24	37	4	10	11	4	1	79	46	24	14	2	5	13	4	2	52
Louisville *Courier-Journal*	38	19	2	7	11	2	6	7	0	45	71	2	5	8	0	9	2	0	24
Miami *Herald*	70	19	5	23	14	4	7	3	1	96	70	11	8	12	2	6	6	2	39
Milwaukee *Journal*	42	15	1	4	9	4	1	5	7	76	43	14	2	7	2	3	5	0	18
New York *Times*	135	61	8	43	30	7	11	9	5	170	102	19	17	8	5	3	4	1	41
Portland *Oregonian*	31	26	2	7	5	3	3	0	0	42	54	5	5	7	5	2	5	1	44
San Francisco *Chronicle*	48	21	11	18	16	3	8	5	1	95	62	3	11	10	1	12	10	4	76
St. Louis *Post-Dispatch*	89	20	9	19	15	2	4	1	6	95	88	10	4	19	2	3	5	2	49
Wall Street Journal	18	10	3	5	8	6	3	1	4	24	22	7	4	0	1	7	9	0	18
Washington *Post*	72	43	26	44	13	11	13	6	6	178	138	36	25	14	12	8	7	5	74

+ = Favorable - = Unfavorable 0 = Neutral

*N = Neutral category includes items that do not refer primarily to one candidate or have clear direction or both.

Table 2: Number of Favorable, Unfavorable and Neutral Stories about Each Candidate in the 17 Newspapers in 1988

	Dukakis			*Bentsen*			*Democrats*			*Bush*			*Quayle*			*Republicans*			
	+	-	0	+	-	0	+	-	0	+	-	0	+	-	0	+	-	0	*N
Atlanta *Constitution*	96	32	0	5	0	0	10	1	4	80	24	3	10	11	0	9	11	3	78
Baltimore *Sun*	147	76	1	13	1	0	19	7	3	181	72	4	31	28	1	16	14	2	118
Chicago *Tribune*	75	28	4	11	0	0	12	9	2	66	14	4	19	13	5	16	19	2	102
Christian Science Monitor	44	17	0	3	0	0	11	2	0	50	8	0	2	2	0	5	3	0	66
Dallas *Morning News*	77	43	0	35	10	2	14	11	0	80	18	0	17	17	2	17	11	1	116
Des Moines *Register*	75	28	1	12	1	1	17	5	1	104	34	2	16	22	1	16	19	2	106
Kansas City *Star*	51	14	1	12	1	0	14	1	2	58	10	1	8	11	0	15	9	0	91
Los Angeles *Times*	127	48	0	31	1	1	9	2	0	125	35	0	44	13	0	22	4	0	143
Louisville *Courier-Journal*	40	25	2	7	0	0	18	6	1	63	17	3	18	10	1	19	13	0	41
Miami *Herald*	67	43	3	15	2	0	7	8	0	80	66	0	21	26	0	16	17	1	157
Milwaukee *Journal*	76	22	0	4	0	0	1	1	1	89	18	0	16	7	0	4	2	0	71
New York *Times*	112	48	6	22	0	0	11	8	0	134	40	1	36	18	1	21	2	0	118
Portland *Oregonian*	132	47	2	37	0	0	26	3	1	127	39	0	37	21	1	14	24	0	159
San Francisco *Chronicle*	102	31	3	22	1	0	25	7	0	130	26	2	27	28	2	31	17	1	133
St. Louis *Post-Dispatch*	106	34	1	22	1	0	31	5	0	110	31	1	28	10	1	26	15	0	149
Wall Street Journal	30	6	2	5	1	0	5	0	0	40	12	0	5	7	0	14	5	0	61
Washington *Post*	135	41	4	13	3	0	24	8	6	128	36	0	17	35	2	49	33	5	156

+ = Favorable - = Unfavorable 0 = Neutral

*N = Neutral category includes items that do not refer primarily to one candidate or have clear direction or both.

Dispatch had more unfavorable than favorable stories about Bush.

In 1988 all seventeen papers had more favorable than unfavorable coverage of both Dukakis and Bush. It was, however, Bentsen who had the most favorable coverage. Not only did all seventeen papers have more favorable than unfavorable stories about Bentsen, but also seven of the seventeen had only favorable stories about Bentsen, with no unfavorable or neutral stories. Quayle, on the other hand, fared even less well than Bush had as the Republican vice presidential candidate in 1984. Seven of the seventeen had more unfavorable than favorable stories about Quayle.

The advantage to the Democrats, however, was minimal because most coverage was not about the vice presidential candidates. Our fourth hypothesis, that most coverage was about the presidential candidates, was clearly confirmed, as can be seen in Table 1. In 1984, there were about eight times as many stories about Reagan as there were about Bush and three times as many stories about Mondale as there were about Ferraro. The most extreme case was the Atlanta

Table 3: Number of Democratic, Republican and Neutral Stories in 17 Newspapers

	1984			*1988*		
	D	*R*	*N*	*D*	*R*	*N*
Atlanta *Constitution*	111	82	78	157	132	88
Baltimore *Sun*	161	122	43	292	312	129
Chicago *Tribune*	140	141	87	144	138	119
Christian Science Monitor	47	61	69	71	76	66
Dallas *Morning News*	122	95	97	172	180	122
Des Moines *Register*	88	84	57	179	170	114
Kansas City *Star*	47	38	47	107	97	95
Los Angeles *Times*	198	134	118	218	242	143
Louisville *Courier-Journal*	132	96	30	105	131	48
Miami *Herald*	188	146	64	197	170	161
Milwaukee *Journal*	102	110	46	132	108	72
New York *Times*	303	290	86	205	246	126
Portland *Oregonian*	107	80	60	279	230	164
San Francisco *Chronicle*	156	160	99	220	226	164
St. Louis *Post-Dispatch*	224	138	80	215	201	152
Wall Street Journal	57	54	39	64	66	63
Washington *Post*	288	273	87	276	246	173

D = Democratic; R = Republican; N = Neutral

Constitution, with eighty-five stories about Reagan and three about Bush.

In 1988 there were nearly seven times as many stories about Dukakis as there were about Bentsen and more than three times as many stories about Bush as there were about Quayle. This is an interesting outcome because there was considerable discussion late in the campaign about what seemed to be a Republican effort to keep Quayle out of the limelight, principally by having him appear in out-of-the-way places. Yet Bentsen was kept out of the limelight even more, and certainly this was no accident. Not only did the vice presidential candidates stay off the beaten path, they also stayed away from the major issues, as the tables on coverage by the individual papers later in the chapter show clearly.

We also hypothesized that coverage would not be related to the editorial endorsement of these papers, and Tables 3 and 4 provide the evidence on that point. We report simply the total number of Democratic, Republican, and neutral stories in Table 3. This means that we

Table 4: Percentage of Democratic and Republican Stories, with Neutral Stories Excluded

	1984		*1988*	
	D	*R*	*D*	*R*
Atlanta *Constitution*	57.5%	42.5%	54.3%	45.7%
Baltimore *Sun*	56.9	43.1	48.3	51.7
Chicago *Tribune*	49.8	50.2	51.1	48.9
Christian Science Monitor	43.5	56.5	48.3	51.7
Dallas *Morning News*	56.2	43.8	48.9	51.1
Des Moines *Register*	51.2	48.8	51.3	48.9
Kansas City *Star*	55.3	44.7	52.5	47.5
Los Angeles *Times*	59.6	40.4	47.4	54.6
Louisville *Courier-Journal*	57.9	42.1	44.5	55.5
Miami *Herald*	56.3	43.7	53.7	46.3
Milwaukee *Journal*	48.1	51.9	55.0	45.0
New York *Times*	51.1	48.9	45.5	54.5
Portland *Oregonian*	57.2	42.8	54.8	45.2
San Francisco *Chronicle*	49.4	50.6	49.3	50.7
St. Louis *Post-Dispatch*	61.9	38.1	51.7	48.3
Wall Street Journal	51.4	48.6	49.2	50.8
Washington *Post*	51.3	48.7	52.9	47.1

D = Democratic; R = Republican

are combining pro-Democratic with anti-Republican under Democratic and pro-Republican and anti-Democratic under Republican.

The Atlanta *Constitution*, the Des Moines *Register*, the Louisville *Courier-Journal*, the Milwaukee *Journal*, the New York *Times*, and the St. Louis *Post-Dispatch* endorsed the Democratic ticket in both years. The Chicago *Tribune*, the Dallas *Morning News,* the Miami *Herald,* the Portland *Oregonian,* and the San Francisco *Chronicle* endorsed the Republican ticket in both years. The Baltimore *Sun,* the *Christian Science Monitor*, the Los Angeles *Times* and the *Wall Street Journal* did not endorse a candidate in either year. The Washington *Post* endorsed the Democratic ticket in 1984 but did not endorse either ticket in 1988. The Kansas City *Star* was the only paper to switch sides, endorsing the Republicans in 1984 and the Democrats in 1988.

The *Star* is thus perhaps the place to start in analyzing the impact of endorsement in coverage. The *Star* was more favorable to the Democrats in 1984, as Table 4 shows, when it endorsed the Republican ticket than it was in 1988 when it endorsed the Democratic ticket.

Looking at the entire array of papers, we see no clear pattern related to endorsements in either year. The seven newspapers whose coverage was most favorable to the Democrats in 1984 included three Democratic papers, two Republican papers, and two that did not endorse anyone. In 1988 two of the three paper most favorable to the Democrats endorsed the Republican ticket.

The tendency for coverage to be divided fairly equally between Democrats and Republicans is shown in Table 4. (Note that neutral stories are excluded from that table.) In 1984 seven of the seventeen papers were within 5 percent of a 50-50 split. In other words, they were somewhere between 45 percent Democratic-55 percent Republican and 55 percent Democratic-45 percent Republican. But in 1988 this tendency was even greater, with only one of the seventeen papers not within 5 percent of 50-50.

Headline use in the two campaigns in shown in Tables 5 and 6. What would concern us here would be an imbalance in one direction with larger heads coupled with an imbalance in the opposite direction with smaller heads. In 1984 the larger imbalances for streamers and spread heads are in favor of the Democrats on the part of two Republican papers – the Dallas *Morning News* and the Portland *Oregonian.* In 1988 there really was nothing striking in the way of an imbalance in those two larger types of heads. We conclude, therefore,

Table 5: Classification of Headlines by Size and Party Favored, 1984

	Streamer			*Spread*			*2-Column*			*Major 1-Col*			*Minor 1-Col.*			*Total*		
	D	*R*	*N*	*D*	*R*	*N*	*D*	*R*	*N*	*D*	*R*	*N*	*D*	*R*	*N*	*D*	*R*	*N*
Atlanta *Constitution*	2	2	3	23	11	25	21	19	25	17	6	29	16	12	43	79	50	125
Baltimore *Sun*	8	8	5	53	34	40	40	31	34	21	16	16	16	7	9	138	96	104
Chicago *Tribune*	8	8	8	37	34	50	34	28	25	12	11	51	6	11	37	97	92	161
Christian Science *Monitor*	4	9	9	4	7	7	6	7	5	1	3	5	25	22	64	40	49	90
Dallas Morning *News*	22	12	33	39	36	21	36	26	27	16	13	11	9	8	5	122	95	97
Des Moines *Register*	4	2	1	18	24	18	28	29	23	10	13	15	13	8	13	73	76	70
Kansas City *Star*	7	2	16	8	11	20	15	10	20	9	5	10	4	3	9	43	31	75
Los Angeles *Times*	6	7	8	56	39	48	53	28	72	24	19	24	20	17	30	159	108	182
Louisville *Courier-Journal*	2	6	9	31	55	33	22	40	36	13	20	11	1	4	0	69	125	89
Miami *Herald*	9	16	13	53	43	28	32	54	44	21	17	39	4	8	13	119	138	137
Milwaukee *Journal*	8	1	12	14	20	38	25	31	31	22	30	22	3	3	10	72	85	113
New York *Times*	3	17	3	54	63	69	48	42	33	28	41	36	62	43	114	195	206	255
Portland *Oregonian*	28	16	22	39	36	25	19	17	8	19	10	5	2	1	0	107	80	60
San Francisco *Chronicle*	16	10	6	59	59	37	49	44	45	21	20	4	21	27	7	166	150	99
St. Louis *Post-Dispatch*	16	10	11	38	43	31	43	67	26	38	39	23	7	13	32	142	172	123
Wall Street Journal	2	0	3	5	11	13	10	14	7	8	9	3	0	0	1	25	34	27
Washington *Post*	18	24	18	63	79	41	74	91	42	29	29	76	3	6	61	187	229	238

D = Democratic; R = Republican; N = Neutral

Table 6: Classification of Headlines by Size and Party Favored, 1988

	Streamer			*Spread*			*2-Column*			*Major 1-Col*			*Minor 1-Col.*			*Total*		
	D	***R***	***N***	***D***	***R***	***N***	***D***	***R***	***N***	***D***	***R***	***N***	***D***	***R***	***N***	***D***	***R***	***N***
Atlanta *Constitution*	12	7	24	17	21	22	28	26	26	30	15	63	14	15	41	101	84	176
Baltimore *Sun*	25	19	25	70	85	83	43	36	44	23	26	24	33	35	138	194	201	314
Chicago *Tribune*	8	5	5	34	45	40	32	21	19	14	15	98	6	2	17	94	88	179
Christian Science Monitor	5	2	10	9	4	13	5	9	24	7	9	11	2	3	100	28	27	158
Dallas *Morning News*	23	12	18	56	61	40	31	34	40	22	16	24	4	3	80	136	126	202
Des Moines *Register*	1	3	5	28	35	35	41	32	26	41	26	37	61	36	55	172	132	158
Kansas City *Star*	1	0	9	24	12	59	25	11	36	14	14	30	5	3	56	69	40	190
Los Angeles *Times*	20	16	14	71	71	43	68	54	56	25	25	7	43	34	42	227	200	162
Louisville *Courier-Journal*	2	2	2	28	53	30	27	29	33	21	16	13	5	6	15	83	106	93
Miami *Herald*	10	7	6	26	23	27	31	36	44	15	15	11	28	25	217	111	106	305
Milwaukee *Journal*	8	4	13	44	53	37	23	34	17	18	14	10	10	17	15	103	122	92
New York *Times*	7	9	21	56	63	46	51	61	32	20	18	7	90	85	18	224	236	124
Portland *Oregonian*	20	12	30	31	26	45	35	27	29	27	23	16	79	83	180	192	171	300
San Francisco *Chronicle*	3	7	11	56	61	63	43	44	47	45	39	27	28	37	76	176	188	224
St. Louis *Post-Dispatch*	9	5	16	40	38	53	49	28	44	34	27	136	16	22	45	148	120	294
Wall Street Journal	0	1	1	5	9	22	21	7	10	1	8	9	8	6	15	35	31	57
Washington *Post*	23	18	28	68	62	52	57	58	51	31	39	33	37	28	107	216	205	271

D = Democratic; R = Republican; N = Neutral

that our hypothesis that allocation of headlines would be equitable is confirmed.

Issue coverage by the papers is shown in Tables 7 and 8. We hypothesized that the coverage would be about how the race was going, not about the issues. The evidence of that is overwhelming. Politics and government was the most frequent category for every paper except the Washington *Post* in 1984 and for every paper except the Dallas *Morning News*, the Portland *Oregonian*, and the San Francisco *Chronicle* in 1988. Candidate strength was the second most frequent category for most papers. The politics and government category consisted largely of stories about what the candidates were doing in their campaigns. This was the focus in both campaigns, and the prime example came in the final three weeks in 1988 when Dukakis announced he was reviving his campaign and making a bid for victory. But the stories were not about issues, not about new ideas that Dukakis was offering, not about how he differed from Bush. They were about how his last-minute bid was going.

What is surprising in both years is the relatively light coverage of economic activity and the virtually nonexistent coverage of health, science, and education, all identified as major concerns for the country in both campaign years. What is equally surprising is how similar coverage was in 1988 to what is was in 1984. We heard discussion of the absence of issues in the campaign in 1988. We did not hear such concern to any appreciable degree in 1984. Yet our figures provide no basis for suggesting that issues were any more a part of the campaign coverage in 1984 than they were in 1988. In both years all of these newspapers devoted a clear majority of their coverage to how the campaign was being conducted, who was ahead, and the strength of the candidates.

Although there was great similarity between newspapers, there are some individual patterns worth noting. The Atlanta *Constitution* (Tables 11 and 12) had three-fourths of its coverage on politics and government and candidate strength in 1984 and nearly that much in 1988. The *Constitution* had only one horserace story in 1984 but had twenty-three in 1988, making it the fourth highest category. Its coverage of Mondale was considerably more favorable than its coverage of Reagan, but its coverage of Ferraro was only slightly favorable. The *Constitution*'s stories on Dukakis and Bush were favorable about three-fourths of the time, but it had more unfavorable than favorable stories about Quayle.

The Baltimore *Sun* (Tables 13 and 14) had twice as many stories in

Table 7: Major Issues in Campaign Stories for the Seventeen Newspapers, 1984

	Politics, Government	War, Defense, Diplomacy	Economic Activity	Crime	Public Moral Problems	Public Health, Welfare	Accidents, Disasters	Science, Invention	Education, Classic Arts	Recreation, Media	Human Interest	Strength of Candidate	Horserace	Total
Atlanta *Constitution*	125	18	25	3	7	2	0	0	4	3	0	65	1	253
Baltimore *Sun*	135	41	8	1	11	6	0	0	10	0	4	105	17	338
Chicago *Tribune*	208	25	22	1	8	1	1	0	2	3	4	62	31	368
Christian Science Monitor	86	17	8	3	7	3	0	4	2	1	0	40	6	177
Dallas Morning *News*	130	36	36	1	10	2	0	1	7	17	3	45	26	318
Des Moines *Register*	96	15	39	3	9	2	0	0	5	13	12	34	11	239
Kansas City *Star*	81	5	6	0	2	3	0	0	3	0	4	20	8	132
Los Angeles *Times*	251	53	28	4	9	5	8	0	7	2	4	61	18	450
Louisville *Courier-Journal*	98	43	19	1	15	10	0	2	15	2	0	40	13	258
Miami *Herald*	149	46	18	2	10	7	0	0	9	18	10	101	28	398
Milwaukee *Journal*	111	18	30	1	9	1	0	1	3	1	4	60	19	258
New York *Times*	208	72	38	10	17	16	3	0	42	30	31	190	22	679
Portland *Oregonian*	79	35	44	2	9	2	0	0	7	1	0	49	20	247
San Francisco *Chronicle*	125	56	45	3	10	4	0	0	11	29	5	42	85	415
St. Louis *Post-Dispatch*	167	38	29	6	11	23	0	0	20	20	9	107	12	442
Wall Street Journal	67	17	6	1	1	3	0	0	8	13	1	32	1	150
Washington *Post*	211	76	66	2	29	10	0	12	24	44	10	228	19	731

Table 8: Major Issues in Campaign Stories for the Seventeen Newspapers, 1988

	Politics, Government	*War, Defense, Diplomacy*	*Economic Activity*	*Crime*	*Public Moral Problems*	*Public Health, Welfare*	*Accidents, Disasters*	*Science, Invention*	*Education, Classic Arts*	*Recreation, Media*	*Human Interest*	*Strength of Candidate*	*Horserace*	***Total***
Atlanta *Constitution*	132	26	15	7	12	19	0	4	10	23	1	104	25	378
Baltimore *Sun*	222	58	49	23	22	46	0	1	9	38	4	215	49	736
Chicago *Tribune*	151	23	28	9	12	12	1	0	5	36	3	111	10	401
Christian Science Monitor	69	15	24	4	9	24	0	2	5	5	0	40	16	213
Dallas Morning *News*	138	25	37	12	15	25	1	5	2	19	0	161	33	474
Des Moines *Register*	148	23	39	10	15	16	0	2	4	31	2	124	49	463
Kansas City *Star*	118	12	22	6	16	15	0	10	8	18	0	48	26	299
Los Angeles *Times*	220	39	66	15	34	10	0	2	5	35	14	116	47	603
Louisville *Courier-Journal*	81	20	17	10	14	21	1	2	5	12	0	72	29	284
Miami *Herald*	192	31	24	19	7	25	1	1	4	37	4	154	30	529
Milwaukee *Journal*	125	16	15	7	18	9	0	1	1	8	10	67	35	312
New York *Times*	190	38	41	17	20	16	0	0	8	8	35	171	33	577
Portland *Oregonian*	182	61	55	16	23	47	1	4	9	24	4	185	60	671
San Francisco *Chronicle*	157	36	34	13	15	36	1	9	5	46	4	185	47	588
St. Louis *Post-Dispatch*	229	27	36	12	15	40	0	3	7	9	13	142	38	571
Wall Street Journal	59	16	34	4	6	7	0	4	3	6	0	32	22	193
Washington *Post*	264	49	58	15	22	33	1	2	10	68	1	144	28	695

Table 9: Emphasis Ranks for Issues in the Seventeen Newspapers, 1984

	Politics, Government	*War, Defense, Diplomacy*	*Economic Activity*	*Crime*	*Public Moral Problems*	*Public Health, Welfare*	*Accidents, Disasters*	*Science, Invention*	*Education, Classic Arts*	*Recreation, Media*	*Human Interest*	*Strength of Candidate*	*Horserace*
Atlanta *Constitution*	1	4	3	7*	5	9	11*	11*	6	7*	11*	2	10
Baltimore *Sun*	1	3	7	10	5	9	11*	11*	6	11*	8	2	4
Chicago *Tribune*	1	4	5	10*	6	10*	10*	13	9	8	7	2	3
Christian Science Monitor	1	3	4	8*	5	8*	12*	7	10	11	12*	2	6
Dallas Morning *News*	1	3*	3*	11	7	10	13	11*	8	6	9	2	5
Des Moines *Register*	1	4	2	10	8	11	12*	12*	9	5	6	3	7
Kansas City *Star*	1	5	4	10*	9	7*	10*	10*	7*	10*	6	2	3
Los Angeles *Times*	1	3	4	10*	6	9	7	13	8	12	10*	2	5
Louisville *Courier-Journal*	1	2	4	13	5*	8	11*	9*	5*	9*	11*	3	7
Miami *Herald*	1	3	5	11	7*	10	12*	12*	9	5*	7*	2	4
Milwaukee *Journal*	1	5	3	9*	6	9*	13	9*	8	9*	7	2	4
New York *Times*	1	3	5	11	9	10	12	13	4	7	6	2	8
Portland *Oregonian*	1	4	3	8	6	11*	9*	11*	7	11*	9*	2	5
San Francisco *Chronicle*	1	3	4	11	8	10	12*	12*	7	6	9	5	2
St. Louis *Post-Dispatch*	1	3	4	11	9	5	12*	12*	6*	6*	10	2	8
Wall Street Journal	1	3	6	8*	8*	7	12*	12*	5	4	8*	2	8*
Washington *Post*	2	3	4	12*	6	10*	12*	9	7	5	10*	1	8

Table 10: Emphasis Ranks for Issues in the Seventeen Newspapers, 1988

	Politics, Government	*War, Defense, Diplomacy*	*Economic Activity*	*Crime*	*Public Moral Problems*	*Public Health, Welfare*	*Accidents, Disasters*	*Science, Invention*	*Education, Classic Arts*	*Recreation, Media*	*Human Interest*	*Strength of Candidate*	*Horserace*
Atlanta *Constitution*	1	3	7	10	8	6	13	11	9	5	12	2	4
Baltimore *Sun*	1	3	4*	8	9	6	13	12	10	7	11	2	4*
Chicago *Tribune*	1	5	4	9	6*	6*	12	13	10	3	11	2	8
Christian Science Monitor	1	6	3*	12	7	3*	12*	11	8*	8*	12*	2	5
Dallas Morning *News*	2	5*	3	9	8	5*	12	10	11	7	13	1	4
Des Moines *Register*	1	6	4	9	8	7	13	11*	10	5	11*	2	3
Kansas City *Star*	1	8	4	11	6	7	12*	9	10	5	12*	2	3
Los Angeles *Times*	1	5	3	8	7	10	13	12	11	6	9	2	4
Louisville *Courier-Journal*	1	5	6	9	7	4	12	11	10	8	13	2	3
Miami *Herald*	1	4	7	8	9	6	12*	12*	10*	3	10*	2	5
Milwaukee *Journal*	1	5	6	10	4	8	13	11*	11*	9	7	2	3
New York *Times*	1	4	3	8	7	9	12*	12*	10*	10*	5	2	6
Portland *Oregonian*	2	3	5	9	8	6	13	11*	10	7	11*	1	4
San Francisco *Chronicle*	2	5*	7	9	8	5*	13	10	11	4	12	1	3
St. Louis *Post-Dispatch*	1	6	5	9	7	3	13	12	11	10	8	2	4
Wall Street Journal	1	5	2	9*	7*	6	12*	9*	11	7*	12*	3	4
Washington *Post*	1	5	4	9	8	6	12*	11	10	3	12*	2	7

* = tie

Table 11: Number and Direction of Stories about Candidates and Issues in the Atlanta *Constitution*, 1984

	Mondale			*Ferraro*			*Democrats*			*Reagan*			*Bush*			*Republicans*			
	+	-	0	+	-	0	+	-	0	+	-	0	+	-	0	+	-	0	*N
Politics, Government	33	4	3	6	3	3	2	1	0	20	10	5	1	0	1	0	1	0	32
War, Defense, Diplomacy	6	0	1	0	0	0	0	0	0	1	3	3	1	0	0	0	0	0	3
Economic Activity	1	0	2	1	0	0	0	0	0	4	9	2	0	0	0	0	0	0	6
Crime	0	0	0	1	0	0	0	0	0	0	0	2	0	0	0	0	0	0	0
Public Moral Problems	0	0	0	1	1	0	0	0	0	1	1	1	0	0	0	0	0	0	2
Public Health, Welfare	1	0	0	0	1	0	0	0	0	0	0	0	0	0	0	0	0	0	0
Accidents, Disasters	0	0	0	0	0	0	0	0	0	0	0	0	0	0	0	0	0	0	0
Science, Invention	0	0	0	0	0	0	0	0	0	0	0	0	0	0	0	0	0	0	0
Education, Classic Arts	2	0	0	0	0	0	1	0	0	1	0	0	0	0	0	0	0	0	0
Recreation, Media	0	0	0	0	0	0	0	0	0	0	0	1	0	0	0	0	0	0	2
Human Interest	0	0	0	0	0	0	0	0	0	0	0	0	0	0	0	0	0	0	0
Strength of Candidate	20	4	2	4	6	1	2	0	0	14	6	0	0	0	0	0	0	0	6
Horserace	0	0	0	0	0	0	0	0	0	1	0	0	0	0	0	0	0	0	0
Total	**63**	**8**	**8**	**13**	**11**	**4**	**5**	**1**	**0**	**42**	**29**	**14**	**2**	**0**	**1**	**0**	**1**	**0**	**51**

+ = Favorable - = Unfavorable 0 = Neutral

*N = Neutral stories

Table 12: Number and Direction of Stories about Candidates and Issues in the Atlanta *Constitution*, 1988

	Dukakis			*Bentsen*			*Democrats*			*Bush*			*Quayle*			*Republicans*			
	+	-	0	+	-	0	+	-	0	+	-	0	+	-	0	+	-	0	*N
Politics, Government	23	8	0	2	0	0	5	0	4	19	10	1	2	0	0	2	6	0	50
War, Defense, Diplomacy	9	3	0	0	0	0	0	0	0	9	2	0	0	0	0	1	0	0	2
Economic Activity	13	0	0	0	0	0	0	0	0	1	0	0	0	0	0	0	0	0	1
Crime	2	0	0	0	0	0	0	0	0	1	2	0	0	0	0	1	1	0	0
Public Moral Problems	1	1	0	0	0	0	1	1	0	3	1	0	0	0	0	0	0	0	4
Public Health, Welfare	6	2	0	1	0	0	0	0	0	4	1	0	0	1	0	0	0	0	4
Accidents, Disasters	0	0	0	0	0	0	0	0	0	0	0	0	0	0	0	0	0	0	0
Science, Invention	0	0	0	0	0	0	0	0	0	0	0	0	0	0	0	1	0	0	3
Education, Classic Arts	2	0	0	2	0	0	0	0	0	2	0	0	0	1	0	0	0	1	2
Recreation, Media	6	2	0	0	0	0	2	0	0	4	1	0	0	2	0	0	0	0	6
Human Interest	1	0	0	0	0	0	0	0	0	0	0	0	0	0	0	0	0	0	0
Strength of Candidate	32	14	0	0	0	0	2	0	0	17	7	2	8	7	0	4	3	2	5
Horserace	1	2	0	0	0	0	0	0	0	20	0	0	0	0	0	0	1	0	1
Total	**96**	**32**	**0**	**5**	**0**	**0**	**10**	**1**	**4**	**80**	**24**	**4**	**10**	**11**	**0**	**9**	**11**	**3**	**78**

+ = Favorable - = Unfavorable 0 = Neutral
*N = Neutral stories

Table 13: Number and Direction of Stories about Candidates and Issues in the Baltimore *Sun*, 1984

	Mondale			*Ferraro*			*Democrats*			*Reagan*			*Bush*			*Republicans*			
	+	-	**0**	+	-	**0**	+	-	**0**	+	-	**0**	+	-	**0**	+	-	**0**	*N
Politics, Government	34	12	1	11	0	0	7	1	0	27	6	5	4	2	0	6	1	0	18
War, Defense, Diplomacy	11	3	2	4	0	0	0	0	0	6	10	2	1	0	0	0	0	0	2
Economic Activity	1	3	1	0	0	0	0	0	0	0	2	1	0	0	0	0	0	0	0
Crime	1	0	0	0	0	0	0	0	0	0	0	0	0	0	0	0	0	0	0
Public Moral Problems	0	1	0	1	7	0	0	1	0	0	0	0	0	1	0	0	0	0	0
Public Health, Welfare	4	0	0	0	0	0	0	0	0	2	0	0	0	0	0	0	0	0	0
Accidents, Disasters	0	0	0	0	0	0	0	0	0	0	0	0	0	0	0	0	0	0	0
Science, Invention	0	0	0	0	0	0	0	0	0	0	0	0	0	0	0	0	0	0	0
Education, Classic Arts	2	0	0	0	0	1	0	0	1	3	3	0	0	0	0	0	0	0	0
Recreation, Media	0	0	0	0	0	0	0	0	0	0	0	0	0	0	0	0	0	0	0
Human Interest	1	0	0	0	0	0	0	0	0	2	0	1	0	0	0	0	0	0	0
Strength of Candidate	17	15	2	8	3	0	0	1	0	21	26	2	4	3	0	0	1	0	2
Horserace	3	3	0	0	0	0	0	0	0	11	0	0	0	0	0	0	1	0	0
Total	**74**	**22**	**4**	**24**	**10**	**1**	**7**	**3**	**1**	**72**	**47**	**11**	**9**	**6**	**0**	**6**	**3**	**0**	**22**

+ = Favorable - = Unfavorable 0 = Neutral
*N = Neutral stories

Table 14: Number and Direction of Stories about Candidates and Issues in the Baltimore *Sun*, 1988

	Dukakis			*Bentsen*			*Democrats*			*Bush*			*Quayle*			*Republicans*			
	+	-	0	+	-	0	+	-	0	+	-	0	+	-	0	+	-	0	*N
Politics, Government	37	20	0	2	0	0	7	5	1	34	19	3	6	1	0	7	8	2	70
War, Defense, Diplomacy	15	5	0	1	0	0	0	0	0	23	3	1	3	0	0	0	1	0	6
Economic Activity	12	5	0	1	0	0	0	0	0	14	4	0	3	1	0	0	2	0	7
Crime	3	5	0	0	0	0	0	0	0	6	5	0	0	0	0	0	0	0	2
Public Moral Problems	1	1	0	1	0	0	0	0	1	8	1	0	3	1	0	3	0	0	2
Public Health, Welfare	12	9	1	0	0	0	1	0	0	11	11	0	0	0	0	0	1	0	0
Accidents, Disasters	0	0	0	0	0	0	0	0	0	0	0	0	0	0	0	0	0	0	0
Science, Invention	0	0	0	0	0	0	0	0	0	1	0	0	0	0	0	0	0	0	0
Education, Classic Arts	3	1	0	1	0	0	0	0	0	2	0	0	0	0	0	0	0	0	2
Recreation, Media	8	4	0	1	0	0	2	0	0	8	4	0	0	2	0	1	0	0	8
Human Interest	0	0	0	0	0	0	0	0	0	1	0	0	1	0	0	0	0	0	2
Strength of Candidate	51	24	0	3	1	0	8	2	1	38	25	2	15	23	1	5	2	0	14
Horserace	5	2	0	1	0	0	1	0	0	35	0	0	0	0	0	0	0	0	5
Total	**147**	**76**	**1**	**13**	**1**	**0**	**19**	**7**	**3**	**181**	**72**	**4**	**31**	**28**	**1**	**16**	**14**	**2**	**118**

+ = Favorable - = Unfavorable 0 = Neutral

*N = Neutral stories

1988 as it did in 1984. Although the major emphasis remained on politics and government and candidate strength, the *Sun* greatly increased the number of stories on economic activity, public health and welfare, and horserace. Its coverage of all candidates was clearly favorable, with Bentsen leading by a 13-1 margin.

The Chicago *Tribune* (Tables 15 and 16) had 74 percent of its stories about politics and government and candidate strength in 1984. Those items remained the top categories in 1988 but accounted for only 65 percent of the stories. The *Tribune* gave favorable coverage to all candidates, including 100 percent favorable coverage of Bentsen.

The *Christian Science Monitor* (Tables 17 and 18) had 71 percent of its coverage about politics and government and candidate strength and 10 percent about war, defense, and diplomacy in 1984. Politics and government and candidate strength remained in the top categories in 1988 but accounted for only 51 percent of the stories. Coverage of economic activity and public health and welfare was substantially greater in 1988 than in 1984. The *Monitor* had a greater emphasis on the presidential candidates as opposed to the vice presidential candidates than most papers. Its coverage of all candidates except Quayle was favorable. For Quayle, there were two favorable and two unfavorable stories.

The Dallas *Morning News* (Tables 19 and 20) had more emphasis on economic activity and war, defense, and diplomacy than most papers in 1984 but did have 55 percent on politics and government and candidate strength. In 1988 the *News* was one of three papers to give more coverage to candidate strength than to any other issue. It still had considerable coverage of economic activity and a substantial increase in the number of stories about public heath and welfare. The *News* gave unfavorable coverage to both Republican candidates for vice president but otherwise covered candidates favorably.

The Des Moines *Register* (Tables 21 and 22) had the second smallest percentage of stories on politics and government in 1984 (40 percent) and tied with the Los Angeles *Times* for the smallest percentage about candidate strength (14 percent). It had an even smaller percentage on politics and government in 1988 (32 percent) but much more on candidate strength (26 percent). That still left the *Register* with a lot of stories on other issues in both years. Economic activity was the one issue that the *Register* focused on most for the two years combined. The *Register* gave favorable coverage to the Democratic candidates both years. It had five favorable and five unfavorable stories about Bush in 1984 and more unfavorable than

Table 15: Number and Direction of Stories about Candidates and Issues in the Chicago *Tribune*, 1984

	Mondale			*Ferraro*			*Democrats*			*Reagan*			*Bush*			*Republicans*			
	+	-	0	+	-	0	+	-	0	+	-	0	+	-	0	+	-	0	*N
Politics, Government	56	5	3	23	2	2	4	0	0	48	3	3	10	1	0	0	0	1	47
War, Defense, Diplomacy	9	0	0	1	0	0	0	0	0	10	4	0	0	1	0	0	0	0	0
Economic Activity	3	0	0	0	0	0	0	0	0	7	6	1	0	0	0	0	0	0	5
Crime	0	0	0	0	0	0	0	0	0	0	0	0	0	0	0	0	0	0	1
Public Moral Problems	0	0	0	1	1	1	0	0	0	0	3	0	1	0	0	0	0	0	1
Public Health, Welfare	0	0	0	0	0	0	0	0	0	1	0	0	0	0	0	0	0	0	0
Accidents, Disasters	0	0	0	0	0	0	0	0	0	0	1	0	0	0	0	0	0	0	0
Science, Invention	0	0	0	0	0	0	0	0	0	0	0	0	0	0	0	0	0	0	0
Education, Classic Arts	1	0	0	0	0	0	0	0	0	0	0	0	0	0	0	0	0	0	1
Recreation, Media	0	0	0	0	0	1	0	0	0	0	1	0	0	0	0	0	0	0	1
Human Interest	1	0	0	0	0	0	0	0	0	1	0	0	0	0	0	0	0	1	1
Strength of Candidate	11	6	1	7	2	0	0	0	0	20	0	3	0	0	1	5	1	0	5
Horserace	1	10	0	0	0	0	0	0	0	12	1	0	0	0	0	0	0	0	7
Total	**82**	**21**	**4**	**32**	**5**	**4**	**4**	**0**	**0**	**99**	**19**	**7**	**11**	**2**	**1**	**5**	**1**	**2**	**69**

+ = Favorable - = Unfavorable 0 = Neutral

*N = Neutral stories

Table 16: Number and Direction of Stories about Candidates and Issues in the Chicago *Tribune*, 1988

	Dukakis			*Bentsen*			*Democrats*			*Bush*			*Quayle*			*Republicans*			
	+	-	0	+	-	0	+	-	0	+	-	0	+	-	0	+	-	0	*N
Politics, Government	17	8	2	6	0	0	10	7	1	14	2	2	7	0	2	13	9	1	50
War, Defense, Diplomacy	6	3	0	0	0	0	0	1	0	9	0	1	0	0	0	0	0	0	3
Economic Activity	10	2	0	0	0	0	1	0	0	7	2	0	1	0	0	0	2	0	3
Crime	6	0	0	0	0	0	0	0	0	3	0	0	0	0	0	0	0	0	0
Public Moral Problems	2	3	0	0	0	0	0	0	0	2	0	0	0	0	0	0	3	0	2
Public Health, Welfare	7	1	0	0	0	0	0	0	0	0	2	0	0	0	0	0	0	0	2
Accidents, Disasters	0	0	0	0	0	0	1	0	0	0	0	0	0	0	0	0	0	0	0
Science, Invention	0	0	0	0	0	0	0	0	0	0	0	0	0	0	0	0	0	0	0
Education, Classic Arts	4	0	0	0	0	0	0	0	0	0	0	0	0	0	0	1	0	0	0
Recreation, Media	1	1	2	0	0	0	0	1	1	2	1	0	1	1	2	0	0	1	22
Human Interest	0	1	0	0	0	0	0	0	0	0	0	1	1	0	0	0	0	0	0
Strength of Candidate	22	9	0	5	0	0	0	0	0	21	7	0	9	12	1	2	5	0	18
Horserace	0	0	0	0	0	0	0	0	0	8	0	0	0	0	0	0	0	0	2
Total	**75**	**28**	**4**	**11**	**0**	**0**	**12**	**9**	**2**	**66**	**14**	**4**	**19**	**13**	**5**	**16**	**19**	**2**	**102**

+ = Favorable - = Unfavorable 0 = Neutral
*N = Neutral stories

Table 17: Number and Direction of Stories about Candidates and Issues in the *Christian Science Monitor*, 1984

	Mondale			*Ferraro*			*Democrats*			*Reagan*			*Bush*			*Republicans*			
	+	-	0	+	-	0	+	-	0	+	-	0	+	-	0	+	-	0	*N
Politics, Government	21	5	6	2	0	2	0	1	0	16	5	12	2	0	1	0	0	0	13
War, Defense, Diplomacy	4	0	0	1	0	0	0	0	0	3	1	1	0	0	0	0	0	0	7
Economic Activity	1	0	1	0	0	0	0	0	0	2	1	0	0	0	0	0	0	0	3
Crime	0	0	1	0	0	0	0	0	0	0	0	0	0	0	0	0	0	0	2
Public Moral Problems	0	0	2	0	1	1	0	0	0	0	0	3	0	0	0	0	0	0	0
Public Health, Welfare	0	0	0	0	0	0	0	0	0	0	1	0	0	0	0	0	0	0	2
Accidents, Disasters	0	0	0	0	0	0	0	0	0	0	0	0	0	0	0	0	0	0	0
Science, Invention	0	0	0	0	0	0	0	0	0	2	0	0	0	0	0	0	0	0	2
Education, Classic Arts	0	0	0	0	0	0	0	0	0	0	0	0	0	0	0	0	0	0	2
Recreation, Media	0	0	0	0	0	0	0	0	0	0	0	0	0	0	0	0	0	0	1
Human Interest	0	0	0	0	0	0	0	0	0	0	0	0	0	0	0	0	0	0	0
Strength of Candidate	4	7	4	1	2	0	2	0	0	12	1	0	3	1	0	2	0	0	1
Horserace	1	1	0	0	0	1	0	0	0	2	0	0	0	0	0	0	0	0	1
Total	**31**	**13**	**14**	**4**	**3**	**4**	**2**	**1**	**0**	**37**	**9**	**16**	**5**	**1**	**1**	**2**	**0**	**0**	**34**

+ = Favorable - = Unfavorable 0 = Neutral

*N = Neutral stories

Table 18: Number and Direction of Stories about Candidates and Issues in the *Christian Science Monitor*, 1988

	Dukakis			*Bentsen*			*Democrats*			*Bush*			*Quayle*			*Republicans*			
	+	-	**0**	+	-	**0**	+	-	**0**	+	-	**0**	+	-	**0**	+	-	**0**	***N**
Politics, Government	19	2	0	0	0	0	10	1	0	5	0	0	0	1	0	4	2	0	25
War, Defense, Diplomacy	4	0	0	0	0	0	0	0	0	5	0	0	0	0	0	0	0	0	6
Economic Activity	3	0	0	0	0	0	0	0	0	9	1	0	0	0	0	0	0	0	11
Crime	0	0	0	0	0	0	0	0	0	1	1	0	0	0	0	0	0	0	1
Public Moral Problems	1	2	0	0	0	0	0	0	0	2	0	0	0	0	0	0	0	0	4
Public Health, Welfare	9	3	0	0	0	0	0	0	0	5	2	0	0	0	0	0	0	0	5
Accidents, Disasters	0	0	0	0	0	0	0	0	0	0	0	0	0	0	0	0	0	0	0
Science, Invention	0	0	0	0	0	0	0	0	0	0	0	0	0	0	0	0	0	0	2
Education, Classic Arts	2	0	0	0	0	0	0	0	0	2	0	0	0	0	0	0	0	0	1
Recreation, Media	2	0	0	0	0	0	0	0	0	0	1	0	0	0	0	0	0	0	2
Human Interest	0	0	0	0	0	0	0	0	0	0	0	0	0	0	0	0	0	0	0
Strength of Candidate	4	7	0	3	0	0	1	1	0	10	3	0	2	1	0	1	0	0	7
Horserace	0	3	0	0	0	0	0	0	0	11	0	0	0	0	0	0	0	0	2
Total	**44**	**17**	**0**	**3**	**0**	**0**	**11**	**2**	**0**	**50**	**8**	**0**	**2**	**2**	**0**	**5**	**3**	**0**	**66**

+ = Favorable - = Unfavorable 0 = Neutral
*N = Neutral stories

Table 19: Number and Direction of Stories about Candidates and Issues in the Dallas *Morning News*, 1984

	Mondale			*Ferraro*			*Democrats*			*Reagan*			*Bush*			*Republicans*			
	+	-	0	+	-	0	+	-	0	+	-	0	+	-	0	+	-	0	*N
Politics, Government	17	6	10	3	1	1	4	3	2	19	10	3	2	1	2	8	2	1	35
War, Defense, Diplomacy	3	1	2	0	0	0	0	0	0	7	17	1	0	0	0	0	0	0	5
Economic Activity	8	4	2	0	1	0	1	0	0	6	9	0	0	0	0	0	0	0	5
Crime	1	0	0	0	0	0	0	0	0	0	0	0	0	0	0	0	0	0	0
Public Moral Problems	2	0	0	2	0	3	0	0	0	0	1	0	1	0	0	0	0	0	1
Public Health, Welfare	0	0	0	0	0	0	0	0	0	0	1	0	0	0	0	0	0	0	1
Accidents, Disasters	0	0	0	0	0	0	0	0	0	0	0	0	0	0	0	0	0	0	0
Science, Invention	0	0	0	0	0	0	0	0	0	0	1	0	0	0	0	0	0	0	0
Education, Classic Arts	0	1	0	0	0	0	0	0	0	2	1	1	0	0	0	0	0	0	2
Recreation, Media	2	2	0	0	0	0	6	0	1	2	0	0	0	0	1	1	1	0	1
Human Interest	0	1	0	2	0	0	0	0	0	0	0	0	0	0	0	0	0	0	0
Strength of Candidate	3	2	0	2	3	3	0	0	0	5	8	0	0	8	4	0	0	0	7
Horserace	3	2	0	0	0	0	0	0	0	15	3	0	0	0	0	0	0	0	3
Total	**39**	**19**	**14**	**9**	**5**	**7**	**11**	**3**	**3**	**56**	**51**	**5**	**3**	**9**	**7**	**9**	**3**	**1**	**60**

+ = Favorable - = Unfavorable 0 = Neutral
*N = Neutral stories

Table 20: Number and Direction of Stories about Candidates and Issues in the Dallas *Morning News*, 1988

	Dukakis			*Bentsen*			*Democrats*			*Bush*			*Quayle*			*Republicans*			
	+	-	0	+	-	0	+	-	0	+	-	0	+	-	0	+	-	0	*N
Politics, Government	18	7	0	7	1	1	7	6	0	8	0	0	6	1	0	8	4	1	64
War, Defense, Diplomacy	6	3	0	2	0	0	3	1	0	4	1	0	0	0	0	0	1	0	4
Economic Activity	8	4	0	6	1	0	0	1	0	6	2	0	0	1	0	0	1	0	7
Crime	3	2	0	0	0	0	0	0	0	3	1	0	0	1	0	0	0	0	2
Public Moral Problems	4	5	0	0	0	0	0	0	0	2	2	0	0	1	0	0	1	0	0
Public Health, Welfare	8	2	0	2	0	0	0	0	0	4	0	0	1	0	0	3	1	0	4
Accidents, Disasters	1	0	0	0	0	0	0	0	0	0	0	0	0	0	0	0	0	0	0
Science, Invention	1	0	0	1	0	0	0	0	0	1	0	0	0	0	0	0	0	0	2
Education, Classic Arts	0	0	0	0	0	0	0	0	0	0	0	0	0	0	0	0	1	0	1
Recreation, Media	3	2	0	0	0	0	0	1	0	3	0	0	0	0	0	1	1	0	8
Human Interest	0	0	0	0	0	0	0	0	0	0	0	0	0	0	0	0	0	0	0
Strength of Candidate	25	16	0	16	8	1	4	2	0	23	12	1	9	13	2	5	1	0	23
Horserace	0	2	0	1	0	0	0	0	0	28	0	0	1	0	0	0	0	0	1
Total	**77**	**43**	**0**	**35**	**10**	**2**	**14**	**11**	**0**	**82**	**18**	**1**	**17**	**17**	**2**	**17**	**11**	**1**	**116**

+ = Favorable - = Unfavorable 0 = Neutral
*N = Neutral stories

Table 21: Number and Direction of Stories about Candidates and Issues in the Des Moines *Register*, 1984

	Mondale			*Ferraro*			*Democrats*			*Reagan*			*Bush*			*Republicans*			
	+	-	0	+	-	0	+	-	0	+	-	0	+	-	0	+	-	0	*N
Politics, Government	10	8	2	10	2	1	0	0	0	24	8	3	2	1	2	4	1	0	18
War, Defense, Diplomacy	3	2	0	0	0	0	0	0	0	6	3	0	0	0	0	0	1	0	0
Economic Activity	14	2	0	0	1	0	0	0	0	9	5	0	1	0	0	1	0	0	6
Crime	0	0	0	0	0	0	0	0	0	0	0	0	0	0	0	0	0	0	3
Public Moral Problems	6	0	0	1	2	0	0	0	0	0	0	0	0	0	0	0	0	0	0
Public Health, Welfare	0	1	0	0	0	0	0	0	0	0	1	0	0	0	0	0	0	0	0
Accidents, Disasters	0	0	0	0	0	0	0	0	0	0	0	0	0	0	0	0	0	0	0
Science, Invention	0	0	0	0	0	0	0	0	0	0	0	0	0	0	0	0	0	0	0
Education, Classic Arts	0	0	0	1	0	0	0	0	0	2	1	0	1	0	0	0	0	0	0
Recreation, Media	0	2	1	0	0	0	0	0	0	5	2	0	1	0	0	0	0	0	2
Human Interest	0	0	3	0	0	2	1	0	0	2	1	1	0	0	1	0	0	0	1
Strength of Candidate	1	3	1	2	3	2	0	0	0	1	9	2	0	4	1	0	0	0	5
Horserace	2	0	0	0	0	0	0	0	0	9	0	0	0	0	0	0	0	0	0
Total	**36**	**18**	**7**	**14**	**8**	**5**	**1**	**0**	**0**	**58**	**30**	**6**	**5**	**5**	**4**	**5**	**2**	**0**	**35**

+ = Favorable - = Unfavorable 0 = Neutral

*N = Neutral stories

Table 22: Number and Direction of Stories about Candidates and Issues in the Des Moines *Register*, 1988

	Dukakis			*Bentsen*			*Democrats*			*Bush*			*Quayle*			*Republicans*			
	+	-	0	+	-	0	+	-	0	+	-	0	+	-	0	+	-	0	*N
Politics, Government	13	5	1	1	0	0	7	2	1	11	5	2	5	1	0	10	12	2	70
War, Defense, Diplomacy	7	0	0	1	0	0	0	1	0	5	0	0	3	0	0	1	1	0	4
Economic Activity	11	5	0	2	0	0	1	1	0	7	4	0	1	0	0	0	1	0	6
Crime	3	1	0	0	1	0	0	0	0	2	3	0	0	0	0	0	0	0	0
Public Moral Problems	0	2	0	0	0	0	0	0	0	3	7	0	1	1	0	0	0	0	1
Public Health, Welfare	5	1	0	0	0	0	2	0	0	3	4	0	0	0	0	0	0	0	1
Accidents, Disasters	0	0	0	0	0	0	0	0	0	0	0	0	0	0	0	0	0	0	0
Science, Invention	0	0	0	1	0	0	0	0	0	1	0	0	0	0	0	0	0	0	0
Education, Classic Arts	1	0	0	1	0	0	0	0	0	0	0	0	0	0	0	0	0	0	2
Recreation, Media	3	0	0	0	0	0	1	1	0	6	2	0	0	1	1	1	4	0	11
Human Interest	0	0	0	0	0	0	0	0	0	0	0	0	1	0	0	1	0	0	0
Strength of Candidate	28	11	0	6	0	1	6	0	0	26	9	0	5	19	0	3	1	0	9
Horserace	4	3	0	0	0	0	0	0	0	40	0	0	0	0	0	0	0	0	2
Total	**75**	**28**	**1**	**12**	**1**	**1**	**17**	**5**	**1**	**104**	**34**	**2**	**16**	**22**	**1**	**16**	**19**	**2**	**106**

+ = Favorable - = Unfavorable 0 = Neutral

*N = Neutral stories

favorable stories about Quayle. Its coverage of Bush in 1988, however, was more favorable than was its coverage of Reagan in 1984.

The Kansas City *Star* (Tables 23 and 24) had 78 percent of its stories about politics and government and candidate strength in 1984 and therefore had little coverage of anything else. It had more than twice as many stories in 1988 as it did in 1984, with marked increases in the number of stories about economic activity, public moral problems, public health and welfare, science and invention, and recreation and mass media. Its coverage of Quayle was slightly unfavorable, but its coverage of all other candidates in both years was favorable.

The Los Angeles *Times* (Tables 25 and 26) had 70 percent of its coverage about politics and government and candidate strength in 1984. Those categories still led in 1988 but accounted for only 55 percent of the total. It had a marked increase in coverage of economic activity, public moral problems, and popular arts and amusements. Its coverage of all candidates was favorable. Mondale, however, got substantially more favorable coverage than Dukakis did, whereas Bush got more favorable than Reagan did.

The Louisville *Courier-Journal* (Tables 27 and 28) had a smaller proportion of politics and government stories than most of the other papers both years, but still was the leading category. The *Courier-Journal* was the only paper in 1984 in which war, defense, and diplomacy was the second most frequent category, but in 1988 the *Courier-Journal*'s emphasis shifted, with war, defense, and diplomacy fifth. Candidate strength and horserace were the second and third most frequent categories. In 1984 the *Courier-Journal* had more unfavorable than favorable stories about three of the four candidates, but in 1988 it had more favorable than unfavorable stories about all four candidates.

The Miami *Herald* (Tables 29 and 30) gave more emphasis to war, defense, and diplomacy than most papers did in 1984. Most of these stories were about Reagan, and most were unfavorable. It had highly favorable coverage of Reagan on economic activity, however. Politics and government and strength of candidate were the two most frequent topics. That was still true in 1988, but recreation and mass media and public health and welfare were the objects of considerably more stories in 1988 than they had been in 1984. Coverage of all four candidates was favorable in 1984, but the coverage of Quayle was unfavorable in 19988. Furthermore, only a 20-0 margin in horserace stories kept the coverage of Bush from being unfavorable.

Table 23: Number and Direction of Stories about Candidates and Issues in the Kansas City *Star*, 1984

	Mondale			*Ferraro*			*Democrats*			*Reagan*			*Bush*			*Republicans*			
	+	-	0	+	-	0	+	-	0	+	-	0	+	-	0	+	-	0	*N
Politics, Government	16	3	4	2	1	3	2	0	1	9	5	3	1	0	0	2	0	0	29
War, Defense, Diplomacy	0	0	0	1	0	0	0	0	0	3	0	0	1	0	0	0	0	0	0
Economic Activity	3	0	1	0	0	0	0	0	0	0	1	0	0	0	0	0	0	0	1
Crime	0	0	0	0	0	0	0	0	0	0	0	0	0	0	0	0	0	0	0
Public Moral Problems	0	0	0	1	0	0	0	0	0	1	0	0	0	0	0	0	0	0	0
Public Health, Welfare	1	1	0	0	0	0	0	0	0	0	0	0	0	0	0	0	0	0	1
Accidents, Disasters	0	0	0	0	0	0	0	0	0	0	0	0	0	0	0	0	0	0	0
Science, Invention	0	0	0	0	0	0	0	0	0	0	0	0	0	0	0	0	0	0	0
Education, Classic Arts	0	0	0	0	0	0	0	0	0	2	0	1	0	0	0	0	0	0	0
Recreation, Media	0	0	0	0	0	0	0	0	0	0	0	0	0	0	0	0	0	0	0
Human Interest	2	0	0	1	0	0	0	0	0	1	0	0	0	0	0	0	0	0	0
Strength of Candidate	7	2	0	2	0	0	0	0	0	5	0	0	2	1	0	0	0	0	1
Horserace	2	0	0	0	0	0	0	0	0	4	0	0	0	0	0	0	0	0	2
Total	**31**	**6**	**5**	**7**	**1**	**3**	**2**	**0**	**1**	**25**	**6**	**4**	**4**	**1**	**0**	**2**	**0**	**0**	**34**

+ = Favorable - = Unfavorable 0 = Neutral

*N = Neutral stories

Table 24: Number and Direction of Stories about Candidates and Issues in the Kansas City *Star*, 1988

	Dukakis			*Bentsen*			*Democrats*			*Bush*			*Quayle*			*Republicans*			
	+	-	**0**	+	-	**0**	+	-	**0**	+	-	**0**	+	-	**0**	+	-	**0**	***N**
Politics, Government	19	3	0	4	1	0	10	1	0	8	2	1	5	0	0	9	6	0	49
War, Defense, Diplomacy	5	0	0	1	0	0	0	0	0	3	1	0	1	0	0	0	0	0	1
Economic Activity	3	2	1	1	0	0	0	0	0	4	1	0	1	0	0	3	2	0	4
Crime	1	0	0	0	0	0	0	0	0	2	1	0	0	0	0	0	0	0	2
Public Moral Problems	3	1	0	1	0	0	0	0	0	3	1	0	0	0	0	0	0	0	7
Public Health, Welfare	3	2	0	0	0	0	1	0	0	6	2	0	0	0	0	0	1	0	0
Accidents, Disasters	0	0	0	0	0	0	0	0	0	0	0	0	0	0	0	0	0	0	0
Science, Invention	4	0	0	0	0	0	0	0	0	3	0	0	0	0	0	0	0	0	3
Education, Classic Arts	3	0	0	0	0	0	0	0	0	2	0	0	0	0	0	1	0	0	2
Recreation, Media	0	1	0	2	0	0	0	0	0	1	0	0	0	1	0	0	0	0	13
Human Interest	0	0	0	0	0	0	0	0	0	0	0	0	0	0	0	0	0	0	0
Strength of Candidate	10	2	0	3	0	0	3	0	2	5	2	0	1	9	0	2	0	0	9
Horserace	0	3	0	0	0	0	0	0	0	21	0	0	0	1	0	0	0	0	1
Total	**51**	**14**	**1**	**12**	**1**	**0**	**14**	**1**	**2**	**58**	**10**	**1**	**8**	**11**	**0**	**15**	**9**	**0**	**91**

\+ = Favorable - = Unfavorable 0 = Neutral
*N = Neutral stories

Table 25: Number and Direction of Stories about Candidates and Issues in the Los Angeles *Times*, 1984

	Mondale			*Ferraro*			*Democrats*			*Reagan*			*Bush*			*Republicans*			
	+	-	0	+	-	0	+	-	0	+	-	0	+	-	0	+	-	0	*N
Politics, Government	61	8	20	25	1	6	9	0	1	27	11	18	8	1	5	8	2	2	38
War, Defense, Diplomacy	15	1	0	2	0	0	0	1	0	17	8	5	1	0	0	0	0	0	3
Economic Activity	5	6	2	3	0	0	0	0	0	4	4	0	0	0	0	1	1	0	2
Crime	0	0	0	0	0	0	0	0	0	4	0	0	0	0	0	0	0	0	0
Public Moral Problems	1	0	0	0	2	0	0	2	0	0	2	0	0	0	0	0	0	0	2
Public Health, Welfare	1	0	0	0	1	0	0	0	0	1	2	0	0	0	0	0	0	0	0
Accidents, Disasters	3	0	0	0	0	0	0	0	0	0	4	0	0	0	0	0	1	0	0
Science, Invention	0	0	0	0	0	0	0	0	0	0	0	0	0	0	0	0	0	0	0
Education, Classic Arts	0	1	0	0	0	1	0	0	0	2	0	0	1	0	0	1	0	0	1
Recreation, Media	0	0	0	0	0	0	0	0	0	1	0	0	0	0	0	0	0	0	1
Human Interest	0	0	0	0	0	0	0	0	0	1	1	1	0	0	0	0	0	0	1
Strength of Candidate	9	2	2	7	1	3	2	0	0	15	10	0	4	1	0	2	0	0	3
Horserace	3	2	0	0	0	0	0	0	0	7	4	0	0	0	0	1	0	0	1
Total	**98**	**20**	**24**	**37**	**4**	**10**	**11**	**4**	**1**	**79**	**46**	**24**	**14**	**2**	**5**	**13**	**4**	**2**	**52**

+ = Favorable - = Unfavorable 0 = Neutral

*N = Neutral stories

Table 26: Number and Direction of Stories about Candidates and Issues in the Los Angeles *Times*, 1988

	Dukakis			*Bentsen*			*Democrats*			*Bush*			*Quayle*			*Republicans*			
	+	-	0	+	-	0	+	-	0	+	-	0	+	-	0	+	-	0	*N
Politics, Government	55	6	0	18	0	0	0	0	0	50	7	0	18	0	0	10	2	0	54
War, Defense, Diplomacy	6	4	0	2	0	0	0	1	0	7	3	0	2	0	0	2	0	0	12
Economic Activity	16	8	0	4	0	0	0	0	0	13	5	0	5	1	0	3	0	0	11
Crime	4	4	0	0	0	0	0	0	0	4	2	0	0	0	0	0	0	0	1
Public Moral Problems	5	4	0	1	0	0	0	0	0	5	14	0	1	0	0	0	1	0	3
Public Health, Welfare	1	1	0	0	0	0	0	0	0	1	1	0	0	0	0	1	0	0	5
Accidents, Disasters	0	0	0	0	0	0	0	0	0	0	0	0	0	0	0	0	0	0	0
Science, Invention	1	0	0	0	0	0	0	0	0	1	0	0	0	0	0	0	0	0	0
Education, Classic Arts	2	0	0	0	0	0	0	0	0	0	1	0	0	0	0	1	0	0	1
Recreation, Media	5	3	0	0	0	0	0	0	0	5	0	0	2	1	0	0	0	0	19
Human Interest	3	0	0	3	0	0	3	0	0	1	0	0	0	0	0	0	0	0	4
Strength of Candidate	23	15	0	2	1	0	4	0	0	19	2	0	16	10	0	4	1	0	19
Horserace	6	3	0	0	0	0	2	1	0	19	0	0	0	1	0	1	0	0	14
Total	**127**	**48**	**0**	**30**	**1**	**0**	**9**	**2**	**0**	**125**	**35**	**0**	**44**	**13**	**0**	**22**	**4**	**0**	**143**

+ = Favorable - = Unfavorable 0 = Neutral

*N = Neutral stories

Table 27: Number and Direction of Stories about Candidates and Issues in the Louisville *Courier-Journal*, 1984

	Mondale			*Ferraro*			*Democrats*			*Reagan*			*Bush*			*Republicans*			
	+	-	0	+	-	0	+	-	0	+	-	0	+	-	0	+	-	0	*N
Politics, Government	17	6	1	1	3	1	4	3	0	17	12	2	1	0	0	6	1	0	23
War, Defense, Diplomacy	3	4	0	0	1	0	0	0	0	10	22	0	0	3	0	0	0	0	0
Economic Activity	2	6	0	0	0	0	0	2	0	2	4	0	0	2	0	1	0	0	0
Crime	0	0	0	0	0	0	0	0	0	1	0	0	0	0	0	0	0	0	0
Public Moral Problems	2	0	0	2	2	1	1	1	0	1	5	0	0	0	0	0	0	0	0
Public Health, Welfare	1	0	1	0	0	0	0	0	0	2	5	0	0	1	0	0	0	0	0
Accidents, Disasters	0	0	0	0	0	0	0	0	0	0	0	0	0	0	0	0	0	0	0
Science, Invention	0	0	0	0	0	0	0	0	0	0	2	0	0	0	0	0	0	0	0
Education, Classic Arts	1	0	0	0	3	0	0	0	0	4	5	0	1	0	0	0	1	0	0
Recreation, Media	0	0	0	0	0	0	0	1	0	0	0	0	0	0	0	0	0	0	1
Human Interest	0	0	0	0	0	0	0	0	0	0	0	0	0	0	0	0	0	0	0
Strength of Candidate	10	3	0	3	1	0	1	0	0	3	15	0	2	2	0	0	0	0	0
Horserace	2	0	0	1	1	0	0	0	0	5	1	0	1	0	0	2	0	0	0
Total	**38**	**19**	**2**	**7**	**11**	**2**	**6**	**7**	**0**	**45**	**71**	**2**	**5**	**8**	**0**	**9**	**2**	**0**	**24**

+ = Favorable - = Unfavorable 0 = Neutral
*N = Neutral stories

Table 28: Number and Direction of Stories about Candidates and Issues in the Louisville *Courier-Journal*, 1988

	Dukakis			*Bentsen*			*Democrats*			*Bush*			*Quayle*			*Republicans*			
	+	-	**0**	+	-	**0**	+	-	**0**	+	-	**0**	+	-	**0**	+	-	**0**	*N
Politics, Government	4	4	1	1	0	0	15	3	1	6	1	1	7	1	0	5	9	0	22
War, Defense, Diplomacy	5	2	0	0	0	0	0	2	0	5	0	1	1	0	0	1	0	0	3
Economic Activity	4	3	1	2	0	0	0	0	0	3	1	0	1	0	0	1	0	0	1
Crime	2	0	0	0	0	0	0	0	0	4	4	0	0	0	0	0	0	0	0
Public Moral Problems	1	3	0	0	0	0	0	0	0	4	2	0	0	2	0	1	1	0	0
Public Health, Welfare	7	5	0	0	0	0	1	0	0	3	3	1	0	0	0	0	0	0	1
Accidents, Disasters	0	0	0	0	0	0	0	0	0	0	0	0	0	0	1	0	0	0	0
Science, Invention	1	0	0	0	0	0	0	0	0	1	0	0	0	0	0	0	0	0	0
Education, Classic Arts	2	0	0	1	0	0	0	0	0	0	0	0	0	0	0	2	0	0	0
Recreation, Media	1	0	0	0	0	0	0	0	0	0	0	0	0	0	0	3	1	0	7
Human Interest	0	0	0	0	0	0	0	0	0	0	0	0	0	0	0	0	0	0	0
Strength of Candidate	12	7	0	2	0	0	2	1	0	12	6	0	9	7	0	5	2	0	7
Horserace	1	1	0	1	0	0	0	0	0	25	0	0	0	0	0	1	0	0	0
Total	**40**	**25**	**2**	**7**	**0**	**0**	**18**	**6**	**1**	**63**	**17**	**3**	**18**	**10**	**1**	**19**	**13**	**0**	**41**

+ = Favorable - = Unfavorable 0 = Neutral

*N = Neutral stories

Table 29: Number and Direction of Stories about Candidates and Issues in the Miami *Herald*, 1984

	Mondale			*Ferraro*			*Democrats*			*Reagan*			*Bush*			*Republicans*			
	+	-	0	+	-	0	+	-	0	+	-	0	+	-	0	+	-	0	*N
Politics, Government	23	7	1	6	4	1	3	1	1	34	19	2	3	5	2	2	4	0	31
War, Defense, Diplomacy	11	0	1	1	0	0	0	0	0	5	20	4	2	1	0	1	0	0	0
Economic Activity	2	1	0	0	0	0	1	0	0	9	3	1	0	0	0	0	0	0	1
Crime	1	0	0	0	1	0	0	0	0	0	0	0	0	0	0	0	0	0	0
Public Moral Problems	1	2	0	2	3	0	0	1	0	0	0	0	1	0	0	0	0	0	0
Public Health, Welfare	3	0	0	0	0	0	0	0	0	1	3	0	0	0	0	0	0	0	0
Accidents, Disasters	0	0	0	0	0	0	0	0	0	0	0	0	0	0	0	0	0	0	0
Science, Invention	0	0	0	0	0	0	0	0	0	0	0	0	0	0	0	0	0	0	0
Education, Classic Arts	2	0	0	0	1	0	0	0	0	2	2	1	0	0	0	0	0	1	0
Recreation, Media	2	0	2	3	0	2	0	0	0	4	3	0	0	0	0	1	0	0	1
Human Interest	1	0	0	2	1	0	0	0	0	0	2	2	0	0	0	0	0	1	1
Strength of Candidate	23	9	1	9	4	1	2	1	0	18	16	1	2	6	0	2	2	0	4
Horserace	1	0	0	0	0	0	1	0	0	23	2	0	0	0	0	0	0	0	1
Total	**70**	**19**	**5**	**23**	**14**	**4**	**7**	**3**	**1**	**96**	**70**	**11**	**8**	**12**	**2**	**6**	**6**	**2**	**39**

+ = Favorable - = Unfavorable 0 = Neutral
*N = Neutral stories

Table 30: Number and Direction of Stories about Candidates and Issues in the Miami *Herald*, 1988

	Dukakis			*Bentsen*			*Democrats*			*Bush*			*Quayle*			*Republicans*			
	+	-	0	+	-	0	+	-	0	+	-	0	+	-	0	+	-	0	*N
Politics, Government	10	8	1	4	1	0	5	7	0	16	15	0	2	3	0	12	8	0	100
War, Defense, Diplomacy	6	3	0	1	0	0	0	0	0	9	5	0	1	0	0	0	1	0	5
Economic Activity	7	1	0	3	0	0	0	0	0	4	3	0	0	0	0	0	2	0	4
Crime	4	1	1	2	0	0	0	0	0	3	3	0	0	0	0	0	3	0	2
Public Moral Problems	1	1	0	0	0	0	0	0	0	1	3	0	0	0	0	0	0	0	1
Public Health, Welfare	4	5	0	2	0	0	1	0	0	4	5	0	0	0	0	0	0	0	4
Accidents, Disasters	1	0	0	0	0	0	0	0	0	0	0	0	0	0	0	0	0	0	0
Science, Invention	0	0	0	0	0	0	0	0	0	1	0	0	0	0	0	0	0	0	0
Education, Classic Arts	2	0	0	0	0	0	0	0	0	0	0	0	0	1	0	1	0	0	0
Recreation, Media	4	4	1	0	0	0	0	0	0	2	4	0	1	0	0	0	0	1	19
Human Interest	0	0	0	0	0	0	0	0	0	3	0	0	1	0	0	0	0	0	0
Strength of Candidate	27	19	0	3	1	0	1	1	0	17	28	0	14	20	0	3	2	0	17
Horserace	1	1	0	0	0	0	0	0	0	20	0	0	2	1	0	0	0	0	5
Total	**67**	**43**	**3**	**15**	**2**	**0**	**7**	**8**	**0**	**80**	**66**	**0**	**21**	**25**	**0**	**15**	**17**	**1**	**157**

+ = Favorable - = Unfavorable 0 = Neutral
*N = Neutral stories

Sixty-two percent of the Milwaukee *Journal*'s stories (Tables 31 and 32) were about politics and government and candidate strength in 1984. Beyond that, economic activity, horserace, war, defense, and diplomacy were the only categories to get appreciable coverage. The pattern was not much different in 1988. Politics and government and candidate strength accounted for 65 percent of the stories, and the only other category besides economic activity, horserace, and war, defense, and diplomacy to receive a significant amount of coverage was public moral problems. Both vice presidential candidates in 1984 had more unfavorable than favorable coverage, but in 1988 all four candidates had more favorable than unfavorable stories.

The New York *Times* (Tables 33 and 34) had the second lowest percentage of stories on politics and government in 1984, 31 percent, but a relatively high percentage, 28 percent, on candidate strength. It had the largest number of stories on education and classic arts and numerous stories on war, defense, and diplomacy, economic activity, recreation and mass media, human interest, public moral problems, and public health and welfare. In 1988, politics and government and candidate strength again were the most frequent categories, with 33 percent and 30 percent, respectively. The major shift was considerably less coverage of education and classic arts and recreation and mass media. All candidates in both years had more favorable than unfavorable coverage, with Bentsen far ahead with twenty-two favorable stories and no unfavorable or neutral stories.

Politics and government and candidate strength were the leading categories for the Portland *Oregonian* in 1984, with 32 percent and 20 percent, respectively (Tables 35 and 36). Third was economic activity, with 18 percent, the highest figure for any of the papers. Only war, defense, and diplomacy and horserace, of the remaining categories, received substantial coverage. Politics and government and candidate strength again were the most frequent categories in 1988, but this time candidate strength was first, by 28 to 27 percent. Economic activity slopped to fourth, with 8 percent, but there was a substantial increase in public health and welfare, recreation and mass media, public moral problems, and crime. In 1984 there were more unfavorable than favorable stories about Bush, but the other three candidates all had more favorable than unfavorable stories. In 1988 all four candidates had more favorable than unfavorable stories.

The San Francisco *Chronicle* (Tables 37 and 38) had more stories on politics and government than any other category in 1984, but second place went to horserace, with 20 percent, the highest figure for

Table 31: Number and Direction of Stories about Candidates and Issues in the Milwaukee *Journal*, 1984

	Mondale			*Ferraro*			*Democrats*			*Reagan*			*Bush*			*Republicans*			
	+	-	0	+	-	0	+	-	0	+	-	0	+	-	0	+	-	0	*N
Politics, Government	18	6	1	0	0	3	1	3	7	22	12	12	1	6	1	3	5	0	10
War, Defense, Diplomacy	2	0	0	0	0	0	0	0	0	6	9	1	0	0	0	0	0	0	0
Economic Activity	6	2	0	2	2	0	0	0	0	9	5	1	0	0	0	0	0	0	3
Crime	0	1	0	0	0	0	0	0	0	0	0	0	0	0	0	0	0	0	0
Public Moral Problems	1	1	0	0	4	0	0	2	0	1	0	0	0	1	0	0	0	0	0
Public Health, Welfare	0	0	0	0	0	0	0	0	0	0	1	0	0	0	0	0	0	0	0
Accidents, Disasters	0	0	0	0	0	0	0	0	0	0	0	0	0	0	0	0	0	0	0
Science, Invention	0	0	0	0	0	0	0	0	0	1	0	0	0	0	0	0	0	0	0
Education, Classic Arts	0	0	0	0	1	0	0	1	0	0	0	0	0	0	0	0	0	0	1
Recreation, Media	0	0	0	0	0	0	0	0	0	0	0	0	0	0	1	0	0	0	0
Human Interest	0	0	0	0	0	1	0	0	0	3	0	0	0	0	0	0	0	0	0
Strength of Candidate	13	3	0	2	2	0	0	0	0	24	15	0	0	0	0	0	0	0	1
Horserace	2	2	0	0	0	0	0	0	0	10	1	0	1	0	0	0	0	0	3
Total	**42**	**15**	**1**	**4**	**9**	**4**	**1**	**5**	**7**	**76**	**43**	**14**	**2**	**7**	**2**	**3**	**5**	**0**	**18**

+ = Favorable - = Unfavorable 0 = Neutral
*N = Neutral stories

Table 32: Number and Direction of Stories about Candidates and Issues in the Milwaukee *Journal*, 1988

	Dukakis			*Bentsen*			*Democrats*			*Bush*			*Quayle*			*Republicans*			
	+	-	0	+	-	0	+	-	0	+	-	0	+	-	0	+	-	0	*N
Politics, Government	34	6	0	1	0	0	1	0	1	28	4	0	4	0	0	4	0	0	42
War, Defense, Diplomacy	3	3	0	1	0	0	0	0	0	3	2	0	2	1	0	0	0	0	1
Economic Activity	3	3	0	0	0	0	0	0	0	6	0	0	0	0	0	0	0	0	3
Crime	0	1	0	0	0	0	0	0	0	2	1	0	0	0	0	0	0	0	3
Public Moral Problems	2	1	0	0	0	0	0	1	0	2	5	0	1	1	0	0	2	0	3
Public Health, Welfare	3	1	0	0	0	0	0	0	0	2	1	0	0	0	0	0	0	0	2
Accidents, Disasters	0	0	0	0	0	0	0	0	0	0	0	0	0	0	0	0	0	0	0
Science, Invention	1	0	0	0	0	0	0	0	0	0	0	0	0	0	0	0	0	0	0
Education, Classic Arts	1	0	0	0	0	0	0	0	0	0	0	0	0	0	0	0	0	0	0
Recreation, Media	0	0	0	0	0	0	0	0	0	7	0	0	1	0	0	0	0	0	0
Human Interest	3	0	0	0	0	0	0	0	0	3	1	0	0	0	0	0	0	0	3
Strength of Candidate	19	7	0	1	0	0	0	0	0	16	4	0	7	5	0	0	0	0	8
Horserace	7	0	0	1	0	0	0	0	0	20	0	0	1	0	0	0	0	0	6
Total	**76**	**22**	**0**	**4**	**0**	**0**	**1**	**1**	**1**	**89**	**18**	**0**	**16**	**7**	**0**	**4**	**2**	**0**	**71**

+ = Favorable - = Unfavorable 0 = Neutral

*N = Neutral stories

Table 33: Number and Direction of Stories about Candidates and Issues in the New York *Times*, 1984

	Mondale			*Ferraro*			*Democrats*			*Reagan*			*Bush*			*Republicans*			
	+	-	0	+	-	0	+	-	0	+	-	0	+	-	0	+	-	0	*N
Politics, Government	41	20	2	12	1	4	2	6	0	40	32	5	7	2	3	2	1	1	27
War, Defense, Diplomacy	12	10	0	0	1	0	1	1	1	14	24	3	1	2	0	0	0	0	2
Economic Activity	9	7	3	0	0	0	0	1	1	9	6	2	0	0	0	0	0	0	0
Crime	0	0	0	0	8	1	0	0	0	0	0	0	0	0	0	0	0	0	1
Public Moral Problems	3	0	0	2	5	0	0	0	0	2	1	0	0	1	1	0	0	0	2
Public Health, Welfare	1	1	0	0	0	0	1	0	0	3	10	0	0	0	0	0	0	0	0
Accidents, Disasters	0	0	0	0	0	0	0	0	0	0	0	1	2	0	0	0	0	0	0
Science, Invention	0	0	0	0	0	0	0	0	0	0	0	0	0	0	0	0	0	0	0
Education, Classic Arts	7	4	0	5	9	1	0	0	1	8	6	2	0	0	0	0	0	0	1
Recreation, Media	8	2	1	1	1	1	0	1	0	4	3	1	0	1	0	0	1	0	5
Human Interest	5	0	0	6	1	0	3	0	1	6	1	3	5	0	0	0	0	0	0
Strength of Candidate	49	17	2	17	4	0	4	0	1	65	19	4	1	1	1	1	2	0	2
Horserace	0	0	0	0	0	0	0	0	0	19	0	0	1	1	0	0	0	0	1
Total	**135**	**61**	**8**	**43**	**30**	**7**	**11**	**9**	**5**	**170**	**102**	**19**	**17**	**8**	**5**	**3**	**4**	**1**	**41**

+ = Favorable - = Unfavorable 0 = Neutral

*N = Neutral stories

Table 34: Number and Direction of Stories about Candidates and Issues in the New York *Times*, 1988

	Dukakis			*Bentsen*			*Democrats*			*Bush*			*Quayle*			*Republicans*			
	+	-	**0**	+	-	**0**	+	-	**0**	+	-	**0**	+	-	**0**	+	-	**0**	***N**
Politics, Government	45	5	2	7	0	0	5	3	0	33	7	0	8	1	0	6	1	0	67
War, Defense, Diplomacy	7	2	1	1	0	0	0	0	0	11	2	0	3	1	0	3	0	0	7
Economic Activity	11	3	1	0	0	0	0	0	0	11	4	0	2	0	0	4	1	0	4
Crime	4	2	0	0	0	0	0	0	0	7	3	0	0	0	0	0	0	0	1
Public Moral Problems	1	0	0	0	0	0	0	0	0	7	9	1	0	0	0	1	0	0	1
Public Health, Welfare	5	1	0	0	0	0	2	0	0	3	2	0	1	1	0	0	0	0	1
Accidents, Disasters	0	0	0	0	0	0	0	0	0	0	0	0	0	0	0	0	0	0	0
Science, Invention	0	0	0	0	0	0	0	0	0	0	0	0	0	0	0	0	0	0	0
Education, Classic Arts	3	1	0	2	0	0	0	0	0	2	0	0	0	0	0	0	0	0	0
Recreation, Media	0	1	0	0	0	0	1	0	0	1	0	0	2	1	0	0	0	0	2
Human Interest	11	3	1	4	0	0	2	1	0	4	0	0	4	0	0	2	0	0	3
Strength of Candidate	23	30	1	8	0	0	1	1	0	32	13	0	16	14	1	5	0	0	26
Horserace	2	1	0	0	0	0	0	1	0	23	0	0	0	0	0	0	0	0	6
Total	**112**	**48**	**6**	**22**	**0**	**0**	**11**	**8**	**0**	**134**	**40**	**1**	**36**	**18**	**1**	**21**	**2**	**0**	**118**

+ = Favorable - = Unfavorable 0 = Neutral

*N = Neutral stories

Table 35: Number and Direction of Stories about Candidates and Issues in the Portland *Oregonian*, 1984

	Mondale			*Ferraro*			*Democrats*			*Reagan*			*Bush*			*Republicans*			
	+	-	0	+	-	0	+	-	0	+	-	0	+	-	0	+	-	0	*N
Politics, Government	9	10	1	1	1	2	3	0	0	13	6	1	2	1	0	0	3	1	25
War, Defense, Diplomacy	3	3	0	0	0	0	0	0	0	8	15	0	1	0	1	0	0	0	4
Economic Activity	5	8	0	1	0	0	0	0	0	6	15	2	0	0	1	0	1	0	5
Crime	0	0	0	0	0	0	0	0	0	1	1	0	0	0	0	0	0	0	0
Public Moral Problems	2	0	0	1	1	0	0	0	0	0	0	0	0	1	0	1	0	0	3
Public Health, Welfare	0	0	0	0	0	0	0	0	0	0	1	0	0	0	0	0	0	0	0
Accidents, Disasters	0	0	0	0	0	0	0	0	0	0	0	0	0	0	0	0	0	0	0
Science, Invention	0	0	0	0	0	0	0	0	0	0	0	0	0	0	0	0	0	0	0
Education, Classic Arts	0	0	0	0	0	0	0	0	0	0	4	1	0	0	0	0	0	0	2
Recreation, Media	0	0	0	0	0	0	0	0	0	0	0	1	0	0	0	0	0	0	0
Human Interest	0	0	0	0	0	0	0	0	0	0	0	0	0	0	0	0	0	0	0
Strength of Candidate	9	1	1	5	2	1	0	0	0	5	10	0	2	5	3	0	1	0	4
Horserace	3	4	0	0	0	0	0	0	0	9	2	0	0	0	0	1	0	0	1
Total	**31**	**26**	**2**	**8**	**5**	**3**	**3**	**0**	**0**	**42**	**54**	**5**	**5**	**7**	**5**	**2**	**5**	**1**	**44**

+ = Favorable - = Unfavorable 0 = Neutral
*N = Neutral stories

Table 36: Number and Direction of Stories about Candidates and Issues in the Portland *Oregonian*, 1988

	Dukakis			*Bentsen*			*Democrats*			*Bush*			*Quayle*			*Republicans*			
	+	-	0	+	-	0	+	-	0	+	-	0	+	-	0	+	-	0	*N
Politics, Government	29	4	1	6	0	0	15	0	0	15	2	0	4	3	0	3	12	0	88
War, Defense, Diplomacy	17	6	0	6	0	0	0	0	0	17	1	0	4	1	0	3	0	0	6
Economic Activity	15	6	0	6	0	0	0	0	0	10	2	0	6	0	0	1	1	0	8
Crime	4	0	0	1	0	0	0	0	0	3	6	0	0	0	0	0	1	0	1
Public Moral Problems	8	0	0	2	0	0	0	1	0	4	0	0	2	0	0	0	0	0	6
Public Health, Welfare	14	4	0	4	0	0	3	0	0	7	6	0	0	0	0	1	0	0	8
Accidents, Disasters	1	0	0	0	0	0	0	0	0	0	0	0	0	0	0	0	0	0	0
Science, Invention	2	0	0	1	0	0	0	0	0	1	0	0	0	0	0	0	0	0	0
Education, Classic Arts	3	1	0	2	0	0	0	0	0	0	0	0	1	0	0	0	0	0	2
Recreation, Media	5	1	0	0	0	0	0	0	0	4	1	0	1	1	0	0	3	0	8
Human Interest	0	0	0	0	0	0	0	0	0	1	0	0	3	0	0	0	0	0	0
Strength of Candidate	29	19	1	9	0	0	6	2	1	24	21	1	16	16	1	5	7	0	27
Horserace	5	6	0	0	0	0	2	0	0	41	0	0	0	0	0	0	1	0	5
Total	**132**	**47**	**2**	**37**	**0**	**0**	**26**	**3**	**1**	**127**	**39**	**1**	**37**	**21**	**1**	**14**	**24**	**0**	**159**

+ = Favorable - = Unfavorable 0 = Neutral
*N = Neutral stories

Table 37: Number and Direction of Stories about Candidates and Issues in the San Francisco *Chronicle*, 1984

	Mondale			*Ferraro*			*Democrats*			*Reagan*			*Bush*			*Republicans*			
	+	-	0	+	-	0	+	-	0	+	-	0	+	-	0	+	-	0	*N
Politics, Government	9	8	3	3	3	1	2	2	0	21	15	1	2	3	0	7	5	1	39
War, Defense, Diplomacy	5	2	0	0	1	0	0	1	0	13	24	0	1	2	0	0	1	0	6
Economic Activity	8	1	1	2	0	0	1	1	0	10	6	0	0	2	1	0	0	0	12
Crime	1	0	0	0	0	0	0	0	0	1	0	0	0	0	0	0	0	1	0
Public Moral Problems	0	0	1	0	6	0	0	0	0	0	0	0	0	0	0	0	1	1	1
Public Health, Welfare	0	0	0	0	0	0	0	0	0	0	4	0	0	0	0	0	0	0	0
Accidents, Disasters	0	0	0	0	0	0	0	0	0	0	0	0	0	0	0	0	0	0	0
Science, Invention	0	0	0	0	0	0	0	0	0	0	0	0	0	0	0	0	0	0	0
Education, Classic Arts	1	0	0	0	0	1	0	0	0	2	2	1	0	0	0	0	0	1	3
Recreation, Media	3	1	2	5	2	0	0	0	1	8	2	1	0	0	0	0	1	0	3
Human Interest	0	1	0	0	0	0	0	0	0	1	0	0	0	0	0	0	1	0	2
Strength of Candidate	6	1	0	7	4	1	0	1	0	3	9	0	5	3	0	0	1	0	1
Horserace	15	7	4	1	0	0	5	0	0	36	0	0	3	0	0	5	0	0	9
Total	**48**	**21**	**11**	**18**	**16**	**3**	**8**	**5**	**1**	**95**	**62**	**3**	**11**	**10**	**1**	**12**	**10**	**4**	**76**

+ = Favorable - = Unfavorable 0 = Neutral
*N = Neutral stories

Table 38: Number and Direction of Stories about Candidates and Issues in the San Francisco *Chronicle*, 1988

	Dukakis			*Bentsen*			*Democrats*			*Bush*			*Quayle*			*Republicans*			
	+	-	0	+	-	0	+	-	0	+	-	0	+	-	0	+	-	0	*N
Politics, Government	15	4	1	3	0	0	14	5	0	20	2	2	5	4	1	14	14	1	52
War, Defense, Diplomacy	7	3	0	1	0	0	0	0	0	8	0	0	6	1	0	3	0	0	7
Economic Activity	8	3	1	2	0	0	0	0	0	9	2	0	4	0	0	0	0	0	5
Crime	3	0	0	0	0	0	0	0	0	2	4	0	1	1	0	0	0	0	2
Public Moral Problems	3	0	1	1	0	0	0	0	0	2	1	0	1	1	0	0	0	0	5
Public Health, Welfare	14	1	0	5	0	0	0	0	0	9	2	0	0	0	0	0	0	0	5
Accidents, Disasters	1	0	0	0	0	0	0	0	0	0	0	0	0	0	0	0	0	0	0
Science, Invention	1	0	0	1	0	0	0	0	0	4	0	0	0	0	0	0	0	0	3
Education, Classic Arts	1	0	0	0	0	0	0	0	0	2	0	0	0	0	0	0	0	0	2
Recreation, Media	14	0	0	1	0	0	0	0	0	5	2	0	2	3	0	1	0	0	18
Human Interest	0	0	0	1	0	0	1	0	0	0	0	0	1	0	0	0	0	0	1
Strength of Candidate	35	19	0	4	1	0	10	2	0	29	13	0	7	17	1	12	3	0	32
Horserace	0	1	0	3	0	0	0	0	0	40	0	0	0	1	0	1	0	0	1
Total	**102**	**31**	**3**	**22**	**1**	**0**	**25**	**7**	**0**	**130**	**26**	**2**	**27**	**28**	**2**	**31**	**17**	**1**	**133**

+ = Favorable - = Unfavorable 0 = Neutral
*N = Neutral stories

any of the papers. The *Chronicle* also had more stories dealing with war, defense, and diplomacy and economic activity than with candidate strength. The 1988 pattern was considerably different, with candidate strength first, 31 percent, the second highest figure for any paper. Politics and government was second and horserace third. Its coverage was more favorable than unfavorable for all candidates both years, but by a narrow margin for the vice presidential candidates in 1984 and for Quayle in 1988. Bentsen, on the other hand, had the most favorable coverage of all.

The St. Louis *Post-Dispatch* (Tables 39 and 40) had a total of 62 percent of its stories about politics and government and candidate strength in 1984. It was considerably above average in the number of stories about public health and welfare and education and classic arts. Its coverage in 1988 was remarkably similar, with the only shift of note being more coverage of economic activity and less of war, defense, and diplomacy. The *Post-Dispatch* coverage of Bush in 1984 was highly unfavorable, with 4 favorable and 19 unfavorable stories, but it was highly favorable of Bush in 1988, with 108 favorable stories and 31 unfavorable. Its coverage of the other candidates in both years was favorable. Although it was the least favorable to Bush in 1984, it was the most favorable to Quayle in 1988.

The *Wall Street Journal* (Tables 41 and 42) had two-thirds of its coverage on politics and government and candidate strength in 1984. It had a higher proportion of stories than average on war, defense, and diplomacy and education and classic arts but, surprisingly, had a lower proportion on economic activity. That changed in 1988 when economic activity was its second most frequent topic, with 17 percent. Politics and government led with 31 percent, and candidate strength was a close third behind economic activity. Ferraro in 1984 and Quayle in 1988 had more unfavorable than favorable stories. Bush and Dukakis had much more favorable coverage than their 1984 counterparts.

The Washington *Post* was the only paper to have candidate strength as its most frequent topic in 1984, with 31 percent. Politics and government was a close second, with 29 percent, and it had more stories in seven categories than any other paper. In 1988 politics and government was its most frequent topic but with only 23 percent. Candidate strength was second, with 21 percent. The other noteworthy changes in 1988 were substantial increases in the number of stories about public health and welfare and crime. The *Post*'s cover-

Table 39: Number and Direction of Stories about Candidates and Issues in the St. Louis *Post-Dispatch*, 1984

	Mondale			*Ferraro*			*Democrats*			*Reagan*			*Bush*			*Republicans*			
	+	-	0	+	-	0	+	-	0	+	-	0	+	-	0	+	-	0	*N
Politics, Government	38	8	4	7	2	1	2	1	0	30	20	4	0	12	0	2	5	0	31
War, Defense, Diplomacy	4	2	1	0	0	0	1	0	0	3	20	1	0	0	0	0	0	1	5
Economic Activity	2	2	1	0	1	1	0	0	0	11	9	0	0	0	1	0	0	1	0
Crime	1	0	0	0	5	0	0	0	0	0	0	0	0	0	0	0	0	0	0
Public Moral Problems	1	0	0	2	1	0	0	0	0	6	1	0	0	0	0	0	0	0	0
Public Health, Welfare	6	1	0	0	0	0	0	0	5	0	8	1	0	2	0	0	0	0	0
Accidents, Disasters	0	0	0	0	0	0	0	0	0	0	0	0	0	0	0	0	0	0	0
Science, Invention	0	0	0	0	0	0	0	0	0	0	0	0	0	0	0	0	0	0	0
Education, Classic Arts	0	1	0	0	2	0	1	0	0	2	10	2	1	0	1	0	0	0	0
Recreation, Media	1	0	1	0	0	0	0	0	0	4	4	0	1	1	0	0	0	0	8
Human Interest	2	0	0	1	0	0	0	0	0	5	0	0	1	0	0	0	0	0	0
Strength of Candidate	33	5	2	9	4	0	0	0	1	26	15	2	1	4	0	1	0	0	4
Horserace	1	1	0	0	0	0	0	0	0	8	1	0	0	0	0	0	0	0	1
Total	**89**	**20**	**9**	**19**	**15**	**2**	**4**	**1**	**6**	**95**	**88**	**10**	**4**	**19**	**2**	**3**	**5**	**2**	**49**

+ = Favorable - = Unfavorable 0 = Neutral
*N = Neutral stories

Table 40: Number and Direction of Stories about Candidates and Issues in the St. Louis *Post-Dispatch*, 1988

	Dukakis			*Bentsen*			*Democrats*			*Bush*			*Quayle*			*Republicans*			
	+	-	0	+	-	0	+	-	0	+	-	0	+	-	0	+	-	0	*N
Politics, Government	26	8	1	8	0	0	22	3	0	34	2	1	0	0	0	16	11	0	87
War, Defense, Diplomacy	4	5	0	0	0	0	1	0	0	7	4	0	0	0	0	1	1	0	3
Economic Activity	8	4	0	5	0	0	1	2	0	5	1	0	0	0	0	1	0	0	9
Crime	4	0	0	1	0	0	0	0	0	2	1	0	0	1	0	0	0	0	3
Public Moral Problems	3	1	0	0	0	0	0	0	0	3	3	0	1	0	0	0	1	0	3
Public Health, Welfare	14	1	0	1	0	0	1	0	0	4	7	0	0	0	0	1	1	0	10
Accidents, Disasters	0	0	0	0	0	0	0	0	0	0	0	0	0	0	0	0	0	0	0
Science, Invention	1	0	0	0	0	0	0	0	0	1	0	0	0	0	0	1	0	0	0
Education, Classic Arts	3	0	0	0	0	0	0	0	0	2	0	0	1	0	0	0	0	0	1
Recreation, Media	4	1	0	0	0	0	0	0	0	0	0	0	0	0	0	0	0	0	4
Human Interest	3	0	0	0	0	0	2	0	0	0	0	0	0	0	0	0	0	0	8
Strength of Candidate	33	13	0	5	1	0	4	0	0	24	13	0	15	9	1	6	1	0	17
Horserace	3	1	0	2	0	0	0	0	0	28	0	0	0	0	0	0	0	0	4
Total	**106**	**34**	**1**	**22**	**1**	**0**	**31**	**5**	**0**	**110**	**31**	**1**	**28**	**10**	**1**	**26**	**15**	**0**	**149**

+ = Favorable - = Unfavorable 0 = Neutral
*N = Neutral stories

Table 41: Number and Direction of Stories about Candidates and Issues in the *Wall Street Journal*, 1984

	Mondale			*Ferraro*			*Democrats*			*Reagan*			*Bush*			*Republicans*			
	+	-	0	+	-	0	+	-	0	+	-	0	+	-	0	+	-	0	*N
Politics, Government	7	4	1	1	4	3	2	0	0	4	12	2	0	0	0	5	8	0	14
War, Defense, Diplomacy	4	0	0	0	0	0	0	0	0	2	6	1	2	0	0	0	0	0	2
Economic Activity	3	0	1	0	0	0	0	0	0	1	0	1	0	0	0	0	0	0	0
Crime	0	0	0	0	1	0	0	0	0	0	0	0	0	0	0	0	0	0	0
Public Moral Problems	0	0	0	0	0	0	0	0	0	0	1	0	0	0	0	0	0	0	0
Public Health, Welfare	0	0	0	0	0	0	0	0	0	2	0	0	0	0	0	0	0	0	1
Accidents, Disasters	0	0	0	0	0	0	0	0	0	0	0	0	0	0	0	0	0	0	0
Science, Invention	0	0	0	0	0	0	0	0	0	0	0	0	0	0	0	0	0	0	0
Education, Classic Arts	1	0	0	0	0	1	0	0	0	4	0	1	0	0	0	0	1	0	0
Recreation, Media	2	1	1	0	1	0	0	1	4	1	0	1	0	0	0	1	0	0	0
Human Interest	0	0	0	1	0	0	0	0	0	0	0	0	0	0	0	0	0	0	0
Strength of Candidate	1	5	0	3	2	2	1	0	0	9	3	1	2	0	1	1	0	0	1
Horserace	0	0	0	0	0	0	0	0	0	1	0	0	0	0	0	0	0	0	0
Total	**18**	**10**	**3**	**5**	**8**	**6**	**3**	**1**	**4**	**24**	**22**	**7**	**4**	**0**	**1**	**7**	**9**	**0**	**18**

+ = Favorable - = Unfavorable 0 = Neutral

*N = Neutral stories

Table 42: Number and Direction of Stories about Candidates and Issues in the *Wall Street Journal*, 1988

	Dukakis			*Bentsen*			*Democrats*			*Bush*			*Quayle*			*Republicans*			
	+	-	**0**	+	-	**0**	+	-	**0**	+	-	**0**	+	-	**0**	+	-	**0**	***N**
Politics, Government	10	0	1	1	1	0	5	0	0	3	2	0	0	0	0	9	1	0	26
War, Defense, Diplomacy	4	1	0	0	0	0	0	0	0	3	1	1	1	1	0	0	0	0	5
Economic Activity	3	4	1	0	0	0	0	0	0	7	1	0	0	0	0	1	2	0	15
Crime	2	0	0	0	0	0	0	0	0	1	1	0	0	0	0	0	0	0	0
Public Moral Problems	0	1	0	0	0	0	0	0	0	2	1	0	0	0	0	0	0	0	2
Public Health, Welfare	4	0	0	0	0	0	0	0	0	0	0	0	0	0	0	0	0	0	3
Accidents, Disasters	0	0	0	0	0	0	0	0	0	0	0	0	0	0	0	0	0	0	0
Science, Invention	1	0	0	0	0	0	0	0	0	1	0	0	0	0	0	0	0	0	2
Education, Classic Arts	2	0	0	0	0	0	0	0	0	1	0	0	0	0	0	0	0	0	0
Recreation, Media	1	0	0	0	0	0	0	0	0	0	1	0	0	0	0	0	0	0	3
Human Interest	0	0	0	0	0	0	0	0	0	0	0	0	0	0	0	0	0	0	0
Strength of Candidate	3	0	0	3	0	0	0	0	0	4	5	0	4	5	0	4	2	0	2
Horserace	0	0	0	1	0	0	0	0	0	18	0	0	0	1	0	1	0	0	1
Total	**30**	**6**	**2**	**5**	**1**	**0**	**5**	**0**	**0**	**40**	**12**	**0**	**5**	**7**	**0**	**14**	**5**	**0**	**61**

+ = Favorable - = Unfavorable 0 = Neutral
*N = Neutral stories

Table 43: Number and Direction of Stories about Candidates and Issues in the Washington *Post*, 1984

	Mondale			*Ferraro*			*Democrats*			*Reagan*			*Bush*			*Republicans*			
	+	-	0	+	-	0	+	-	0	+	-	0	+	-	0	+	-	0	*N
Politics, Government	21	16	5	13	3	5	5	2	2	29	45	17	6	3	2	3	3	2	29
War, Defense, Diplomacy	10	7	2	5	0	0	0	0	0	17	18	3	5	1	0	0	0	0	8
Economic Activity	8	9	6	2	1	0	0	0	0	18	8	3	2	1	3	0	1	0	4
Crime	1	0	0	1	0	0	0	0	0	0	0	0	0	0	0	0	0	0	0
Public Moral Problems	2	0	1	1	1	3	0	0	1	7	6	1	1	2	1	1	0	0	1
Public Health, Welfare	1	0	0	0	0	0	0	0	0	1	3	1	3	0	0	0	0	0	1
Accidents, Disasters	0	0	0	0	0	0	0	0	0	0	0	0	0	0	0	0	0	0	0
Science, Invention	1	0	0	3	0	0	0	0	0	2	3	0	3	0	0	0	0	0	0
Education, Classic Arts	2	2	0	1	2	0	0	0	0	3	9	1	1	1	0	0	0	0	2
Recreation, Media	4	0	3	2	1	0	0	0	0	2	4	2	0	0	1	1	2	1	21
Human Interest	1	0	0	1	0	0	0	0	0	3	1	1	0	0	1	0	0	1	1
Strength of Candidate	19	9	9	14	5	3	8	4	3	85	40	7	4	5	4	2	1	1	5
Horserace	2	0	0	1	0	0	0	0	0	11	1	0	0	1	0	1	0	0	2
Total	**72**	**43**	**26**	**44**	**13**	**11**	**13**	**6**	**6**	**178**	**138**	**36**	**25**	**14**	**12**	**8**	**7**	**5**	**74**

+ = Favorable - = Unfavorable 0 = Neutral
*N = Neutral stories

Table 44: Number and Direction of Stories about Candidates and Issues in the Washington *Post*, 1988

	Dukakis			*Bentsen*			*Democrats*			*Bush*			*Quayle*			*Republicans*			
	+	-	0	+	-	0	+	-	0	+	-	0	+	-	0	+	-	0	*N
Politics, Government	36	12	0	7	1	0	13	6	5	79	26	7	7	2	1	34	24	4	79
War, Defense, Diplomacy	19	4	0	1	0	0	0	0	0	15	1	0	2	0	0	2	0	1	4
Economic Activity	17	4	0	0	0	0	1	0	0	13	2	0	0	1	0	1	2	0	17
Crime	8	0	0	0	0	0	0	0	0	6	1	0	0	0	0	0	0	0	0
Public Moral Problems	5	3	1	0	0	0	1	1	0	2	0	0	0	1	0	1	2	0	5
Public Health, Welfare	9	4	1	0	0	0	0	0	0	9	6	0	0	0	0	0	1	0	3
Accidents, Disasters	1	0	0	0	0	0	0	0	0	0	0	0	0	0	0	0	0	0	0
Science, Invention	0	0	0	0	0	0	0	0	0	0	0	0	0	0	0	1	0	0	1
Education, Classic Arts	4	0	0	0	0	0	0	0	0	1	0	0	0	0	0	0	0	0	5
Recreation, Media	9	3	2	0	0	2	3	0	0	7	4	0	0	3	0	2	2	0	30
Human Interest	1	0	0	0	0	0	0	0	0	0	0	0	0	0	0	0	0	0	0
Strength of Candidate	26	10	0	5	0	0	6	1	0	24	15	0	8	28	1	8	2	0	10
Horserace	0	1	0	0	0	0	0	0	0	25	0	0	0	0	0	0	0	0	2
Total	**135**	**41**	**4**	**13**	**3**	**0**	**24**	**8**	**6**	**128**	**36**	**0**	**17**	**35**	**2**	**49**	**33**	**5**	**156**

+ = Favorable - = Unfavorable 0 = Neutral
*N = Neutral stories

age was favorable for all four candidates in 1984. In 1988, however, it had the least favorable coverage of Quayle of any paper, with 17 favorable stories and 35 unfavorable stories. Most of these stories were in the candidate-strength category. On the other hand, its coverage of Bush was 78 percent favorable.

There thus seems to be overall considerable similarity between newspapers. Politics and government, candidate strength, war, defense, and diplomacy, horserace, and economic activity tended to be the most frequently covered issues. There were two patterns, however, for these newspapers in that for some, those five topics were virtually all that was covered, whereas others, notably the Louisville *Courier-Journal*, the Miami *Herald*, the New York *Times,* the San Francisco *Chronicle*, the St. Louis *Post-Dispatch* and the Washington *Post*, provided substantial coverage of several other issues in both years.

Finally, although considerably more was said about the absence of issues and issue coverage in 1988 than in 1984, there is little evidence that issues played a smaller part in 1988. In fact, most of the evidence points the other way. Overall, there was more issue coverage in 1988 than in 1984, although the difference was not large.

Notes

1. Guido H. Stempel III, "The Prestige Press Covers the 1960 Presidential Campaign," *Journalism Quarterly*, 38:157-163 (Spring 1961); *idem*, "The Prestige Press in Two Presidential Elections," *Journalism Quarterly*, 42:15-21 (Spring 1965); *idem*, "The Prestige Press Meets the Third-Part Challenge," *Journalism Quarterly*, 46:699-706 (Winter 1969); Guido H. Stempel III and John W. Windhauser, "The Prestige Press Revisited: Coverage of the 1980 Presidential Campaign," *Journalism Quarterly*, 61:49-55 (Spring 1984).
2. Anon., "Nation's Editors Pick 15 'Superior Papers,'" *Editor & Publisher*, April 12, 1960, p. 14.

3

Watching the Campaigns on Network Television

John W. Windhauser and Dru Riley Evarts

Hundreds of people in Sacramento were waving flags as they listened to President Ronald Reagan talk of going forward again in America. Only the Republicans, he claimed, would keep the American economy healthy. Four years later in 1988, the president returned to Sacramento with the same campaign theme.

Giving a thumbs-up sign to the crowd of supporters in downtown Los Angeles, Mondale said that "Polls don't vote; people vote." An estimated audience of 20,000 shouted approval. Again, four years later, Michael Dukakis repeated a similar remark to a group of supporters in the closing days of the campaign. "People vote, polls don't." He then reminded his audience that in 1948 President Harry Truman came from behind. Spectators waved signs that read: "Poll me, CBS" and "Retire Reagan." These events were aired on the nightly news.

In the 1960s Marshall McLuhan labeled television a global village that would eventually captivate the people and become the center of their attention.[1] Each night the three television network news programs participate in an information ritual as a part of that focus. They try with varying success to gain the competitive audience edge and at the same time, chase each other with similar news presentations.[2]

From the first televised coverage of the 1948 political conventions to the present,[3] television coverage has been recognized as a medium for politicians.[4] Although television's role in politics was somewhat dormant during the 1950s,[5] the 1960 presidential race marked television as an image-maker.[6] Few people, for example, remember what issues were discussed during the 1960 television debates, but they recall that former President John F. Kennedy looked the best. The impression counted.[7]

For years the newspaper press was regularly criticized for campaign coverage. Those inconsistent charges, however, were not aimed at television news until after the 1968 presidential race when former vice-president Spiro Agnew attacked television news reports.[8] Other complaints were echoed later by former *TV Guide* columnist Edith Efron,[9] but were debunked when a reanalysis of television news programs revealed marginal news advantages for either party.

Since the 1968 race, only a few studies have looked at television news coverage of presidential races, with most of those studies focusing only on either the 1972[10] or the 1976 race.[11] The newspaper medium dominated the literature in both the 1980[12] and the 1984[13] campaigns. Although this little attention might give the wrong impression of the importance of television news content, other studies clearly have indicated that audiences sought information,[14] including political and public affairs,[15] from television and that this need started in the 1950s.[16] More importantly, both showmanship and imagery were key factors in election victories.[17]

With these ideas in mind, we decided to include network television news coverage of the 1984 and 1988 presidential campaigns in our study. Additionally, we wanted to determine whether the Democratic or Republican parties and their candidates had news advantages over each other. Our three hypotheses, which suggested balanced television news and issue coverage between the Democratic and Republican party and a lack of favoritism for either party, paralleled the three hypotheses suggested for the leading daily newspapers reported in Chapter 2.

Hypothesis 1: Coverage would be fairly well balanced between the two political parties and between their candidates seeking either the presidential or vice presidential office. Studies of television news coverage of former races suggests that television news is fairly unbiased or balanced[18] and variations in coverage reflect the differences in the candidates and their campaigns.[19] A few other studies report considerable agreement in network television news patterns.[20]

Hypothesis 2: Campaign issues would focus more on the candidates and their supporters and on politics rather than substantive issues. Although the few television studies reported some emphasis on issues,[21] most of those studies overlooked the candidates and their supporters as possible campaign issues. Campaign studies of newspapers[22] suggest that image rather than substance dominates. With television considered an "image maker,"[23] we would expect little substance on issues in television news reports.

Hypothesis 3: Visual presentations of the two parties would be similar and would center on activities of the race and "image" building. Despite the added angle that visuals give to a television news story, little attention has focused on how the candidates and their parties are portrayed. A few related studies in television campaign advertising suggest that candidates are packaged with "images" or "appeals" rather than issues.[24] In studies of presidential and other political advertisements placed in newspapers, "image" and identifications rule the appeals.[25]

All network evening news programs, including the weekends, were included in the sample for both years.[26] The unit of analysis was the news story segment.[27] For each segment, the news was coded as to the direction, the candidate, or the party and the various visuals or "sound bites."[28] The coding procedures are described in Chapter 1.

Results of the Study

The Overall Campaign

Both the ABC and CBS news programs in the 1984 race carried more news segments on the Republicans than on the Democrats, and NBC's coverage slightly favored the Democrats. The results also showed that the news segments on all three news programs were favorable for the four candidates.

Four years later, all three news programs aired more stories about the Democrats, more than doubled their neutral coverage, and reported more negative stories. But the data also revealed that the story segments on all three news programs were favorable toward the presidential candidates, with the Democrats having the edge. Coverage was negative toward the Democratic vice presidential candidate in 1984, and four years later it was aimed toward the Republican vice presidential nominee.

Generally, the Democrats in both races, rather than the Republicans, had significantly higher proportions of positive coverage; the news edge favored the Republicans, however. Few issues, other than politics and the strength of the candidates, were stressed. The video visuals used with the news reports reflected those telegenic messages.

Table 45: Number of Favorable, Unfavorable and Neutral Stories about Each Candidate in the 1984 and in the 1988 Presidential Races on the Three Evening News Programs

	ABC			*CBS*			*NBC*		
1984	+	-	0	+	-	0	+	-	0
Mondale	101	8	5	116	16	1	100	11	4
Ferraro	21	8	3	43	16	4	30	12	4
Democratic	6	1	2	4	2	1	1	0	0
Reagan	107	13	17	166	51	5	99	21	13
Bush	26	2	0	25	6	5	18	5	4
Republicans	1	1	2	5	0	2	1	0	0
Neutral	0	0	43	0	0	29	0	0	32
1988									
Dukakis	88	34	25	121	50	13	94	38	13
Bentsen	16	1	0	20	2	3	14	4	3
Democratic	10	4	2	15	3	0	14	4	4
Bush	89	33	21	118	48	8	97	32	6
Quayle	14	15	3	25	27	2	19	16	2
Republican	14	10	4	19	33	1	24	20	1
Neutral	0	0	140	0	0	104	0	0	108

NOTE: + = Favorable; - = Unfavorable; 0 = Neutral. The neutral category includes items which did not refer either to one candidate or have a clear direction.

All four presidential candidates received considerably more coverage than their vice presidential colleagues, as shown in Table 45. Overall coverage for both parties was favorable. In 1984 Reagan was the subject of nearly five times more stories than Bush was. Mondale was the subject of almost three times as many stories as was Ferraro. A similar pattern existed for the two vice presidential candidates in the 1988 race.

In looking at only favorable and unfavorable news items, we found that all three network news programs carried a higher percentage of positive segments toward Mondale in 1984, as shown in Table 45. Bush, as a 1988 presidential candidate, held that slight advantage.

At least 90 percent of the 1984 campaign television news about Mondale, 72 percent about Ferraro, 81.4 percent about Reagan, and 84.1 percent about Bush was favorable. About 79.1 percent of the general Democratic stories and 87.5 percent of the Republican stories were favorable. All three news programs carried a higher percentage of positive stories about Mondale than about Reagan.

Of the four 1984 candidates, Bush could have been considered the invisible candidate. He had limited coverage on CBS and NBC. ABC aired almost an equal number of stories about Bush and Ferraro. The other two network news programs carried almost twice as many stories about Ferraro.

Unlike the case in the 1984 race, in 1988 coverage was highly negative toward both parties, with the Republicans having the largest proportions. Of the four candidates, Bentsen had the least amount of coverage, and most of that was positive news. Discussions of Bentsen by either Bush or Quayle were almost nil. Quayle's campaign strategy was to question and attack Dukakis's ideas and programs and to ignore Bentsen. Bentsen campaigned against Quayle's credentials and the fact the Quayle could be a "heartbeat" away from the presidency.

Another noticeable coverage change from 1984 to 1988 was the increase of neutral items. Two factors might explain the shift. First, the news programs, especially ABC, started focusing on issues in different areas of the country. Next, the news items that featured both parties were balanced.

In 1984 ABC news aired only 12 percent or 43 neutral stories about the race, but in 1988 that coverage increased to 140 stories or 27 percent of the news. During the final weeks of the campaign, ABC took its evening news program across the country. Peter Jennings reported what voters thought about the race, the issues, and the candidates in cities such as Johnstown, Pennsylvania; San Antonio, Texas; Cleveland, Ohio; and Peoria, Illinois. Major topics included environment versus employment, values and the candidates, gun control, and the Pledge of Allegiance.

The increase of neutral stories on CBS went from 29 to 104. In 1984 only 6 percent of the total news segments were neutral, but that distribution shifted to 17 percent in 1988. Similar to both ABC and CBS news, NBC had large increases in 1988 in its coverage of neutral stories. In 1984, 32, or 9 percent, of NBC's total issues were neutral. That number reached 21 percent of 513 issues in the 1988 campaign.

As in Chapter 2, in Table 45, the directional categories were combined into three groups: Democratic, Republican, and neutral. Table 46 shows this distribution for both the 1984 and 1988 races. The Democratic category included all of the pro-Democratic and the anti-Republican categories. Similarly, the Republican group included all of the pro-Republican and the anti-Democratic groupings.

Table 46: Number of Democratic, Republican and Neutral Stories Aired about Each Candidate in the 1984 and in the 1988 Presidential Races on the Three Evening News Programs

	Democratic	*Republican*	*Neutral*
1984			
ABC Evening News	144	151	72
CBS Evening News	220	230	47
NBC Evening News	157	141	57
1988			
ABC Evening News	172	156	195
CBS Evening News	264	217	131
NBC Evening News	190	186	137

Finally, the neutral category included the neutral story segments about all of the candidates and those neutral stories about the campaign in general (Table 47).

Neither the Democrats nor the Republicans had a majority of the news segments aired, as Table 47 illustrates. In 1988 the coverage of both parties on NBC was an almost even 50-50 split, whereas the Democrats held the advantage on ABC and CBS. The Republicans in 1984 had a slight news edge on ABC and CBS, but the Democrats held that position on NBC.

Some of that favorable coverage on CBS could be attributed to the live interviews of both Dukakis and Bentsen on the CBS Evening News and the news of those interviews. For nearly six minutes, Dan Rather interviewed Bentsen without asking an embarrassing question.

Another fifteen minutes of favorable, multiple news coverage was given to Dukakis. Within this time frame, Dukakis explained his "M-1 tank ride" and described Bush as the candidate who wrapped himself with the American flag and the Pledge of Allegiance. Again, Rather avoided probing questions and kept Dukakis's interview on a positive news slant. Republican advisers for Bush and Quayle turned down CBS requests for live interviews of the evening news. In return, CBS reported those refusals as negative news.

Issue Dominance on Nightly News Programs

Election issue presentations on all three network news programs

Table 47: Percentage of Democratic and Republican Stories with Neutral Stories Excluded in the 1984 and in the 1988 Presidential Races on the Three Network Television Evening News Programs

	Democratic	*Republican*
1984		
ABC Evening News	48.8	51.2
CBS Evening News	48.9	51.1
NBC Evening News	52.7	47.3
1988		
ABC Evening News	52.4	47.6
CBS Evening News	54.9	45.1
NBC Evening News	50.5	49.5

were alike for both political parties and for both election races. Issues in 1984 focused mainly on politics and government, defense and diplomacy, and candidate strength, as shown in Table 48. These three categories controlled at least 77 percent of all issues reported. Nearly 79 percent of CBS's and NBC's issue coverage dealt with these topics, followed by 71 percent for ABC. Four years later, these categories still explained 72 percent of CBS's coverage and 68 percent for ABC and 69 percent for NBC (Table 48).

In looking at the two races, crime-, economic-, and media-oriented themes shifted in the ranks. The Bush campaign kept Willie Horton, prison furloughs, and illegal drugs at the top of his crime agenda. Whenever Bush was endorsed by a police group, he portrayed Dukakis as a "soft-on-crime" governor. As evidence of his hard position on crime, Dukakis cited crime statistics and programs in Massachusetts and questioned Bush and his colleagues about their dealings with Gen. Manuel Noriega of Panama and illegal drugs. Crime issues increased from six topics to 68.

Common Democratic economic slogans ranged from "good jobs at good wages" and "bring prosperity home" to "making America number one." The GOP candidate responded with his slogans of a "flexible freeze," "no new taxes," and "are you better off." In campaign appearances, Reagan stressed Bush's economic policies as extensions of his own.

The heavy network news coverage on advertisements used by the parties and the campaigns as staged media events explained the drastic issue changes between the 1984 and 1988 race. Campaign ads were shown in news packages as "sound bites." The revolving door

Table 48: Major Campaign Issues in the 1984 and in the 1988 Presidential Races by Network Television Newscast

	1984 Race			*1988 Race*		
	ABC	**CBS**	**NBC**	**ABC**	**CBS**	**NBC**
Politics, Government	105	204	139	209	199	195
War, Defense, Diplomacy	53	63	46	29	47	36
Economic Activity	19	17	11	36	31	30
Crime	3	0	3	27	30	31
Public Moral Problems	10	14	21	14	24	17
Public Health Welfare	7	7	7	27	26	24
Accidents, Disasters	2	0	0	2	0	1
Science	2	0	0	3	0	1
Education, Classic Arts	5	13	5	3	5	1
Recreation, Media	3	7	3	26	34	29
Human Interest	6	2	1	2	0	0
Strength of Candidate	104	127	97	117	194	124
Horserace	48	43	22	28	22	24
Total	**367**	**497**	**355**	**523**	**612**	**513**

of prison furloughs became a regular news feature of crime and furlough programs.

Another Bush ad aired several times as news with a diplomacy and defense theme was Bush with Mikhail Gorbachev near the White House. A voice-over said: "This is no time to train somebody in how to meet with the Russians. This is the time for strength and experience."

Ads also became news when ads of opponents were shown in a candidate's ads. For instance, Dukakis watches himself ride in an armored tank. The Democratic candidate then turns off the television set and says to the viewer, "haven't seen anything like it in twenty-five years of public life. George Bush's negative television ads, distorting my record, full of lies, and he knows it."

Although little attention was given to other topics, the overall priorities for each news show were similar, as indicated by the rankings in Table 49 and the high rank-order correlations. Those correlations ranged in 1984 from a +0.965 between CBS and NBC to a +0.917 between ABC and NBC. The rank-order correlation between ABC and CBS was +0.957. In 1988, a +0.957 correlation existed between CBS and NBC, followed by a +0.93 between ABC and NBC and +0.886 between ABC and CBS.

Almost identical patterns of dominant issues were found in

Table 49: Major Campaign Issues Ranked in the 1984 and in the 1988 Presidential Races by Network Television Newscast

	1984 Race			*1988 Race*		
	ABC	CBS	NBC	ABC	CBS	NBC
Politics, Government	1	1	1	1	1	1
War, Defense, Diplomacy	3	3	3	4	3	3
Economic Activity	5	5	6	3	5	5
Crime	10.5	12	9.5	6.5	6	4
Public Moral Problems	6	6	5	9	8	9
Public Health, Welfare	7	8.5	7	6.5	7	7.5
Accidents, Disasters	12.5	12	12.5	12.5	12	11
Science	12.5	12	12.5	10.5	12	11
Education, Classic Arts	9	7	8	10.5	10	11
Recreation, Media	10.5	8.5	9.5	8	4	6
Human Interest	8	10	11	12.5	12	13
Strength of Candidate	2	2	2	2	2	2
Horserace	4	4	4	5	9	7.5

coverage of the 1984 race but not in 1988 between the Democratic and Republican parties on each news program. On NBC the three main topics made up 83 percent of the Democratic and 75 percent of the Republican issue coverage. But it was considerably lower in 1988, with the Democrats at 72 percent and the Republicans at 67 percent. The top groupings in 1984 accounted for about 80 percent of the coverage for both parties on CBS and nearly 70 percent in 1988. Compared to the other two news programs, ABC differed in both races with its issue emphasis. In both election races about 74 percent of the Democratic and 68 percent of the Republican issues were grouped in the same three areas.

Reporting the Issue Agendas

Predictably, the two presidential candidates in both elections ruled the issues in their parties just as they had dominated the news segment coverage. Among the three television news programs studied, the issues in both races were fairly consistent. Overall, the Democrats were favored with positive issue themes, as indicated in Table 50.

In both races, as the campaign moved toward election day, the

Table 50: Percentage of Campaign Issues by Direction and Party for Each Network Television News Programs

	1984 Race			*1988 Race*		
	ABC	**CBS**	**NBC**	**ABC**	**CBS**	**NBC**
Favorable Democratic	82.6	80.3	80.9	63.3	68.7	64.9
Unfavorable Democratic	11.0	16.7	14.2	21.1	24.2	24.5
Neutral Democratic	6.4	3.0	4.9	15.6	7.1	10.6
Total	**155**	**203**	**162**	**180**	**227**	**188**
Favorable Republican	79.3	74.0	73.3	57.6	57.7	64.5
Unfavorable Republican	9.5	21.5	16.1	28.6	38.4	31.3
Neutral Republican	11.2	4.5	10.6	13.8	3.9	4.2
Total	**169**	**265**	**161**	**203**	**281**	**217**

candidate strength and horserace references increased, with the Republicans gaining the edge. The band-wagon approach was stressed by the three news shows in visuals accompanying issue coverage. The variety of issues came mainly from the debates or from selected events. Candidates talked more about how to govern and the campaigns rather than what they were going to do.

In the 1984 race Mondale had a considerably higher proportion of favorable issues aired on each network than did Reagan, and Mondale accounted for most of the positive news about the Democrats. Issue coverage was slightly mixed for Bush and Ferraro and almost nonexistent for either party in general.

The highest proportion of favorable issue references for Mondale concerned political activity, defense and diplomacy, and candidate-strength categories. Mondale's weakest area was the horserace. Nearly all of the few positive mentions came early in the campaign or were near presidential debates.

As expected, Reagan in 1984 and Bush in 1988 dominated the horserace issue with favorable comments. The couple of negative notices toward Reagan's chances of winning occurred when Mondale had favorable horserace highlights. Other strong areas for both Republican presidential candidates were political activity and candidate-strength themes. From the 1988 Labor Day kickoff through the eve of the campaign, the horserace messages and the opinion polls favored Bush.

In 1984 both vice presidential candidates, Bush and Ferraro, had strong positive support in their issue showing of political activities, along with strong, favorable endorsements from supporters. Whenever talk about winning was an issue, Bush's mentions were highly positive, whereas Ferraro's were the opposite.

Ferraro in 1984 and Quayle in 1988 had negative comments about their abilities. Unflattering remarks about Ferraro came from her so-called Democratic supporters and clergy of the Catholic church. They attacked Ferraro's views about abortion and her family's financial affairs. Quayle could not avoid questions of his grades, his leadership abilities, and his youth. The most haunting remark for Quayle came in his debate with Bentsen when Quayle told the television audience, "I have as much experience in Congress as Jack Kennedy did when he sought the presidency." Bentsen replied, "Senator, I served with Jack Kennedy. Jack Kennedy was a friend of mine. Senator, you're no Jack Kennedy." That sound bit echoed the Democratic negative campaign theme toward Quayle.

Rather than focus attention of Bentsen, Quayle directed his critical comments mostly toward Dukakis. "I don't know Michael Dukakis. I never served with Michael Dukakis. Michael Dukakis is not a good friend of mine. But I know this, Michael Dukakis is no Harry Truman."

The Issue Agenda by Network

Nearly three-fourths of the 155 Democratic issues on ABC concerned Mondale, and nearly 89 percent of those themes were favorable. Favorable items with the highest proportions dealt with political activity (81 percent), defense and diplomacy (95 percent), and candidate strength (97 percent). The horserace category (31 percent) had the highest proportion of unfavorable references toward Mondale.

In 1988, 81 percent of the 180 Democratic issues emphasized Dukakis, but only 60 percent of that coverage was favorable. Unlike Mondale, Dukakis lacked high positive coverage of his campaign. Proportionally, defense and diplomacy themes had the largest positive coverage (73 percent), followed by candidate strength (63 percent) and political activity (53 percent). All of the horserace references favored Bush.

Reagan in 1984 had a majority (81 percent) on ABC of the 169 Republican issues. About 78 percent of the 137 issues about Reagan were favorable, 9 percent were negative, and the others were neutral.

His strongest areas were grouped into the candidate-strength (86.7 percent) and the horserace (96.3 percent) categories. The economic activity (20 percent) and the defense and diplomacy (40 percent) groups had the highest proportion of negative themes.

As a presidential candidate in 1988, Bush had 70 percent of the 203 Republican issues, but his coverage was similar to Dukakis in that only 62 percent of those issues were positive. From the start of the campaign, the horserace (100 percent), public moral problems (100 percent), and media-oriented (100 percent) themes favored Bush. With negative hints and news segments throughout the campaign about Bush's character, his supporters, and actions of his associates, the positive strength references were only 66 percent.

Only 65.6 percent of the thirty-two issues dealing with Ferraro on ABC were favorable, with the strongest proportions in the candidate-strength group (85.7 percent of fourteen issues). Public moral problems (80 percent) and public health (33.3 percent) contained the highest proportion of negative themes. These two areas had only eight issues. About 9 percent of the issues associated with Ferraro were neutral. Four years later, Bentsen, with 17 issue references, had 94 percent as positive and the rest neutral. All of Bentsen's personal strength and 89 percent of the nine political references were positive.

In 1984, about 93 percent of the Republican's twenty-eight vice presidential references on ABC were positive, with the highest proportions of favorable percentages in the candidate-strength (100 percent) and the horserace (100 percent) groups. Highest proportions of negative themes were in the defense and diplomacy (14.3 percent) and public health (33.3 percent) areas. The few Democratic (9) or Republican (4) party issues were mainly political activities, candidate-strength, or horserace references. Only 44 percent of Quayle's thirty-two references in 1988 were favorable, and most of them were in the political activities (six of eight issues) and the personal strength (eight of fourteen issues) groups. The issue distributions on ABC News for 1984 and 1988 are shown in Tables 51 and 52.

In CBS's 1984 coverage, nearly 66 percent of the 203 Democratic issues were about Mondale with 87 percent of those references as favorable. Political activity (91.5 percent), defense and diplomacy (75 percent), and candidate-strength (86.5 percent) had the highest proportions of desirable themes. The several negative ones were found in the horserace (22 percent) and defense and diplomacy (25 percent) groups.

With 81 percent of 227 Democratic issues aired, Dukakis re-

Table 51: Number and Direction of News Segments in 1984 about Candidates and Issues Aired on ABC News

	Mondale			*Ferraro*			*Democrats*			*Reagan*			*Bush*			*Republicans*			
	+	-	0	+	-	0	+	-	0	+	-	0	+	-	0	+	-	0	*N
Politics, Government	25	3	3	3	1	2	4	1	1	23	2	8	3	0	0	1	1	0	24
War, Defense, Diplomacy	21	1	0	0	0	0	0	0	1	7	6	2	6	1	0	0	0	0	8
Economic Activity	7	0	0	0	0	0	0	0	0	7	2	1	0	0	0	0	0	0	2
Crime	0	0	0	0	0	0	0	0	0	1	0	1	1	0	0	0	0	0	0
Public Moral Problems	1	0	0	1	4	0	0	0	0	0	0	0	0	0	0	0	0	0	4
Public Health, Welfare	1	0	0	2	1	0	0	0	0	0	0	0	2	1	0	0	0	0	0
Accidents, Disasters	1	0	0	0	0	0	0	0	0	0	0	1	0	0	0	0	0	0	0
Science, Invention	1	0	0	0	0	0	0	0	0	1	0	0	0	0	0	0	0	0	0
Education, Classic Arts	0	0	1	1	0	0	0	0	0	3	0	0	0	0	0	0	0	0	0
Recreation, Media	1	0	0	0	0	0	0	0	0	0	0	0	0	0	0	0	0	0	2
Human Interest	3	0	0	0	1	0	0	0	0	0	0	0	0	0	0	0	0	0	2
Strength of Candidate	31	0	1	12	1	1	2	0	0	39	2	4	11	0	0	0	0	0	0
Horserace	9	4	0	2	0	0	0	0	0	26	1	0	3	0	0	0	0	2	1
Total	**101**	**8**	**5**	**21**	**8**	**3**	**6**	**1**	**2**	**107**	**13**	**17**	**26**	**2**	**0**	**1**	**1**	**2**	**43**

+ = Favorable - = Unfavorable 0 = Neutral
*N = Neutral category includes items that do not refer primarily to one candidate or have clear direction.

Table 52: Number and Direction of News Segments in 1988 about Candidates and Issues Aired on ABC News

	Dukakis			*Bentsen*			*Democrats*			*Bush*			*Quayle*			*Republicans*			
	+	-	0	+	-	0	+	-	0	+	-	0	+	-	0	+	-	0	*N
Politics, Government	21	6	13	8	0	1	10	3	1	27	8	12	6	0	2	10	5	3	73
War, Defense, Diplomacy	11	4	0	0	0	0	0	0	0	6	2	1	0	0	0	0	1	0	4
Economic Activity	5	3	2	0	0	0	0	1	0	2	1	4	0	0	0	1	0	0	17
Crime	7	2	3	0	0	0	0	0	0	5	5	1	0	0	0	0	0	0	4
Public Moral Problems	4	2	0	0	0	0	0	0	0	1	4	0	0	0	0	0	1	1	1
Public Health, Welfare	3	2	1	0	0	0	0	0	0	2	2	1	0	2	0	1	0	0	13
Accidents, Disasters	1	0	0	0	0	0	0	0	1	0	0	0	0	0	0	0	0	0	0
Science, Invention	1	0	0	0	0	0	0	0	0	1	0	0	0	0	0	0	0	0	1
Education, Classic Arts	2	0	0	0	0	0	0	0	0	0	0	0	0	0	0	0	0	0	1
Recreation, Media	1	0	2	2	0	0	0	0	0	0	2	1	0	0	0	2	0	0	16
Human Interest	0	0	0	0	0	0	0	0	0	0	0	0	0	0	0	0	0	0	2
Strength of Candidate	31	14	4	6	0	0	0	0	0	19	9	1	8	13	1	0	3	0	8
Horserace	1	1	0	0	0	0	0	0	0	26	0	0	0	0	0	0	0	0	0
Total	**88**	**34**	**25**	**16**	**0**	**1**	**10**	**4**	**2**	**89**	**33**	**21**	**14**	**15**	**3**	**14**	**10**	**4**	**140**

+ = Favorable – = Unfavorable 0 = Neutral
*N = Neutral category includes items that do not refer primarily to one candidate or have clear direction.

ceived more coverage in 1988 than Mondale did in 1984. Only 66 percent of those themes were positive toward Dukakis. Nearly all of the issues reported for Dukakis lacked an overwhelming favorable slant. Highest categories were personal strength (71 percent), political activities (66 percent) and defense and diplomacy (57 percent). Early in the campaign, Dukakis had several positive "ahead" emphases. Bush claimed all of the other favorable references about "winning."

Of the three news programs, CBS in 1984 was the most favorable toward Ferraro. Whereas 31 percent of the 203 Democratic issues focused on her, nearly 70 percent of this coverage was favorable, with the highest favorable items in the candidate-strength and political activity areas. Most references in the horserace and the public moral problems groups were negative.

In 1988, Bentsen had only 11 percent of all total Democratic issues (227) and 80 percent of his coverage was favorable. Highest positive items were for the candidate-strength group, which featured 80 percent of the main issues stressed about Bentsen. Of the 18 general Democratic issues, 83 percent were favorable, and nearly all were politically oriented topics.

With 265 Republican issues on CBS, Reagan had 84 percent, 75 percent of which were favorable. The highest proportions of negative coverage were found in the candidate-strength (33.3 percent) and the defense and diplomacy (26 percent) groups. The horserace (96 percent) and economic activity (78 percent) areas had the highest frequencies and proportions of favorable references.

In 1984, vice presidential candidate Bush, with 13.6 percent of the Republican issues on CBS, had a lower proportional amount (69 percent) of favorable references, as did Reagan (75 percent). Highest percentages of positive references for Bush were in the political activity (72.7 percent), defense and diplomacy (50 percent), candidate strength (57 percent) and horserace (100 percent) areas.

The proportion of favorable coverage on CBS changed little for Bush in 1988 when he was the presidential candidate. Although Bush had 62 percent of the 281 Republican issues, only 68 percent was considered favorable. Highest frequencies for Bush were found in the political, personal strength, and horserace categories. All 19 of the horserace themes were favorable, but 69 percent of the 36 political and 65 percent of the personal strength themes were positive. Most of Bush's negative themes in the 1988 race also dealt with his personal characteristics, his style, and his supporters.

Table 53: Number and Direction of News Segments in 1984 about Candidates and Issues Aired on CBS News

	Mondale			*Ferraro*			*Democrats*			*Reagan*			*Bush*			*Republicans*			
	+	-	0	+	-	0	+	-	0	+	-	0	+	-	0	+	-	0	*N
Politics, Government	54	5	0	20	3	3	4	1	1	53	11	3	16	1	5	3	0	2	19
War, Defense, Diplomacy	12	4	0	3	0	0	0	0	0	26	10	2	2	2	0	0	0	0	2
Economic Activity	5	0	0	1	0	0	0	0	0	7	2	0	1	0	0	0	0	0	1
Crime	0	0	0	0	0	0	0	0	0	0	0	0	0	0	0	0	0	0	0
Public Moral Problems	1	0	0	2	6	0	0	0	0	2	1	0	0	0	0	0	0	0	2
Public Health, Welfare	1	0	0	0	0	0	0	0	0	4	1	0	0	0	0	0	0	0	1
Accidents, Disasters	0	0	0	0	0	0	0	0	0	0	0	0	0	0	0	0	0	0	0
Science, Invention	0	0	0	0	0	0	0	0	0	0	0	0	0	0	0	0	0	0	0
Education, Classic Arts	2	1	0	2	2	0	0	0	0	3	1	0	0	0	0	0	0	0	2
Recreation, Media	2	0	0	0	0	0	0	0	0	4	0	0	0	0	0	0	0	0	1
Human Interest	0	0	0	0	0	0	0	0	0	0	2	0	0	0	0	0	0	0	0
Strength of Candidate	32	4	1	11	2	0	0	1	0	44	22	0	4	3	0	2	0	0	1
Horserace	7	2	0	4	3	1	0	0	0	23	1	0	2	0	0	0	0	0	0
Total	**116**	**16**	**1**	**43**	**16**	**4**	**4**	**2**	**1**	**166**	**51**	**5**	**25**	**6**	**5**	**5**	**0**	**2**	**29**

+ = Favorable – = Unfavorable 0 = Neutral
*N = Neutral category includes items that do not refer primarily to one candidate or have clear direction.

Table 54: Number and Direction of News Segments in 1988 about Candidates and Issues Aired on CBS News

	Dukakis			*Bentsen*			*Democrats*			*Bush*			*Quayle*			*Republicans*			
	+	-	0	+	-	0	+	-	0	+	-	0	+	-	0	+	-	0	*N
Politics, Government	23	5	7	1	0	1	13	2	0	25	6	5	4	3	1	13	19	1	70
War, Defense, Diplomacy	13	9	1	2	0	0	0	0	0	12	1	1	0	0	0	0	5	0	3
Economic Activity	12	3	0	0	0	0	0	0	0	5	5	0	0	1	0	0	1	0	4
Crime	9	6	1	1	0	0	0	0	0	7	5	0	0	0	0	0	0	0	1
Public Moral Problems	3	2	0	0	0	0	0	1	0	4	4	0	3	1	0	0	4	0	2
Public Health, Welfare	10	5	0	0	0	0	0	0	0	1	6	0	0	0	0	0	0	0	4
Accidents, Disasters	0	0	0	0	0	0	0	0	0	0	0	0	0	0	0	0	0	0	0
Science, Invention	0	0	0	0	0	0	0	0	0	0	0	0	0	0	0	0	0	0	0
Education, Classic Arts	1	1	0	0	0	0	0	0	0	1	1	0	0	0	0	1	0	0	1
Recreation, Media	5	2	2	1	0	2	0	0	0	4	0	0	0	0	0	1	1	0	16
Human Interest	0	0	0	0	0	0	0	0	0	0	0	0	0	0	0	0	0	0	0
Strength of Candidate	45	16	2	15	2	0	2	0	0	40	20	2	18	22	1	2	3	0	4
Horserace	0	1	0	0	0	0	0	0	0	19	0	0	0	0	0	2	0	0	0
Total	**121**	**50**	**13**	**20**	**2**	**3**	**15**	**3**	**0**	**118**	**48**	**8**	**25**	**27**	**2**	**19**	**33**	**1**	**104**

\+ = Favorable - = Unfavorable 0 = Neutral
*N = Neutral category includes items that do not refer primarily to one candidate or have clear direction or both.

Table 55: Number and Direction of News Segments in 1984 about Candidates and Issues Aired on NBC News

	Mondale			*Ferraro*			*Democrats*			*Reagan*			*Bush*			*Republicans*			
	+	-	0	+	-	0	+	-	0	+	-	0	+	-	0	+	-	0	*N
Politics, Government	48	2	1	9	2	2	1	0	0	23	4	9	8	2	3	0	0	0	25
War, Defense, Diplomacy	16	2	3	3	0	0	0	0	0	12	4	1	3	1	0	0	0	0	1
Economic Activity	3	0	0	1	0	0	0	0	0	5	1	0	0	0	0	0	0	0	1
Crime	1	0	0	0	0	0	0	0	0	0	0	1	1	0	0	0	0	0	0
Public Moral Problems	3	0	0	8	3	0	0	0	0	2	0	2	1	0	0	0	0	0	2
Public Health, Welfare	0	0	0	1	2	0	0	0	0	3	1	0	0	0	0	0	0	0	0
Accidents, Disasters	0	0	0	0	0	0	0	0	0	0	0	0	0	0	0	0	0	0	0
Science, Invention	0	0	0	0	0	0	0	0	0	0	0	0	0	0	0	0	0	0	0
Education, Classic Arts	0	0	0	0	0	0	0	0	0	3	1	0	0	0	0	0	0	0	1
Recreation, Media	0	0	0	0	0	0	0	0	0	1	0	0	0	0	0	0	0	0	2
Human Interest	0	0	0	0	0	0	0	0	0	1	0	0	0	0	0	0	0	0	0
Strength of Candidate	27	5	0	8	4	2	0	0	0	36	9	0	3	2	1	0	0	0	0
Horserace	2	2	0	0	1	0	0	0	0	13	0	0	3	0	0	1	0	0	0
Total	**100**	**11**	**4**	**30**	**12**	**4**	**1**	**0**	**0**	**99**	**21**	**13**	**18**	**5**	**4**	**1**	**0**	**0**	**32**

+ = Favorable - = Unfavorable 0 = Neutral
*N = Neutral category includes items that do not refer primarily to one candidate or have clear direction.

Table 56: Number and Direction of News Segments in 1988 about Candidates and Issues Aired on NBC News

	Dukakis			*Bentsen*			*Democrats*			*Bush*			*Quayle*			*Republicans*			
	+	-	0	+	-	0	+	-	0	+	-	0	+	-	0	+	-	0	*N
Politics, Government	24	4	4	6	0	2	12	3	3	27	5	5	9	1	0	15	7	1	67
War, Defense, Diplomacy	8	8	1	0	0	0	0	0	0	12	0	1	1	0	0	0	1	0	4
Economic Activity	8	3	2	2	0	0	0	0	0	5	6	0	0	0	0	1	0	0	3
Crime	6	3	3	1	0	1	0	0	0	3	8	0	0	0	0	0	2	0	4
Public Moral Problems	1	0	0	0	0	0	0	0	0	1	1	0	0	0	0	1	8	0	5
Public Health, Welfare	8	3	1	0	0	0	0	0	0	3	4	0	0	0	0	0	0	0	5
Accidents, Disasters	1	0	0	0	0	0	0	0	0	0	0	0	0	0	0	0	0	0	0
Science, Invention	0	0	0	0	0	0	0	0	0	1	0	0	0	0	0	0	0	0	0
Education, Classic Arts	1	0	0	0	0	0	0	0	0	0	0	0	0	0	0	0	0	0	0
Recreation, Media	1	1	1	0	0	0	2	1	1	2	0	0	0	0	0	2	2	0	16
Human Interest	0	0	0	0	0	0	0	0	0	0	0	0	0	0	0	0	0	0	0
Strength of Candidate	36	14	1	5	4	0	0	0	0	22	8	0	9	15	2	4	0	0	4
Horserace	0	2	0	0	0	0	0	0	0	21	0	0	0	0	0	1	0	0	0
Total	**94**	**38**	**13**	**14**	**4**	**3**	**14**	**4**	**4**	**97**	**32**	**6**	**19**	**16**	**2**	**24**	**20**	**1**	**108**

+ = Favorable – = Unfavorable 0 = Neutral

*N = Neutral category includes items that do not refer primarily to one candidate or have clear direction.

Democratic and Republican party issue themes in the 1984 race highlighted politics and strengths of parties and supporters. But in 1988 CBS aired most of its party coverage toward politics, with the Democrats having the positive edge. Nearly 87 percent of the fifteen political issues were favorable compared with 39 percent of the thirty-three political issues involving the Republicans. CBS in 1984 avoided accidents, science, and crime issues. Tables 53 and 54 indicate these findings.

More than 70 percent of the 162 Democratic issues reported in 1984 as the main story theme on NBC focused on Mondale, and 87 percent of that coverage was favorable. The highest proportions and frequencies of issue themes were found in the political activity (94 percent) and the candidate-strength (84.4 percent) groups. The horserace (50 percent) group was negative toward Mondale. NBC lacked coverage of Mondale for main story issues. Of the 188 Democratic issues in 1988, 77 percent concerned Dukakis, and 65 percent of those issues were favorable. As in 1984, the highest frequencies and favorable issue groups in 1988 were political and personal strength categories. Favorable issues in the political group were 75 percent (24 out of 32) and in the candidate-strength categories were 71 percent (36 out of 51). Both of the horserace issues about Dukakis were negative.

In 1984, Ferraro had 28 percent of the Democratic issues on NBC, and slightly more than 65 percent of those issues were considered positive. The distribution for Bentsen was only 12 percent of the 188 Democratic issues. However, he received almost the same favorable coverage (64 percent) in 1988 as Ferraro (65 percent) had in 1984. Negative issues for Ferraro were found mostly in public moral problems (27 percent), public health (67 percent), and candidate-strength (29 percent) categories. Only one story emphasized Ferraro's chances of losing. Favorable issues had political activity (69 percent), diplomacy (100 percent), and candidate-strength (57 percent) themes. Politics (75 percent), economic activity (100 percent), and personal strength (58 percent) categories in 1988 had the highest proportions of positive references about Bentsen.

Reagan in 1984 dominated with 82.6 percent of the main Republican issues of the 161 that were aired on NBC. Nearly 83 percent of those themes were favorable. The highest proportions and frequencies of unfavorable issue themes were in the political activity (11 percent) and defense and diplomacy (23.5 percent) groups. Favorable areas were candidate-strength (80 percent), horserace (100 percent) and political activity (64 percent).

Although Reagan claimed more than 82 percent of the Republican issues, Bush, as a 1988 presidential candidate, had only 62 percent of the 217 Republican themes. Nearly 72 percent of them were positive. Highest negative themes toward Bush were crime (73 percent) and economic activities (55 percent). Both groups had 11 issues. Other categories with high frequencies were defense and diplomacy (13), politics (37), and personal strength (30). At least 92 percent of the defense and diplomacy group and 73 percent of the politics and personal strength themes were positive. All 21 horserace issues favored Bush. Issue results for NBC are shown in Tables 55 and 56.

Visual Coverage of the Parties and the Candidates

Although the Republicans clearly governed the volume of news segments in both races, the Democrats held this edge for the visuals. In both election races, each network news program used more than one-fourth of its visual appeals to identify candidates.In 1984 both ABC and NBC used significantly more slides than did CBS. CBS limited its visuals to videotape. The few slides shown by CBS were used to identify candidates. Both ABC and NBC, which had more than twice the slides used by CBS, also used slides mostly for identification. The couple of other slides were personal strength or crowd scenes.

In their visuals of the four 1988 candidates, all three used slides only for identification purposes. Identification visuals, as in the 1984 campaigns, accounted for more than a quarter of the total visuals. ABC had the highest network use of those visuals, 33.3 percent of 219 identities, even though CBS showed more photos (230). NBC used 177 identifications of the candidates.

Videotape was used as the main visual element for displaying activities of the 1988 campaign and was used heavily for identifications. At least 43 percent of the identification visuals on ABC were shown on tape, compared with 51 percent on CBS and 52 percent on NBC. The other scenes depicted crowds, supporters, and the personal styles of the candidates, as shown in Table 57.

Besides the identification visuals, crowds, special-interest groups, and scenes with political supporters were the appeals used most frequently for both parties. The last three accounted for almost half

Table 57: Percentage Distribution of Visual Appeals by Political Party Aired on Each Television News Program for 1984 and 1988

	ABC		*CBS*		*NBC*	
1984	*D*	*R*	*D*	*R*	*D*	*R*
Identification	25.1	30.5	29.2	28.1	24.1	25.1
Family	0.8	2.2	0.9	1.5	0.8	2.8
Style	17.6	16.9	20.4	18.7	20.1	24.1
Supporters	21.6	24.6	17.6	22.7	16.5	21.3
Crowds	20.8	14.8	27.3	21.7	19.7	16.1
Special-interest groups	14.1	11.0	4.6	7.4	18.9	10.4
Totals	**255**	**236**	**216**	**203**	**249**	**211**
1988						
Identification	32.4	34.5	23.1	29.5	29.6	29.1
Family	2.5	5.1	2.4	2.4	4.8	3.0
Style	18.0	15.2	17.0	15.1	17.7	16.1
Supporters	16.3	14.8	14.9	14.9	9.3	11.9
Crowds	21.9	20.6	26.5	22.3	28.1	28.0
Special-Interest Groups	8.9	9.8	16.1	15.8	10.5	11.9
Totals	**361**	**296**	**464**	**417**	**334**	**268**

of all the visuals shown; nearly one-fourth of the other visuals were shown only for identifying the candidates. Only four large proportional differences favored the Democrats. The Democrats had significantly more identification and crowd visuals on ABC and special-interest groups on NBC.

The Democratic and Republican parties had similar visuals during the 1984 presidential campaign. Without question, considerable agreement existed among the network news programs for the campaign visual news package.

In both races, CBS had the closest 50-50 split in its use of visual appeals. It visuals clearly favored the Democrats, however, as shown in Tables 58 and 59. Both ABC and NBC also gave the Democrats a slight lead in their visual usage, although this usage was not a significant advantage in their 1984 presentations. At least 70 percent of the identification visuals on ABC and NBC were neutral. But more than 70 percent of the Democratic visual identifications in 1984 on CBS were favorable, and a little less than half were negative toward the Republicans. The regular, heavy use of video visuals instead of slides to identify the candidates on CBS accounted for the limited use of neutral identification appeals.

A majority of the visuals in the other five categories were favorable for both parties on ABC and NBC, and for the Democratic party on CBS. CBS visuals in the supporters, personal style, and crowd categories were slanted against the Republican candidates. Few visuals of any of the candidates and their families were used.

By the 1988 race, ABC used 69 percent of its visual coverage for the Democrats, and 71 percent was favorable. CBS had 52.7 percent, with 85.5 percent favorable, and NBC showed 55.5 percent, with 79 percent positive. On all three news programs, nearly all of the other issues were neutral photos of the candidates. Personal style and crowd scenes favored both Dukakis and Bush.

The few negative supporters or crowd visuals aimed toward Dukakis were the ones that showed abortion demonstrators. Bush faced opposition in scenes with union workers and Democratic supporters at Bush rallies. More special-interest group visuals were associated with Bush than with Dukakis. Quayle had the few negative personal-style images.

Conclusions and Discussion

Speaking to a 1984 election rally on a Monday night in Houston, Bush told about the tears in his eyes when he asked 9,706 immigrants in Miami's Orange Bowl on September 17, 1984, to swear allegiance to the United States. He told the Houston crowd that he and Reagan want to unite America. Bush launched his political career in Houston.

The same evening Ferraro paid tribute to her mother at her alma mater in New York City. She stressed the importance of family and of women in politics. The listless crowd of 15,000 listened.

Both events escaped the evening news programs.

Four years later, Democratic vice presidential candidate Lloyd Bentsen told a group of college students in Los Angeles that the Republicans were making "a great national election into a carnival sideshow." On the same day, Quayle gave another "safe" talk to college students in Illinois, saying that he wanted to work with younger people for the country's future. Again, both news events escaped the three evening news programs.

In only a few instances during both election races did the vice presidential candidates attract network news coverage of their activities. For Ferraro and Quayle, those events were not the "staged" ones.

Table 58: Number of Democratic Visuals Aired in 1984 and in 1988 by Subject Category and by Direction for Each Television News Program

	1984				*1988*			
ABC News	+	–	*0*	*Totals*	+	–	*0*	*Totals*
Identification	14	2	48	**64**	25	2	90	**117**
Family	2	0	0	**2**	9	0	0	**9**
Style	40	4	1	**45**	62	3	0	**65**
Supporters	46	9	0	**55**	58	1	0	**59**
Crowds	48	5	0	**53**	74	4	1	**79**
Special-interest groups	33	3	0	**36**	31	1	0	**32**
CBS News								
Identification	33	10	20	**63**	45	1	61	**107**
Family	2	0	0	**2**	11	0	0	**11**
Style	36	8	0	**44**	78	1	0	**79**
Supporters	33	5	0	**38**	66	3	0	**69**
Crowds	47	10	2	**59**	123	0	0	**123**
Special-Interest Groups	9	1	0	**10**	74	1	0	**75**
NBC News								
Identification	6	0	54	**60**	33	3	63	**99**
Family	2	0	0	**2**	16	0	0	**16**
Style	41	8	1	**50**	56	2	1	**59**
Supporters	34	7	0	**41**	31	0	0	**31**
Crowds	47	1	1	**49**	91	3	0	**94**
Special-Interest Groups	38	7	2	**47**	35	0	0	**35**

When Ferraro talked about her abortion views, the bishop of New York criticized her views on the evening hews. Academic records and talks of "praying for Bush's good health" plagued Quayle. Neither Ferraro nor Quayle could shake those negative television news themes.

Voters would learn little about the issues in either race if they followed only television's news coverage of these and other campaign events. Action scenes of crowds and supporters provided the campaign realities. Style overruled substance.

From the first to the last day on the campaign trail, coverage of the presidential candidates was staged whenever possible for the evening news. Most of those events occurred early in the day. Each event usually contained an emotional link for the candidate and for the people in that area. Talks focused more on generalities rather than

Table 59: Number of Republican Visuals Aired in 1984 and in 1988 by Subject Category and by Direction for Each Television News Program

	1984				1988			
ABC News	+	–	0	Totals	+	–	0	Totals
Identification	17	4	51	**72**	12	2	88	**102**
Family	4	1	0	**5**	14	0	1	**15**
Style	30	10	0	**40**	39	6	0	**45**
Supporters	54	3	1	**58**	42	2	0	**44**
Crowds	33	1	1	**35**	54	3	4	**61**
Special-Interest Groups	24	2	0	**26**	27	2	0	**29**
CBS News								
Identification	26	8	23	**57**	39	0	84	**123**
Family	3	0	0	**3**	10	0	0	**10**
Style	21	16	1	**38**	55	8	0	**63**
Supporters	28	15	3	**46**	54	8	0	**62**
Crowds	30	11	3	**44**	92	1	0	**93**
Special-Interest Groups	12	2	1	**15**	65	1	0	**66**
NBC News								
Identification	13	0	40	**53**	18	3	57	**78**
Family	5	0	1	**6**	7	0	1	**8**
Style	30	21	0	**51**	39	4	0	**43**
Supporters	40	5	0	**45**	29	3	0	**32**
Crowds	29	1	4	**34**	70	3	2	**75**
Special-Interest Groups	18	2	2	**22**	29	3	0	**32**

specifics. When the candidates avoided the issues in the 1988 campaign, all three news programs started covering issues, which partly explained the large number of neutral stories.

Few substantial issues were reported on the nightly news, but the network television news programs did have agreement on the overall distribution of those issues and the main ones emphasized for each party. Four of every five issues in both election-year races dealt with politics, diplomacy, or the strength of the candidates and their supporters. Such themes were reported in almost every nightly news program. Strength features of the candidates and their parties were the main topics stressed in other election studies of local,[29] general,[30] state,[31] and presidential races.[32]

One explanation of these issue patterns might be the apparent nature of television news. Unlike print news, television news is woven of both video and talk. Simplicity is stressed for a 10- to 60-second story with many sound bites, which helps explain the heavy use of identification visuals and action-type crowd videos about both campaigns.

The technology of the television medium, it seems, often forces the television press to become allies with the candidates they are covering. The heavy emphasis on reporting and showing what is happening now sacrifices the in-depth and follow-up stories, especially when the candidates campaign throughout the country. Close-ups of campaign activities with sight, sound, action, and a simple story line tell the campaign story. Candidates providing these elements for the television press will have the higher chance of being televised and will avoid major, regular discussion of issues. This occurred in the 1984 race. Four years later, television coverage focused on the "negativism" of both campaigns and increased the visuals by showing more scenes.

CBS news provided the extra coverage of the candidates, although that coverage came toward the end of the 1988 race. All four candidates were given an opportunity to be interviewed by Dan Rather on the CBS evening news. Only Dukakis and Bentsen accepted the invitation and were interviewed. Although the interviews focused on a variety of issues, the overall coverage and tone of the interviews tended to be favorable, and this reflected the extra coverage given to the Democrats by CBS news.

CBS also made news by reporting the failure of the Republican candidates to be interviewed on the nightly news. Republicans responded that their candidates had little to gain from such encounters when Bush was ahead in all of the national polls and in the electoral college.

All three network news programs used similar issue and visual campaign coverage. Despite the abundance of possible campaign stories and the available resources of the three television network news programs and their affiliates, the television press was fairly even in its overall coverage of the 1984 campaign. Similar patterns were found in four previous election races.[33]

The high proportion and number of neutral news segments in the 1988 race resulted from all three networks highlighting issues, rather than candidates, and having balanced coverage whenever both parties were reported in the same news segment. Newscaster Peter Jennings, for example, spent time visiting selected cities and talking with people in those towns about what concerned them. In a small

Northern California town, the residents of Eureka told Jennings their concerns about the environment and the economy. The people were torn between these two major issues.

Without question, the results of this study show considerable volume advantages in news and issues for the Republicans, mainly Reagan, and that edge in 1984 was fairly consistent. The Democrats in both campaigns had more visuals and had higher favorable proportions of coverage, and the Democrats, mainly Mondale and Dukakis, held the decisive edge with more favorable issue themes, news, and visual coverage. Both Bush and Bentsen, as vice presidential candidates, also held those favorable edges over their opponents, even though overall coverage of the vice presidential candidates in either race was marginal.

In 1988 the negative tone of the campaign was obvious in the high proportions of negative story segments focusing on three of the four candidates. Bentsen was the only person to escape most of those injurious comments. Both Quayle and Dukakis became unpleasant personality issues for their party.

Although these results suggest consistency in news coverage, they illustrate that a higher volume of news coverage in either election race did not necessarily mean favorable coverage. More importantly, when the directional categories were combined, the differences in volume and proportional differences in coverage between the parties were not that distinct. Such findings are consistent with other news studies of political campaigns and closely match the patterns reported in the few television news studies of the previous six presidential races.[34]

For a clear indicator of imbalance, coverage and the direction of that coverage should consistently support one party. This did not happen in either race. Imbalanced coverage should occur from one presidential campaign to the next election race. This, too, did not happen.

First, in 1984 Reagan clearly dominated the nightly news programs throughout the race. Part of that campaign coverage could be attributed to his incumbency and to his personal appeal. But the coverage was not always favorable. Extra coverage came from the television press.

Throughout the 63-day campaign, Reagan did not hold a press conference. Instead, his talks and activities were scheduled to make news for television. The crowds, campaign activities, and the supporters provided the extra news-segment coverage for the nightly news packages. Extra coverage also came from the television press people who tried to trap Reagan with his remarks and style. Those stories focused on Reagan's negative aspects. This, in turn, meant more news-segment coverage. Mondale had a higher proportion of favorable news segments than did Reagan. Again, although some imbalances existed, they obviously did not reflect bias.

Second, similar patterns occurred in 1988. Although the Democrats held the overall favorable edge, the Republicans had the volume. Neither party had high, strong positive news presentations. If imbalance occurred, the visuals should have been slanted. Again, this did not happen.

Finally, with a planned approach of one campaign theme a day for the evening news, Bush varied little from his 1988 agenda. Even in the last days when he was without doubt ahead in the race, he campaigned as the "underdog."

Most of the findings confirm the three hypotheses of coverage similarities and reject the hypothesis of balanced coverage between the two parties. But the evidence for balanced coverage in either race was not beyond doubts. The volume edge in news segments did not mean favorable treatment of news, issues, or visuals. Other factors, such as the personal abilities of the candidates to make news and the availability of news time for interviews, diluted charges of slanted or imbalanced news toward any network news program.

The news appeal of Reagan in both campaigns helped the Republicans, compared to the effect of the poor images and styles of the Democratic presidential candidates. Those Democratic components merely added leverage to the Republicans' strategy of "one theme per day."

Besides the coverage consistency, the other two major findings were that television news editors were similar to newspaper editors[35] in using the most accessible material available throughout the campaign and that television news coverage, along with newspaper coverage,[36] focused heavily on what candidates are rather than on what they would do.

Notes

1. Marshall McLuhan, *The Gutenberg Galaxy: The Making of Typographic Man* (Toronto: The University of Toronto Press, 1962); idem. *Understanding Media: The Extensions of Man* (New York: New American Library, 1964); Marshall McLuhan and E.S. Carpenter, *Explorations in Communication* (Boston: The Beacon Press, 1960); Marshall McLuhan and Quentin Fiore, *The Medium is the Message* (New York: Random House, 1967).
2. David L. Altheide, "Three-in-One News: Network Coverage of Iran," *Journalism Quarterly*, 59:482-486 (Autumn 1982); Joseph R. Dominick, "Business Coverage in Network Newscasts," *Journalism Quarterly*, 58:179-185 (Summer 1981); Joe S. Foote and Michael E. Steele, "Degree of Conformity in Lead Stories in Early Evening Network TV Newscasts," *Journalism Quarterly*, 63:19-23 (Spring 1986); Joseph S. Fowler and Stuart W. Showalter, "Evening Network News Selection: A Confirmation of News Judgment," *Journalism Quarterly*, 51:712-715 (Winter 1974); James B. Lemert, "Content Duplication by the Networks in Competing Evening Newscasts," *Journalism Quarterly*, 51:238-244 (Summer 1974); Milan D. Meeske and Mohamad Hamid Javaheri, "Network Television Coverage of the Iranian Hostage Crisis," *Journalism Quarterly*, 59:641-645 (Winter 1982); Daniel Riffe, Brenda Ellis, Momo K. Rogers, Roger L. Van Ommeren, and Kieran A. Woodman, "Gatekeeping and the Network News Mix," *Journalism Quarterly*, 63:315-321 (Summer 1986); Gerald C. Stone and Elinor Grusin, "Network TV as the Bad News Bearer," *Journalism Quarterly*, 61:517-523, 592 (Autumn 1984); Larry W. Thomas and Laslo V. Boyd, "Television News Coverage of Six Federal Regulatory Agencies," *Journalism Quarterly*, 61:160-164 (Spring 1984).
3. John Ehrlichman, *Witness to Power* (New York: Simon and Schuster, 1982); James Keogh, *President Nixon and the Press* (New York: Funk and Wagnalls, 1972); Richard M. Nixon, *Six Crises* (Garden City, N.Y.: Doubleday, 1962); *idem*, *Memoirs of Richard Nixon* (New York: Grosset and Dunlap, 1978); Theodore H. White, *Breach of Faith* (New York: Dell, 1976); "Text of Senator Nixon's Broadcast Explaining Supplementary Expense Fund," New York *Times*, Sept. 24, 1952.
4. Samuel L. Becker and Elmer W. Lower, "Broadcasting in Presidential Campaigns," in Sidney Kraus, ed., *The Great Debates* (Bloomington: Indiana University Press, 1962), pp. 25-55; Samuel

L. Becker and Elmer W. Lower, "Broadcasting in Presidential Campaign, 1960-1976," in Kraus, ed., *The Great Debates*, pp. 11-40; Gladys Engel Lang and Kurt Lang, *Politics and Television* (Chicago: Quadrangle, 1968); *idem*, *Politics and Television, Re-Viewed* (Beverly Hills, Calif.: Sage, 1984); Martin Mayer, "Right Before Your Eyes," *About Television* (New York: Harper and Row, 1972); Herbert Simon and Frederick Stern, "The Effect of Television Upon Voting Behavior in Iowa in the 1952 Presidential Election," *American Political Science Review*, 44:470-477 (June 1955).

5. Herbert Hyman and Paul B. Sheatsley, "The Political Appeal of President Eisenhower," *Public Opinion Quarterly*, 17:443-460 (Winter 1953-1954).

6. Pierre Salinger, *With Kennedy* (New York: Doubleday, 1966); Theodore H. White, *The Making of the President 1960* (New York: Atheneum, 1961).

7. Elihu Katz and Jacob J. Feldman, "The Debates in the Light of Research: A Survey of Surveys," in Kraus, *The Great Debates*, pp. 173-223; Fred Fedler, Ron Smith, and Mike Meeske, "*Time*, *Newsweek*, and the Kennedys: A Study of Three Presidential Elections," paper presented to the Association for Education in Journalism, Athens, Ohio, July 1982; Samuel Lubell, "Personalities vs. Issues," in Kraus, *The Great Debates*, pp. 151-162; White, *The Making of the President 1960*.

8. New York *Times*, Nov. 14, 1969, p. 24; *Broadcasting*, Dec. 1, 1969, p. 56

9. Edith Efron, *The News Twisters* (Los Angeles: Nash Publishing, 1971).

10. Terry F. Buss and C. Richard Hofstetter, "The Logic of Television News Coverage of Political Campaign Information," *Journalism Quarterly*, 54:341-349 (Summer 1977); Dru Evarts and Guido H. Stempel III, "Coverage of the 1972 Campaign by TV, News Magazines, and Major Newspapers," *Journalism Quarterly*, 51:645-653, 669 (Winter 1974); Robert S. Frank, "The Grammar of Film in Television News," *Journalism Quarterly*, 51:245-250 (Summer 1974); C. Richard Hofstetter, *Bias in the News* (Columbus: Ohio State University Press, 1976); C. Richard Hofstetter and Cliff Zukin, "TV Network News and Advertising in the Nixon and McGovern Campaigns," *Journalism Quarterly*, 56:106-115, 152 (Spring 1979); Dennis T. Lowry, "Measures of Network Bias in the 1972 Presidential Campaign," *Journal of Broadcasting*, 18:387-402 (Fall 1974); Gary D. Malaney and Terry F. Buss, "AP Wire Reports vs. CBS TV

News Coverage of a Presidential Campaign," *Journalism Quarterly*, 56:602-610 (Autumn 1973); Thomas E. Patterson and Robert D. McClure, *The Unseeing Eye: The Myth of Television Power in National Elections* (New York: G.P. Putnam's Sons, 1976).

11. Thomas E. Patterson, *The Mass Media Election* (New York: Praeger, 1980).

12. Guido H. Stempel III and John W. Windhauser, "The Prestige Press Revisited: Coverage of the 1980 Presidential Campaign," *Journalism Quarterly*, 61:49-55 (Spring 1984); James Glen Stovall, "Foreign Policy Issue Coverage in the 1980 Presidential Campaign," *Journalism Quarterly*, 59:531-540 (Winter 1982); *idem*, "The Third-Party Challenge of 1980: News Coverage of the Presidential Candidates," *Journalism Quarterly*, 62:266-271 (Summer 1985).

13. Jeff Merron and Gary D. Gaddy, "Editorial Endorsements and News Play: Bias in Coverage of Ferraro's Finances," *Journalism Quarterly*, 63:127-137 (Spring 1986); Michael J. Robinson and Austin Ranney, eds., *The Mass Media in Campaign '84* (Washington, D.C.: American Enterprise Institute for Public Policy Research, 1985).

14. Paul A. Atkins and Harry Elwood, "TV News Is First Choice in Survey of High Schools," *Journalism Quarterly*, 55:596-599 (Autumn 1978); Dan G. Drew and Stephen D. Reese, "Children's Learning from a Television Newscast," *Journalism Quarterly*, 61:83-88 (Spring 1984); Ronald J. Faber, Stephen D. Reese, and H. Leslie Steeves, "Spending Time with the News Media: The Relationship between Reliance and Use," *Journal of Broadcasting and Electronic Media*, 29:445-450 (Fall 1985); Ronald J. Faber, Jane D. Brown, and Jack M. McLeod, "Coming of Age in the Global Village: Television and Adolescence," *Inter Media* (New York: Oxford University Press, 1986), pp. 550-572; Lucy L. Henke, "Perceptions and Use of News Media by College Students," *Journal of Broadcasting and Electronic Media*, 29:431-436 (Fall 1985); Lucy L. Henke, Thomas R. Donohue, Christopher Cook, and Diane Cheung, "The Impact of Cable on Traditional TV News Viewing, *Journalism Quarterly*, 61:174-178 (Spring 1984); Richard R. Martin, John T. McNelly, and Fausto Izearay, "Is Media Exposure Unidimensional? A Socioeconomic Approach," *Journalism Quarterly*, 53:619-625 (Winter 1976); Robert W. Pittman, "Communication with the TV Generation," speech at the 100th American Newspaper Publishers Association Annual Convention, San Francisco, April 1986; Donna Rouner, "Active Television Viewing and the Cultivation Hypothesis," *Jour-*

nalism Quarterly, 61:168-174 (Spring 1984); Merrill Samuelson, Richard F. Carter, and Lee Ruggels, "Education, Available Time, and Use of Mass Media," *Journalism Quarterly*, 40:491-496, 617 (1963); "The Times Poll, Public and Press – Two Viewpoints," Los Angeles *Times*, Aug. 11, 1985; John W. Windhauser, Mark Barden, and Time Viner, "How Mississippians Use Their Newspapers and Other Media," paper presented to the Mississippi Press Association, Biloxi, Miss., June 1981; John W. Windhauser and Dan L. Lattimore, "Use of the Mass Media on a College Campus," *College Press Review*, 12:22-23 (Winter 1973); W. Gill Woodall, Dennis K. Davis, and Haluk Sahin, "From the Boob Tube to the Black Box: Television News Comprehension from an Information Processing Perspective," *Journal of Broadcasting*, 27:1-23 (Winter 1983).

15. Charles K. Atkin, John Galloway, and Oguz Nayman, "News Media Exposure, Public Knowledge and Campaign Interest," *Journalism Quarterly*, 53:231-237 (Summer 1976); Lee B. Becker and David Demers, "Motivations, Media Use, and Electoral Decision Making," paper presented to the Association for Education in Journalism, Athens, Ohio, July 1982; Steven H. Chaffee, L. Scott Ward, and Leonard P. Tipton, "Mass Communication and Political Socialization," *Journalism Quarterly*, 47:647-659, 666 (Autumn 1970); Peter Clarke and Eric Fredin, "The Media and Political Reasoning," paper presented to the Association for Education in Journalism, College Park, Md., August 1976; Gary Kebbel, "The Importance of Political Activity in Explaining Multiple Media Use," *Journalism Quarterly*, 62:559-566 (Autumn 1985); Margaret K. Latimer, "The Newspaper: How Significant for Black Voters in Presidential Elections?" *Journalism Quarterly*, 60:16-23, 47 (Spring 1983); William A. Lucas and William C. Adams, "Talking, Television, and Voter Indecision," *Journal of Communication*, Autumn 1978, pp. 120-131; Jarol B. Manheim, "Can Democracy Survive Television?" *Journal of Communication*, Spring 1976, pp. 84-90; Robert D. McClure and Thomas E. Patterson, "Print vs. Network News," *Journal of Communication*, Spring 1976, pp. 23-28; M. Mark Miller and Stephen D. Reese, "Media Dependency as Interaction: Effects of Exposure and Reliance on Political Activity and Efficacy," *Communication Research*, 9:227-248 (April 1982); Garrett J. O'Keefe, "Political Malaise and Reliance on Media," *Journalism Quarterly*, 57:122-128 (Spring 1980); Churchill L. Roberts, "Media Use and Difficulty of Decision in the 1976 Presidential Campaign," *Journalism Quarterly*, 56:794-802 (Winter 1979); Alan M. Rubin, "Child

and Adolescent Television Use and Political Socialization," *Journalism Quarterly*, 55:125-129 (Spring 1979); Arthur Schlesinger Jr., "Politics and Television," in Barry Cole, ed., *Television Today* (New York: Oxford University Press, 1981), pp. 283-288.

16. Elihu Katz, "Platforms and Windows: Broadcasting's Role in Election Campaigns," *Journalism Quarterly*, 48:304-314 (Summer 1971); Dennis S. Rutkus, "Presidential Television," *Journal of Communication*, 26:73-78 (Spring 1976); Michael J. Robinson, "Television and American Politics: 1956-1976," *The Public Interest*, Summer 1977, pp. 3-39; Robert Rudd and Marjorie J. Fish, "Depth of Issue Coverage in Television," *Journal of Broadcasting and Electronic Media*, 33:197-202 (Spring 1989); James Glen Stovall, "Coverage of 1984 Presidential Campaign," *Journalism Quarterly*, 65:443-449, 484 (Summer 1988).

17. Daniel M. Gaby, "Politics and Public Relations," *Public Relations Journal*, October 1980, pp. 11-12; Kathleen Hall Jamieson, *Packaging the Presidency: A History and Criticism of Presidential Campaign Advertising* (New York: Oxford University Press, 1984); Stanley Kelly Jr., *Professional Public Relations and Political Power* (Baltimore: John Hopkins Press, 1961); Gladys Engel Lang and Kurt Lang, *The Battle for Public Opinion* (New York: Columbia University Press, 1983); Richard W. Lee, ed., *Politics and the Press* (Washington D.C.: Acropolis, 1970); "Good Questions and Bad Answers," *Newsweek*, March 26, 1984, p. 59; Bruce I. Newman, "Political Candidates Can Use Marketing Research Tools to Build Comprehensive Campaign Strategy," *Marketing News*, May 13, 1984; Dan Nimmo, *The Presidential Persuaders* (Englewood Cliffs, N.J.: Prentice-Hall, 1970); *idem*, *Political Communication and Public Opinion in America* (Santa Monica, Calif.: Goodyear, 1978); Dan Nimmo and Robert L. Savage, *Candidates and Their Images: Concepts, Methods and Findings* (Pacific Palisades, Calif.: Goodyear, 1976); Dan Nimmo, *Popular Images of Politics* (Englewood Cliffs, N.J.: Prentice-Hall, 1974); M. Timothy O'Keefe and Kenneth G. Sheinkopf, "The Voter Decides: Candidate Image or Campaign Issue?" *Journal of Broadcasting*, 28:403-412 (Fall 1974); H.L. Reiter, *Parties and Elections in Corporate America* (New York: St. Martin's Press, 1987); William J. Small, *Political Power and the Press* (New York: W.W. Norton, 1972); Larry J. Sabarto, *The Rise of Political Consultants* (New York: Basic Books, 1981); Roger Streitmatter, "The Impact of Presidential Personality on News Coverage in Major Newspapers," *Journalism Quarterly*, 62:66-73 (Spring

1985); "The Other Campaign: Press vs. Candidates," *U.S. News and World Report*, Mar. 12, 1984, pp. 24-25.

18. Evarts and Stempel, "Coverage of the 1972 Campaign"; Lowry, "Measures of Network Bias"; Robinson and Ranney, *The Mass Media.*

19. Frank, "The Grammar of Film"; Hofstetter, "Bias in the News; C. Richard Hofstetter and Terry F. Buss, "Bias in Television News Coverage of Political Events: A Methodological Analysis," *Journal of Broadcasting*, 22:517-530 (Fall 1978); Malaney and Buss, "AP Wire Reports"; Meadow, "Cross-Media Comparison"; Patterson, *The Mass Media*; Patterson and McClure, *The Unseeing Eye*; Guido H. Stempel III, "Media Evaluation: The State of the Art," paper presented to the Association for Education in Journalism, Carleton University, Canada, August 1975; Robert L. Stevenson and Mark T. Greene, "A Reconsideration of Bias in the News," *Journalism Quarterly*, 57:115-121 (Spring 1980); Alden Williams, "Unbiased Study of Television News Bias," *Journal of Communication*, Autumn 1975, pp. 190-199.

20. See note 2.

21. Wenmouth Williams Jr., Mitchell Shapiro, and Craig Cutbirth, "The Impact of Campaign Agendas on Perceptions of Issues in 1980 Campaign," *Journalism Quarterly*, 60:226-231 (Summer 1983). See also notes 10 and 11.

22. James W. Markham, *Press Coverage of the 1958 State Elections in Pennsylvania: A Measure of Performance*, report of a study sponsored by the School of Journalism at Pennsylvania State University, 1959; *idem*, "Press Treatment of the 1958 State Elections in Pennsylvania," *The Western Political Quarterly*, 14:912-924 (December 1961); James W. Markham and Guido H. Stempel III, *Pennsylvania Daily Press Coverage of the 1956 Election Campaign: A Measure of Performance*, report of a study sponsored by the School of Journalism, Pennsylvania State University, 1957; John W. Windhauser, "How the Metropolitan Press Covered the 1970 General Election Campaigns of Ohio," *Journalism Quarterly*, 54:332-340 (Summer 1977).

23. Edwin Diamond and Stephen Bates, *The Spot: The Rise of Political Advertising on Television* (Cambridge, Mass.: MIT Press, 1984); Thomas Griffith, "TV's Condescending Coverage," *Time*, Aug. 20, 1984, p. 105; Lang and Lang, *Politics and Television, Re-Viewed*; Gladys Engel Lang and Kurt Lang, "The Television Personality in Politics," *Public Opinion Quarterly*, 20:107-116 (Spring

1956); Joe McGinniss, *The Selling of the President, 1968* (New York: Trident Press, 1969); Leslie Phillips, "Winning Politics: It's No Longer about the Issues," *USA Today*, Aug. 8, 1986, p. 4A. See also note 17.

24. Richard A. Joslyn, "The Content of Political Spot Ads," *Journalism Quarterly*, 57:92-97 (Spring 1980); James G. Benze and Eugene Declerq, "Content of Television Political Spot Ads for Female Candidates," *Journalism Quarterly*, 62:278-283, 288 (Summer 1985).

25. Ronald Gene Humke, Raymond L. Schmitt, and Stanley E. Grupp, "Candidates, Issues, and Party in Newspaper Political Advertisements," *Journalism Quarterly*, 52:499-504 (Autumn 1975); James J. Mullen, "Newspaper Advertising in the Johnson-Goldwater Campaign," *Journalism Quarterly*, 45:219-225 (Summer 1968); *idem*, "Newspaper Advertising in the Kennedy-Nixon Campaign," *Journalism Quarterly*, 40:3-11 (Winter 1963); Walter Thomas Viner, "A Content Analysis of Political Advertisements Appearing in Daily Mississippi Newspapers During the 1980 Campaign Session," Master's thesis, University of Mississippi, Oxford, 1982; John W. Windhauser and Dan L. Lattimore, "Use of Political Advertisements in Local Election Campaigns," paper presented to the Association for Education in Journalism, Fort Collins, Col., August 1973.

26. The 1984 and the 1988 television data reported in this study included more news programs than listed in the Television News Archives at Vanderbilt University. Besides taping the weekday news programs, we taped the network news programs for the weekends in various sections of the country. By doing this, we avoided regional and national programming conflicts of football games. I want to thank the following people who helped with this news project: J. Nicholas DeBonis, Elinor Grusin, Gigi Guyton, Bertha C. Most, Marlene M. Windhauser, and Mary E. Windhauser, as well as Dru Riley Evarts of Ohio University, for the preliminary coding of the 1984 CBS News data, and Jacklyn Freeman of the Television News Archives, Vanderbilt University, for locating and sending tapes of missing news programs.

27. A news segment was defined as a single news item that focused on a specific event and setting within a campaign news package. Whenever it changed, the item was coded as a separate story segment. Each news segment was coded as to the direction of the segment, the candidate in it, the major issue, and the major visuals or "sound bites" used. A news segment could have several visuals but would have only one main issue theme.

28. The six visuals used were: 1.) identification, a visual of the candidate; 2.) family, the candidate with his or her family; 3.) style, portrayal of a candidate's strengths or weaknesses; 4.) supporters, people who showed either positive or negative support for a candidate; 5.) crowds, the candidate with groups of people who lacked an apparent association with the candidate and his or her party; and 6.) special-interest groups, the candidate with organized, social, political, occupational, or demographic groups such as elderly, students, women, veterans, dock workers, and church organizations.
29. John W. Windhauser, "Reporting of Campaign Issues in Ohio Municipal Election Races," *Journalism Quarterly*, 54:332-340 (Summer 1977).
30. Windhauser, "How the Metropolitan Press Covered the 1970 General Election Campaigns in Ohio."
31. Markham, *Coverage of the 1958 State Elections in Pennsylvania*; *idem*, "Press Treatment of the 1958 State Elections in Pennsylvania."
32. Markham and Stempel, *Pennsylvania Daily Press Coverage of the 1956 Election Campaign:*; David S. Myers, "Editorials and Foreign Affairs in the 1964 Presidential Campaign," *Journalism Quarterly*, 45:211-218 (Summer 1968); *idem*, "Editorials and Foreign Affairs in the 1968 Presidential Campaign," *Journalism Quarterly*, 47:57-64 (Spring 1970); *idem*, "Editorials and Foreign Affairs in the 1972 Presidential Campaign," *Journalism Quarterly*, 51:251-257, 296 (Summer 1974); *idem*, "Editorials and Foreign Affairs in the 1976 Presidential Campaign," *Journalism Quarterly*, 55:92-99 (Spring 1978); idem, "Editorials and the Economy in the 1976 Presidential Campaign," *Journalism Quarterly*, 55:755-760 (Winter 1978); *idem*, "Editorials and the Economy in the 1980 Presidential Campaign," *Journalism Quarterly*, 59:414-419 (Autumn 1982); *idem*, "Editorials and Foreign Affairs in Recent Presidential Campaigns," *Journalism Quarterly*, 59:541-547 (Autumn 1982); James Glen Stovall, "Foreign Policy Issue Coverage in the 1980 Presidential Campaign," *Journalism Quarterly*, 62:266-271 (Summer 1985).
33. See notes 10, 11, and 12.
34. See notes 10, 11, and 12.
35. See notes 29, 30, 31, and 32.
36. See Chapter 2.

4

How the News Magazines Covered the 1984 and 1988 Campaigns

Guido H. Stempel III

The three news magazines — *Newsweek*, *Time*, and *U.S. News and World Report* — are among the best known print media in this country. *Newsweek* and *Time* have larger circulations than any daily newspaper. The three magazines combined have 9.8 million circulation and, with pass-along readership, reach between a fourth and third of the families in this country.

All three have distinctive images. *Time*'s image was for colorful writing, but the color was obtained by extravagant use of adjectives that made writing opinionated and sometimes stilted. *Time* also became associated with the Republican views of its publisher and co-founder, Henry Luce. *Newsweek* attempted to capitalize on the image of *Time* as opinionated by claiming in massive promotional campaign that it was the news magazine that "separated fact from opinion." But *Newsweek* also gained the reputation of being liberal, partly because of what it wrote and partly because it was owned by the Washington *Post*. *U.S. News and World Report*, founded by the renowned conservative David Lawrence, became recognized as a major outlet for conservative political thought.

All three have been much discussed, often criticized, and occasionally studied seriously by scholars. Those studies, however, rarely have focused on political campaign coverage. Only twice has the coverage of a presidential campaign by the news magazines been made.

The first such study was of the 1960 campaign. It covered the primary and convention period but not the campaign itself. The major finding of that study was that the news magazine tended to favor the middle-of-the-road candidates.[1] It did not find marked differences between the magazines nor evidence of bias on the part of any one of the magazines.

The second study was of the 1972 campaign by two of the authors of the present study. That study was of the campaign itself. We expected to find some difference between the magazines because of the differences in political orientation mentioned above. We found nothing of the sort.[2] *Newsweek*, the most liberal of the three magazines, was more favorable to the Republicans than the other two magazines. *U.S. News and World Report* was slightly more favorable to the Republicans than was *Time*. But perhaps most important, the coverage by the three magazines varied only slightly. The analysis was of sentences, and the study found that 57.6 percent of the sentences in *Newsweek* favored the Republicans, 56.9 percent of the sentences in *U.S. News and World Report* favored the Republicans, and 52.3 percent of the sentences in *Time* favored the Republicans.

That study also included six major newspapers and the three television networks, and found that coverage in the newspapers and on the television networks slightly favored the Democrats, in contrast to the Republican leaning of the coverage of news magazines. We concluded that this probably reflected the fact that the Republicans led by a wide margin in the polls from the start and had fewer problems in their campaign than the Democrats did. Weekly publication would tend to deal with this overall picture and thus differ from the daily media in their coverage.

On the basis of that study and the similarities between the 1972 and 1984 campaigns, we hypothesized that the news magazines would lean to the Republican side in 1984 and 1988. Although the incumbency advantage was not a factor in 1988, we still hypothesized that the news magazines would lean to the Republican side. We also hypothesized, our 1972 results notwithstanding, that the order of favorability to the Republicans would be *U.S. News and World Report*, *Time*, and *Newsweek*. Finally, we hypothesized that the news magazines, like other media, would emphasize politics and government and candidate strength among the thirteen categories.

Our study in 1984 began with the issues dated September 3 and included all of the issues during the campaign period, ending with the issues of November 5. In 1988 we started with the issues dated September 5 and ended with the issues of November 7. All stories dealing with the presidential campaign were included in the analysis. The coding included the following:

1. Classification of the major issue in the story, using the 13

categories described in Chapter 1

2. Classification of the story by the candidate the story deals with primarily, using the same procedure used in classifying newspapers described in Chapter 2

3. Classification of the story as favorable, unfavorable, or neutral with respect to the candidate, done in the same way as it was done for the newspapers

Results of the Study

Our expectation that coverage would favor the Republicans in both years for the three magazines combined was correct, but what was more striking was the large number of neutral articles. In 1984 there were more neutral or balanced stories (45.3 percent) than either Democratic or Republican stories. In 1988 there was just about an equal number of Democratic stories, Republican stories, and neutral stories. See Tables 60 and 61.

For 1984 New*sweek* had the highest percentage of neutral stories, 51.4, compared to 42.2 percent of the stories in *Time* and 41.7 percent of the stories in *U.S. News and World Report*. For 1988, *Newsweek* again led in proportion of neutral stories, with 40.3 percent, whereas *Time* had 35.2 percent, and *U.S. News and World Report* had 25.0 percent

The main reason that there were so many neutral or balanced stories is the form that the stories typically took. Campaign roundups included both candidates and thus had an ample amount of both pro-Democratic and pro-Republican material. Such stories also included some transitional or context-setting sentences that were totally neutral. But beyond this, there was a clear attempt to balance a story even if it dealt with only one party or one candidate. All of the magazines had stories about Dukakis in October, for example, and those stories invariably pointed to both successes and failures of the campaign. Even the paragraphs that dealt with a success had a tendency to state "on the other hand" and point to a negative or qualifying aspect. Likewise, the paragraphs that dealt with failures usually did not proclaim them to be total failures. In news magazine coverage, every cloud had a silver lining.

Coverage favored the Republicans to a larger extent in 1984 than it did in 1988, and in 1988, one of the magazines – *Time* – actually gave the Democrats more favorable coverage than it gave the

Table 60: Number and Direction of Stories about Candidates in Three News Magazines, 1984 and 1988

	Mondale			*Ferraro*			*Democrats*			*Reagan*			*Bush*			*Republicans*			
1984	+	-	0	+	-	0	+	-	0	+	-	0	+	-	0	+	-	0	*N
Newsweek	3	8	4	1	1	4	0	0	3	14	4	6	0	2	1	3	0	0	20
Time	9	8	5	5	1	0	0	0	0	9	4	1	2	0	0	0	0	0	21
U.S. News & World Report	6	6	5	4	0	2	0	0	1	19	0	4	0	0	2	0	0	0	11

	Dukakis			*Bentsen*			*Democrats*			*Bush*			*Quayle*			*Republicans*			
1988	+	-	0	+	-	0	+	-	0	+	-	0	+	-	0	+	-	0	*N
Newsweek	10	6	0	0	0	0	2	0	0	14	3	0	2	1	0	1	1	0	27
Time	10	0	0	0	0	0	0	0	0	10	1	0	0	2	0	1	0	0	13
U.S. News & World Report	7	12	0	0	0	0	0	0	0	16	7	0	1	13	1	1	0	0	18

+ = Favorable – = Unfavorable 0 = Neutral
*N = Neutral category includes items that do not refer primarily to one candidate or have clear direction.

Table 61: Number of Democratic, Republican, and Neutral Stories in News Magazines, 1984 and 1988

	Democratic	*Republican*	*Neutral*
1984			
Newsweek	10	26	38
Time	17	20	27
U.S. News & World Report	10	25	25
1988			
Newsweek	17	23	27
Time	13	11	13
U.S. News & World Report	27	30	19

Republicans. Excluding neutral stories, 45.8 percent of the stories in *Time* had favored the Republicans. Contrary to our expectations, it was *Newsweek* that was most favorable to the Republicans in 1988, with 57.5 percent of the stories (neutral stories excluded) favoring the Republicans. For *U.S. News and World Report*, the figure was 52.6 percent. Overall, with neutral stories excluded, 52.9 percent of the stories in 1988 favored the Republicans.

The Republican margin was more clear-cut in 1984 when, excluding neutral stories, 61.8 percent of the stories favored the Republicans. *Newsweek* was most favorable, with 72.3 percent favoring the Republicans, compared with 71.4 percent for *U.S. News and World Report* and 54.0 percent for *Time*.

In neither campaign did the order of the magazines in favorability to the Republicans match our hypothesis. What this means is that the perceived political orientation of the three magazines was not reflected in their coverage of either campaign.

We also found in both campaigns that coverage did not focus very heavily on vice-presidential candidates. There were, overall, more than four-and-one-half as many stories about the presidential candidates as the vice-presidential candidates. In 1984 there were three times as many stories about Mondale as about Ferraro and nearly nine times as many about Reagan as about Bush. In 1988, none of the magazines had a story about Bentsen. This does not mean that he wasn't mentioned but that he was an incidental player in a story about one of the other candidates. For all of the talk about Quayle, only *U.S. News and World Report* had much coverage about him, with fifteen stories, thirteen of them negative. There were thus about two stories for Quayle for every three about Bush in *U.S. News and World*

Report. For the other two magazine, the ratio was about 5 to 1.

Our expectation that coverage would focus on politics and government and candidate strength was clearly confirmed. The first indication is that for each of the magazines, as Tables 62 to 64 indicate, there were in each campaign between five and seven issue categories that had zero frequencies — no stories dealing with those issues. In 1984, 75.9 percent of the stories in all three magazines were about politics and government or candidate strength. In 1988 the figure was 69.4 percent for those two categories combined.

If one looks at our figures for newspapers or television, one finds a similar kind of emphasis on those two categories. The significance of this is in part what it indicates about categories that were not present. Although economic activity was a major issue in both years, for example, or at least seemed to be, only 6 percent of the stories in the two years combined dealt with it. At that, it got twice as much coverage as science and invention, despite the scientific and technology questions that face the country.

It also should be noted that there is a tendency for coverage to be positive rather than negative. Overall, there were almost twice as many positive as negative stories. On the other hand, *U.S. News and World Report* had more unfavorable than favorable stories about both parties in 1988 — 12-7 against the Democrats and 20-18 against the Republicans. That, however, was in sharp contrast to their performance in 1984 of 10-6 for the Democrats and 19-0 for the Republicans. The only other instance of more unfavorable than favorable coverage was *Newsweek*'s coverage of the Democrats in 1984, with nine of thirteen stories unfavorable.

If you look at the coverage by topics for each news magazine as shown in Tables 62 to 64, you will see a lot more similarity than difference between magazines and between campaigns. We have already mentioned the preponderance of coverage of politics and government and candidate strength. One difference between campaigns is considerably more horserace coverage in 1984 than there was in 1988. This is not to state that the news magazines ignored who was winning or seemed to be winning in 1988, but that this was in some instances subordinated by other concerns in a given story.

There also was considerably more coverage of economic activity as an issue in *U.S. News and World Report* than in the other two magazines, but it was not a great deal of coverage — fourteen stories in the eighteen issues of the magazine. That's about one-third of the number of stories *U.S. News and World Report* had in both politics

Table 62: Number and Direction of Stories about Candidates and Issues in *Newsweek*, 1984 and 1988

	Mondale			*Ferraro*			*Democrats*			*Reagan*			*Bush*			*Republicans*			
1984	+	-	0	+	-	0	+	-	0	+	-	0	+	-	0	+	-	0	*N
Politics, Government	1	4	0	0	0	0	0	0	3	7	1	4	0	0	0	3	0	0	12
War, Defense, Diplomacy	0	0	0	0	0	0	0	0	0	0	0	0	0	2	0	0	0	0	3
Public Moral Problems	0	0	0	0	1	2	0	0	0	0	0	0	0	0	1	0	0	0	4
Science, Invention	0	0	0	0	0	0	0	0	0	0	0	1	0	0	0	0	0	0	0
Recreation, Media	0	0	0	0	0	1	0	0	0	0	1	0	0	0	0	0	0	0	1
Strength of Candidate	2	4	4	1	0	1	0	0	0	7	2	1	0	0	0	0	0	0	0

Note: No stories in 1984 about economic activity, crime, public health and welfare, accidents and disasters, education and classic arts, human interest, or horserace.

	Dukakis			*Bentsen*			*Democrats*			*Bush*			*Quayle*			*Republicans*			
1988	+	-	0	+	-	0	+	-	0	+	-	0	+	-	0	+	-	0	*N
Politics, Government	2	3	0	0	0	0	2	0	0	8	0	0	0	0	0	1	0	0	15
War, Defense, Diplomacy	0	0	0	0	0	0	0	0	0	1	1	0	0	0	0	0	0	0	1
Economic Activity	1	0	0	0	0	0	0	0	0	0	0	0	0	0	0	0	0	0	3
Public Moral Problems	0	0	0	0	0	0	0	0	0	0	0	0	0	1	0	0	0	0	2
Public Health, Welfare	0	0	0	0	0	0	0	0	0	0	0	0	0	0	0	0	0	0	1
Human Interest	0	0	0	0	0	0	0	0	0	0	0	0	1	0	0	0	0	0	0
Strength of Candidate	6	3	0	0	0	0	0	0	0	5	2	0	1	0	0	0	1	0	4
Horserace	1	0	0	0	0	0	0	0	0	0	0	0	0	0	0	0	0	0	1

+ = Favorable – = Unfavorable 0 = Neutral
Note: No stories in 1988 about crime, accidents and disasters, science and invention, education and classic arts, or recreation and media.
*N = Neutral category includes items that do not refer primarily to one candidate or have clear direction.

Table 63: Number and Direction of Stories about Candidates and Issues in *Time*, 1984 and 1988

	Mondale			*Ferraro*			*Democrats*			*Reagan*			*Bush*			*Republicans*			
1984	+	-	0	+	-	0	+	-	0	+	-	0	+	-	0	+	-	0	*N
Politics, Government	6	3	2	0	0	0	0	0	0	6	1	1	0	0	0	0	0	0	16
Economic Activity	0	0	2	0	0	0	0	0	0	0	1	0	0	0	0	0	0	0	0
Public Moral Problems	0	0	0	0	0	0	0	0	0	0	0	0	2	0	0	0	0	0	3
Recreation, Media	0	0	0	1	0	0	0	0	0	0	0	0	0	0	0	0	0	0	1
Strength of Candidate	3	1	1	4	1	0	0	0	0	0	2	0	0	0	0	0	0	0	1
Horserace	0	4	0	0	0	0	0	0	0	3	0	0	0	0	0	0	0	0	0

Note: No stories in 1984 about war, defense, and diplomacy, crime, public health and welfare, accidents and disasters, science and invention, human interest, or education and classic arts.

	Dukakis			*Bentsen*			*Democrats*			*Bush*			*Quayle*			*Republicans*			
1988	+	-	0	+	-	0	+	-	0	+	-	0	+	-	0	+	-	0	*N
Politics, Government	6	0	0	0	0	0	0	0	0	3	1	0	0	0	0	0	0	0	5
War, Defense, Diplomacy	1	0	0	0	0	0	0	0	0	0	0	0	0	0	0	0	0	0	0
Public Health, Welfare	1	0	0	0	0	0	0	0	0	0	0	0	0	0	0	0	0	0	1
Human Interest	0	0	0	0	0	0	0	0	0	0	0	0	0	0	0	0	0	0	4
Strength of Candidate	2	0	0	0	0	0	0	0	0	5	0	0	0	2	0	1	0	0	1
Horserace	0	0	0	0	0	0	0	0	0	2	0	0	0	0	0	0	0	0	2

+ = Favorable – = Unfavorable 0 = Neutral
Note: No stories in 1988 about economic activity, crime, public moral problems, accidents and disasters, science and invention, recreation and media, or education and classic arts.
*N = Neutral category includes items that do not refer primarily to one candidate or have clear direction.

Table 64: Number and Direction of Stories about Candidates and Issues in *U.S. News and World Report*, 1984 and 1988

1984	*Mondale*			*Ferraro*			*Democrats*			*Reagan*			*Bush*			*Republicans*			
	+	-	0	+	-	0	+	-	0	+	-	0	+	-	0	+	-	0	*N
Politics, Government	1	0	2	0	0	0	0	0	1	4	0	1	0	0	1	0	0	0	8
War, Defense, Diplomacy	0	0	1	0	0	0	0	0	0	0	0	1	0	0	0	0	0	0	1
Economic Activity	2	2	0	0	0	0	0	0	0	0	0	0	0	0	1	0	0	0	0
Public Moral Problems	0	0	0	0	0	1	0	0	0	0	0	1	0	0	0	0	0	0	0
Recreation, Media	0	0	0	0	0	0	0	0	0	0	0	0	0	0	0	0	0	0	0
Human Interest	0	0	0	0	0	1	0	0	0	0	0	0	0	0	0	0	0	0	0
Strength of Candidate	3	1	2	4	0	0	0	0	0	6	0	1	0	0	0	0	0	0	2
Horserace	0	3	0	0	0	0	0	0	0	9	0	0	0	0	0	0	0	0	0

Note: No stories in 1984 about crime, public health and welfare, science and invention, education and classic arts, or accidents and disasters.

1988	*Dukakis*			*Bentsen*			*Democrats*			*Bush*			*Quayle*			*Republicans*			
	+	-	0	+	-	0	+	-	0	+	-	0	+	-	0	+	-	0	*N
Politics, Government	2	3	0	0	0	0	0	0	0	4	0	0	0	0	0	1	0	0	14
War, Defense, Diplomacy	3	2	0	0	0	0	0	0	0	2	2	0	0	0	1	0	0	0	0
Economic Activity	0	5	0	0	0	0	0	0	0	0	3	0	0	0	0	0	0	0	1
Crime	0	0	0	0	0	0	0	0	0	0	0	0	0	0	0	0	0	0	1
Public Health, Welfare	1	0	0	0	0	0	0	0	0	1	0	0	0	0	0	0	0	0	0
Recreation, Media	1	0	0	0	0	0	0	0	0	0	0	0	0	2	0	0	0	0	2
Strength of Candidate	0	2	0	0	0	0	0	0	0	7	1	0	1	11	0	0	0	0	0
Horserace	0	0	0	0	0	0	0	0	0	2	1	0	0	0	0	0	0	0	0

+ = Favorable – = Unfavorable 0 = Neutral
Note: No stories in 1988 about public moral problems, accidents and disasters, science and invention, education and classic arts, or human interest.
*N = Neutral category includes items that do not refer primarily to one candidate or have clear direction.

and government and in candidate strength.

One factor in issue coverage was that these magazines did some coverage of issues independent of the candidates. Early in the campaign, they discussed what the issues were, but they did that without a clear indication of where each candidate stood on some of those issues.

Conclusions

Our first hypothesis, that coverage would favor the Republicans, was confirmed overall, although it was not true for *Time* in 1988. Clearly, the main feature of the news magazines' coverage was that neutral and balanced stories dominated. Neither side had any appreciable advantage in either year, and in 1988 there were almost equal numbers of Democratic, Republican, and neutral stories.

Our second hypothesis, that the order of favorability to the Republicans would be *U.S. News and World Report*, *Time*, and *Newsweek*, was not the case at all. *Time* was third in both years, *Newsweek* was most favorable to the Republicans in 1984 and the second most favorable was *U.S. News and World Report.*

Our third hypothesis, that most of the stories would deal with politics and government and candidate strength, was strongly confirmed, with almost three-fourths of the stories in those two categories. Like the newspapers and television news, the news magazines focused on the candidates and the political process, not issues. Although the absence of issues in the campaign itself became an issue in 1988, we did not find much difference in the patterns of coverage in 1984 and 1988. Issues were not really there in 1984 either, but that fact drew less comment then. For the news magazines, as for other media, this raises the question of whether campaigns as they are conducted should control coverage. Having more coverage of the issues will require initiative by the news magazines to get responses from the candidates beyond those occurring in the normal course of campaign activities.

Notes

1. Bruce H. Westley, Charles E. Higbie, Timothy Burke, David J. Lippert, Leonard A. Maurer, and Vernon A. Stone, "The News Magazines and the 1960 Convention," *Journalism Quarterly*, 40:525-531, 547 (Autumn 1963).
2. Dru Evarts and Guido H. Stempel III, "Coverage of the 1972 Campaign by TV, News Magazines, and Major Newspapers," *Journalism Quarterly*, 51:645-648, 676 (Winter 1974).

5

The Editorial Pages of Leading Newspapers in 1984

David S. Myers

A study of editorial comment cannot account directly for the role of specific issues or sets of issues in a presidential campaign and election. Neither does research of this nature indicate the effect of these editorials on the public, since editorial pages appeal primarily to the attentive public, a relatively small group. It is probable, however, that those who do read a paper's opinion page are the most influential thinkers in their communities. Indirectly through the process of opinion leadership, therefore, editorials may exert additional influence.

The principal objective of this chapter and the next is to discuss the amount and partisan direction of editorial space devoted to the 1984 and 1988 presidential election campaigns by seventeen leading newspapers around the country.

The leading newspapers varied in their editorial endorsements in 1984. Those that supported Walter Mondale were the Atlanta *Constitution*, the Des Moines *Register*, the Louisville *Courier-Journal*, the Milwaukee *Journal*, the New York *Times,* the St. Louis *Post-Dispatch*, and the Washington *Post.* Those endorsing Ronald Reagan were the Chicago *Tribune*, the Dallas Morning *News*, the Kansas City *Star*, the Miami *Herald*, the Portland *Oregonian*, and the San Francisco *Chronicle* . The Baltimore *Sun*, the *Christian Science Monitor*, the Los Angeles *Times*, and the *Wall Street Journal* were uncommitted, although partisan editorial comment in the Los Angeles *Times* leaned toward the Democrats, whereas that of the *Wall Street Journal* supported the Republicans.

The study covered the sixty-four day period from the editions of September 3, Labor Day, to November 5, the last full day of the campaign. Election editorials were classified as pro-Democratic, anti-Republican, pro-Republican, anti-Democratic, and neutral. Column lines were recorded to determine the emphasis of partisan direction and to ascertain which issues were discussed most frequently.

Number and Partisan Direction of Editorials

The number of election editorials on the 1984 presidential campaign and election by the leading newspapers varied between 16 (San Francisco *Chronicle* and 64 (Washington *Post*). Of the total 605 election editorials, 5.0 percent were pro-Democratic, 28.1 percent were anti-Republican, 5.1 percent were pro-Republican, 7.3 percent were anti-Democratic, and 54.5 percent were neutral. The percentage of neutral editorials is high, which suggests some indecision on the part of editorial writers. Of the partisan editorials, 72.7 percent were in the Democratic column (pro-Democratic plus anti-Republican editorials), and 27.3 percent were Republican (pro-Republican plus anti-Democratic editorials). What is significant is that, overwhelmingly, the partisan comments were anti-Republican.[1] These were primarily a criticism of Reagan's economic policies, especially the question of the budget deficit, and to a lesser extent a general concern about his hard-line stands on foreign policy matters.

To facilitate analysis, we divided election editorials initially into the categories of domestic affairs, foreign affairs, and mixed (i.e., those containing both domestic and foreign affairs items). Generally, the percentage patterns were similar among the papers. With the exception of the Baltimore *Sun* and the Los Angeles *Times*, the papers wrote more editorials dealing with domestic affairs than foreign affairs. This is not unusual, because papers normally write a number of editorials about the election process in general, which are considered in the domestic affairs column. Also, in most presidential campaigns, and 1984 was no exception, there is a greater number of specific domestic than foreign affairs issues.

When the editorials were considered in terms of printed lines (Table 65), all papers but the Des Moines *Register* (domestic affairs), the Kansas City *Star* (domestic affairs), the San Francisco *Chronicle* (foreign affairs), and the Washington *Post* (foreign affairs) increased their percentages in both major categories. This was true primarily because the lines of mixed editorials were added and to a lesser extent because domestic affairs editorials tended to be slightly longer than

Table 65: Percentage of Editorial Lines about Two General Subject Areas in 17 Prestige Newspapers during the 1984 Presidential Election

	Domestic Affairs	*Foreign Affairs*	*Total No. of Lines*
Atlanta *Constitution*	59.7%	40.3%	1,601
Baltimore *Sun*	50.4	49.6	2,784
Chicago *Tribune*	61.4	38.6	1,493
Christian Science Monitor	68.1	31.9	2,557
Dallas *Morning News*	68.2	31.8	4,314
Des Moines *Register*	67.8	32.2	3,255
Kansas City *Star*	80.5	19.5	1,449
Los Angeles *Times*	50.1	49.9	1,854
Louisville *Courier-Journal*	59.4	40.6	2,279
Miami *Herald*	58.4	41.6	1,844
Milwaukee *Journal*	62.3	37.7	1,970
New York *Times*	62.2	37.8	2,400
Portland *Oregonian*	64.8	35.2	2,044
St. Louis *Post-Dispatch*	57.0	43.0	3,115
San Francisco *Chronicle*	56.2	43.8	762
Wall Street Journal	52.1	47.9	3,679
Washington *Post*	67.7	32.3	3,878
Average	**61.7%**	**38.3%**	**Total 41,278**

foreign affairs editorials. Also, all papers now dealt more with domestic affairs than with foreign affairs.

In attempting to assess the relative importance of issues in the campaign, it was important to determine the partisan direction of papers on both domestic affairs and foreign affairs matters so that a general comparison could be made. Interestingly, with little variation, the percentages of partisan direction of both domestic affairs and foreign affairs editorials followed that of the total number of election editorials. Regarding domestic affairs editorials, the neutral category was highest, with 59.8 percent, whereas anti-Republican sentiment (24.9 percent) easily surpassed the other partisan categories (5.5 percent pro-Democratic, 3.2 percent pro-Republican, 6.6 percent anti-Democratic).

A similar pattern emerged when the partisan direction of domestic affairs editorials was based on the number of printed lines (Table 66). The anti-Republican comments remained essentially the same, the neutral category declined, and each of the other partisan columns increased somewhat. As expected, anti-Republican sentiment was most noticeable in the papers that endorsed Mondale.

Table 66: Percentage of Partisan Editorial Lines about Domestic Affairs in 17 Prestige Newspapers during the 1984 Presidential Campaign

	Democratic		*Republican*		*Neutral*
	pD	*aR*	*pR*	*aD*	
Atlanta *Constitution*	0.0%	58.2%	0.0%	0.0%	41.8%
Baltimore *Sun*	3.0	7.8	0.0	11.6	77.6
Chicago *Tribune*	4.2	18.0	10.9	10.8	56.1
Christian Science Monitor	0.0	0.0	0.0	0.0	100.0
Dallas *Morning News*	0.0	4.8	14.9	38.4	41.9
Des Moines *Register*	6.5	56.1	0.0	0.0	37.4
Kansas City *Star*	0.0	35.4	0.3	0.0	64.3
Los Angeles *Times*	19.4	11.0	0.0	0.0	69.6
Louisville *Courier-Journal*	8.4	44.6	3.6	0.0	43.4
Miami *Herald*	13.8	18.1	19.3	0.0	48.8
Milwaukee *Journal*	16.2	53.6	0.0	0.0	30.2
New York *Times*	18.7	27.1	0.0	3.1	51.1
Portland *Oregonian*	9.0	13.3	20.1	0.0	57.6
St. Louis *Post-Dispatch*	15.4	49.0	0.0	0.0	35.6
San Francisco *Chronicle*	13.8	0.0	39.0	0.0	47.2
Wall Street Journal	0.0	0.7	6.6	40.1	52.6
Washington *Post*	13.1	21.0	2.3	2.3	61.3
Number of Lines	**1,942**	**6,199**	**1,417**	**2,266**	**13,655**
	7.6%	**24.3%**	**5.6%**	**8.9%**	**53.6%**
Total Lines	**8,141**		**3,683**		
	31.9%		**14.5%**		

* pD = pro-Democratic; aR = anti-Republican; pR = pro-Republican; aD = anti-Democratic

When the partisan direction of foreign affairs editorials was based on printed lines (Table 67), a similar pattern emerged. There was, however, a slight drop in the neutral and anti-Republican columns and a more than doubling of anti-Democratic sentiment. Although the latter is interesting, the change is relatively insignificant, because the percentage of space in that column is still low.

Domestic Affairs Issues and Election Editorial Discussion

A number of different domestic affairs issues appeared in the editorials of the leading newspapers on the 1984 presidential campaign. The discussion of domestic affairs in general, however, drew most of the attention (39.5 percent) of all domestic affairs and mixed

Table 67: Percentage of Partisan Editorial Lines about Foreign Affairs Issues in 17 Prestige Newspapers during the 1984 Presidential Campaign

	Democratic		*Republican*		*Neutral*
	pD	*aR*	*pR*	*aD*	
Atlanta *Constitution*	10.7%	43.0%	16.6%	8.7%	21.0%
Baltimore *Sun*	0.0	25.9	8.7	8.1	57.3
Chicago *Tribune*	0.0	25.7	10.7	2.1	61.5
Christian Science Monitor	0.0	0.0	6.1	0.0	93.9
Dallas *Morning News*	0.0	0.0	15.8	45.3	38.9
Des Moines *Register*	0.0	66.3	3.1	0.0	30.6
Kansas City *Star*	0.0	30.4	0.0	0.0	69.6
Los Angeles *Times*	11.1	31.4	9.1	0.0	48.4
Louisville *Courier-Journal*	0.0	34.3	17.0	0.0	48.7
Miami *Herald*	0.0	10.8	27.1	0.0	62.1
Milwaukee *Journal*	12.9	84.4	0.0	0.0	2.7
New York *Times*	9.7	40.6	0.0	0.0	49.7
Portland *Oregonian*	3.9	53.1	6.3	0.0	36.7
St. Louis *Post-Dispatch*	4.9	53.5	0.0	0.0	41.6
San Francisco *Chronicle*	0.0	9.6	20.1	0.0	70.3
Wall Street Journal	0.0	2.7	7.8	39.4	50.1
Washington *Post*	5.2	40.4	0.0	0.0	54.4
Number of Lines	**515**	**4,934**	**1,287**	**1,496**	**7,567**
	3.3%	**31.2%**	**8.1%**	**9.5%**	**47.9%**
Total Lines	**5,449**		**2,783**		
	34.5%		**17.6%**		

* pD = pro-Democratic; aR = anti-Republican; pR = pro-Republican; aD = anti-Democratic

editorials). Next came discussion of the debates – domestic affairs (17.4 percent) and the economy (15.2 percent). When these percentages were compared with those based on the number of printed lines (Table 68), there were slight decreases in the total percentages of space devoted to general domestic affairs matters and to the debates and a corresponding increase in the economic issue area.

Some of the editorials in the general domestic affairs category combined several issues, and others discussed topics such as the importance of registering to vote and voting, public opinion polls, and the presidential race generally. Most significant and most numerous, however, were the editorials that stressed the leadership qualities (or lack thereof) of the candidates. Consistent with the endorsement patterns, more papers gave higher marks to Mondale than to Reagan, and most of the comment was anti-Reagan. Although they acknowl-

Table 68: Percentage of Editorial Lines about 12 Specific Domestic Affairs Issues in 17 Prestige Newspapers during the 1984 Presidential Campaign

	Abortion	Agriculture	Civil Rights	Debates – Domestic	Economy	Ethics	General	Labor	Religion	Social Security	Supreme Court Appointments	Miscellaneous*	No. of Lines
Atlanta *Constitution*	5.9%	0.0%	0.0%	10.8%	9.4%	18.2%	33.8%	0.0%	12.8%	9.1%	0.0%	0.0%	**955**
Baltimore *Sun*	0.0	4.3	0.0	18.0	4.6	0.0	48.6	0.0	8.8	4.0	4.6	7.1	**1,402**
Chicago *Tribune*	0.0	15.3	0.0	9.8	10.8	5.7	28.9	0.0	9.3	5.7	7.0	7.5	**916**
Christian Science Monitor	0.0	0.0	0.0	20.8	23.7	4.0	33.5	0.0	6.7	3.9	0.0	7.4	**1,742**
Dallas *Morning News*	0.0	0.0	0.0	25.0	26.5	1.4	36.9	3.5	3.4	3.3	0.0	0.0	**2,940**
Des Moines *Register*	0.0	15.2	9.0	5.4	20.3	6.5	21.1	0.0	9.7	5.1	0.0	7.7	**2,208**
Kansas City *Star*	5.4	5.8	0.0	7.1	6.3	18.5	17.8	7.8	19.2	0.0	5.1	7.0	**1,166**
Los Angeles *Times*	0.0	0.0	6.5	8.4	34.6	0.0	46.2	0.0	0.0	4.3	0.0	0.0	**928**
Louisville *Courier-Journal*	0.0	6.1	0.0	22.3	22.8	3.5	40.6	0.0	0.0	4.7	0.0	0.0	**1,353**
Miami *Herald*	7.8	7.1	0.0	17.5	7.4	5.9	40.5	0.0	0.0	0.0	0.0	13.8	**1,076**
Milwaukee *Journal*	2.1	0.0	0.0	17.9	25.4	0.0	50.0	0.0	4.6	0.0	0.0	0.0	**1,227**
New York *Times*	0.0	0.0	0.0	20.9	25.7	4.1	26.5	0.0	12.1	7.2	3.5	0.0	**1,493**
Portland *Oregonian*	0.0	0.0	0.0	17.7	5.2	3.7	52.0	0.0	6.0	5.0	0.0	10.4	**1,325**
St. Louis *Post-Dispatch*	0.0	2.6	0.0	14.7	16.4	15.9	37.0	0.0	4.2	2.3	4.3	2.6	**1,777**
San Francisco *Chronicle*	16.4	0.0	0.0	19.6	0.0	0.0	44.4	0.0	11.9	0.0	0.0	7.7	**428**
Wall Street Journal	0.7	0.0	1.0	8.0	20.1	11.4	48.7	0.0	1.0	9.1	0.0	0.0	**1,918**
Washington *Post*	0.0	2.4	0.0	18.7	16.0	2.1	49.4	6.8	0.0	2.5	0.0	2.1	**2,625**
Total Lines	**313**	**868**	**258**	**4,069**	**4,540**	**1,477**	**9,801**	**373**	**1,443**	**1,033**	**316**	**988**	**25,479**
% of Total	**1.2**	**3.4**	**1.0**	**16.0**	**17.8**	**5.8**	**38.5**	**1.5**	**5.7**	**4.0**	**1.2**	**3.9**	

* The miscellaneous category combines eight issues: Campaign finance (*Christian Science Monitor* and Washington *Post*: 131 lines; 0.5% of the total); Crime (Kansas City *Star* and Miami *Herald*: 155; 0.7%); Drugs (*Christian Science Monitor*: 52; 0.2%); Environment (Des Moines *Register*, Miami *Herald*, Portland *Oregonian*, and St. Louis *Post-Dispatch*: 234; 0.9%); Family values (Baltimore *Sun* and San Francisco *Chronicle*: 75; 0.3%); Housing (Portland *Oregonian*: 82; 0.3%); Natural resources (Chicago *Tribune*: 69; 0.3%); Urban problems (Baltimore *Sun* and Des Moines *Register*: 171; 0.7%)

edged Reagan's charm and the role he played in revitalizing the attitudes of the American people, the majority of editorials said that he lacked compassion and the understanding of issues necessary to provide positive direction in the next four years. The Atlanta *Constitution*, for example, noted that Reagan's charm was "his most formidable asset," and that whether he "lets fly with a warm burst of bonhomie or smothers a crowd with some straight-from-the-heart sincerity, the man can work wonders." It asserted, however, that the "charm that so deftly enhances the presidential personality is rather glaringly absent from presidential statecraft."[2]

The *Constitution* gave the president "high marks for a rebirth of good feeling in the country," but stated that "this is not enough." Some of Reagan's best-sounding approaches, it suggested, "have served as a cover for objectives that most Americans would reject out of hand if the goals were put to us bluntly."[3] Mondale was depicted as running "the only kind of campaign he knows how to run," one that was "clean, tough, and issues-oriented." It acknowledged, however, that because he had to deal with the Reagan image of "Good Humor man to the nation," Mondale grew "frazzled" and at times "wearily groped for words ... as he tried to explain that President Reagan is ill-informed."[4]

The Des Moines *Register* stated that Reagan was "an extraordinary leader," who "brought to the presidency a gift for making people feel good, for making problems seem manageable." It noted that Reagan also "had a clear idea of what he wanted to do – and much of it he did," changing the nation's mood and reshaping its agenda. It charged, however, that in running for reelection, he "has not offered a clear idea of where he wants to go from here or how he wants to go about it." It called Mondale "an honorable man who has conducted an honorable campaign" and expressed "much more confidence ... in Mondale's ability to administer a government that gives a fair chance to all."[5] Similarly, the Milwaukee *Journal* credited Reagan's domestic policies as having contained "some positive elements" and noted that he had made "intangible contributions – lifting the spirit of the country, inspiring optimism and restoring popularity to the office of the president." On the negative side, it believed that "one of Reagan's most distressing traits is his uneven grasp of facts that are essential to sound leadership."[6] It also criticized the president for being "unspecific about the shape of domestic policies in a second term."[7] It supported Mondale based on his policies and because he was "highly informed, sharply analytical and intellectually vigorous."[8]

The New York *Times* and the St. Louis *Post-Dispatch* also were positive on some aspects of the Reagan presidency. The former acknowledged that the president "has in some ways done a good job" and "deserves credit because the country feels so much better than it did four years ago." It stated that Reagan "has a gift for symbolism and salesmanship; when he salutes the flag and the troops, he embodies a wide renewal of pride in the country." It called much of his domestic program "repugnant," however, and charged that his popularity has been paid for "with the pain of millions of people thrown out of work in the last four years and with hundreds of billions of dollars Government must borrow in the next four." The *Times* believed that Mondale as president "would offer an enlightened and humane conception of what Government should and should not do." It mentioned the less tangible standards for judging candidates, "theatrical skill" and the "capacity to inspire," noting that Reagan is "the master salesman, the Music Man of American politics." It characterized Mondale as having "all the dramatic flair of a trigonometry teacher" but noted that "there's power in his plainness."[9] The St. Louis *Post-Dispatch* agreed with other papers that the president's "unquenchable optimism has rubbed off on much of the public" and that "the amiable tone he has set for his administration has been infectious and good for the country."[10] It criticized Reagan, however, for not telling the nation "what it can expect from him with regard to the leading issues of the day." It noted that Mondale "is providing answers and taking chances that the voters will agree with him"[11] and that he "has demonstrated a keen understanding of the issues before the public."[12]

The Washington *Post* and the Louisville *Courier-Journal* were less willing to acknowledge the president's positive contributions. The former stated that Reagan made achievements in some areas but that "his administration, minus the push-pull effect of Democratic and Republican cross-pressures, would have been an unmitigated disaster in many areas where it has succeeded." Furthermore, it charged that his "too easy slide to glory this time around has accentuated all those elements of detailed smugness and superficiality that most mar his administration." Although it noted that he "is praised for restoring values," it is believed that "these values now have been reduced to slogans and propaganda" Mondale was depicted as "decent," "diligent," "hard-working," "steady," "bright," and "qualified," and "in contrast to his opponent he has been serious, straightforward and genuinely engaged in the issues that the next president will have to deal with."[13] The Louisville *Courier-Journal* believed that during the campaign Reagan "has relied ... on the imagery of nostalgia," but that Mondale "in every major area of public concern ... has offered honest and thoughtful solutions to problems Mr. Reagan chooses to ignore." It acknowledged that "Mr. Mondale lacks Mr. Reagan's mastery of televised imagery and rhetorical flourishes that pass for leadership these days," but emphasized that Mondale was "a man whose career in public life has been built on decency and a concern for all Americans."[14]

Pro-Reagan comment on the leadership issue was found in the Miami *Herald*, the Dallas *Morning News*, and the *Wall Street Journal*. The latter noted that Reagan "has presided over the budding but nonetheless real assertion of American will abroad and the resurgence of confidence and patriotism at home."[15] The Miami *Herald* suggested that the "one test of a leader is whether people follow" and asserted that "by that test, Mr. Reagan has proved to be an extraordinary leader," having revived the nation's spirit and reordered its priorities in a way that may leave its imprint on American history."[16] The Dallas Morning *News* asserted that "President Reagan has shown exceptional skill and ability."[17]

Finally, the Chicago *Tribune* and the *Christian Science Monitor* were neutral on the issue. The *Tribune*, although endorsing President Reagan, was not enthusiastic in its support. Its comments were considered neutral because they were critical of both candidates. It stated that "if we had to begin life today as an advocate of either Ronald Reagan and the Republicans or Walter Mondale and the Democrats, we'd be reluctant to leave the womb." Furthermore, although acknowledging that both candidates were "decent, well-intentioned and honorable men," it believed that their campaigns "have left us with the feeling that we have a choice between Mr. Reagan asleep at the switch or Mr. Mondale groping wildly in the dark for it."[18] The *Christian Science Monitor* called 1984 "a status quo election," because there "is no great animus, no head of steam, no political energy stirring over basic questions of national direction."[19] It suggested that what the president may have had going for him was "a public longing for a successful two-term presidency." It believed that "the race has tested public interest, partly because it has been so long, partly because serious issues has been left half buried, and partly because the outcome has never seemed deeply in doubt."[20]

Relatively little domestic comment was written about the vice-presidential candidates, Geraldine Ferraro and George Bush. This was somewhat surprising since 1984 marked the first year that a woman was nominated by a major party to run for the position. What was written was in the context of a comparison between the two candidates. The comments on Ferraro were mixed. With two exceptions, the editorials that mentioned Bush were favorable. The Chicago *Tribune*, for example, asserted that Ferraro "is no more qualified for the awesome role of president than 400 or so other members of the House of Representatives, and even the best qualified of whom might have a hard time sticking up with George Bush in knowledge and experience." Picking Ferraro, it suggested "was a gesture toward a just cause – the equality of women in politics."[21] The Dallas Morning *News* stated that she "gives her party's ticket the charisma and personality that her running mate cannot."[22] The Miami *Herald* referred to the Democratic candidate as a "gutsy campaigner, but her credentials are no match for Mr. Bush's," whom it described as "an able leader fully qualified by experience and ability to serve as president."[23] The Milwaukee *Journal* believed that Ferraro conducted her campaign "with grace, grit and intelligence" and that she "has accomplished something significant and worthy" in that she "has measurably changed the way people think about women and politics."[24] The New York *Times* said that the choice of Ferraro "as the first woman on a national ticket unleashed a welcome wave of energy," but conceded that she "is not as ready to be president as George Bush."[25] The St. Louis *Post-Dispatch* believed that both Bush and Ferraro "are a credit to their campaigns."[26] But the *Wall Street Journal* described Ferraro as "a woman with no apparent qualifications."[27]

Finally, the Washington *Post* and the Des Moines *Register* were favorable to Ferraro and highly critical of Bush. The former described Ferraro as "smart, strong, and resourceful" and as having "demonstrated many of the virtues indispensable to the job she could inherit at a moment's notice."[28] It described Bush, however, as trying to "outdo Mr. Reagan as a garbler of facts and a misstater of other people's positions."[29] When he speaks, the paper asserted, Bush shows "something that threatens to trash whatever esteem his impressive resume and his private personal grace has earned him ... he seems to reveal himself ... as blustering, opportunistic, craven and hopelessly ineffective all at once." If this is the real Mr. Bush, the *Post* stated, "it hardly bodes well for his capacity to be an effective president."[30] The Des Moines Register acknowledged "some concerns about whether Geraldine Ferraro's six years in Congress are adequate preparation for the responsibility she seeks, but at least she says where she stands." It claimed that Bush's views "are invisible behind his eager parroting of Reagan's values and priorities."[31]

The economy was the major specific domestic issue discussed by editorial writers, and virtually all of the discussion dealt with the budget deficit. Primary emphasis was on Mondale's proposals,[32] of which the majority of the press approved, and criticism of Reagan's alleged lack of a specific policy direction. The Atlanta *Constitution*, for example, judged Mondale's plan as "reasonable and credible" and "far more square with voters than Ronald Reagan has been." It called the president's support of a constitutional amendment to balance the budget "especially galling" and amounting to "nothing more than airily passing a law against deficits."[33] The Des Moines *Register* believed that there was "nothing very catchy" in Mondale's proposals but that it "is a journeyman, straightforward budget outline that would combine tax increases and spending restraints in an attempt to get federal deficits under control." It was critical of Reagan for not providing voters with his own ideas: "Such is the arrogance of an incumbent with a 15-point lead."[34] The Los Angeles *Times* stated that the Democratic candidate "courageously and responsibly defied political precedent" by promising to raise taxes. It believed that Mondale's proposals "are not the only way to solve the deficit problem, but they would do the trick" and that they "deserve a serious answer from the White House."[35] It noted that the administration "likes to talk about the 'opportunity society' that its policies are creating," but that "unless something is done about the huge federal budget deficit ... the opportunities will prove illusory."[36]

Commenting on Mondale's plan, the Louisville *Courier-Journal* stated that it "takes guts for a politician to propose tax increases in an election year." It believed that Mondale "deserves credit" for offering specifics and noted that "until or unless the president acknowledges that deficits are a danger and proposes how to deal with them, Mr. Mondale's tax and spending chart is the only game in town."[37] Later, it reiterated its concern about the apparent unwillingness of the president to confront the deficit problem: "Mr. Reagan, whistling past the graveyard, pretends it doesn't exist. Perhaps he knows better, perhaps not. Either prospect is frightening."[38] Similarly, the Miami *Herald* noted that Mondale was "confronting painful realities, not ducking them" and stated that his deficit-reduction program "appears to be sensible, if limited." The best part of his program, it believed, "is that he dares to propose one, a stark and laudatory contrast to his opponent," who "gave the nation its deficit dilemma, but ... refuses to tell voters hoe he would end it." Reagan's program, it charged, "consists of a jaunty wave and a cocksure grin."[39] The Milwaukee *Journal* declared that the president's "reckless fiscal policies" were "woefully deficient" and had caused the present deficit problem.[40] It added that "his blithe tolerance of immense budget deficits poses a serious threat to the economy's future and, therefore, is "a failure of overriding proportions."[41] The *Journal* believed that Mondale "has done his duty." Although it suggested that details of Mondale's plan "may legitimately be debated. .. on balance the program is responsible."[42] The Portland *Oregonian* said Mondale was treating the issue "with the seriousness it deserves," whereas Reagan, "with a cynicism of raw distillation, continues to dodge the issue."[43]

The New York *Times* also suggested that Mondale's plan "isn't perfect, but that's a small failing compared with President Reagan's failure to propose any plan at all." It believed that the Democratic candidate "merits a badge of political courage for acknowledging that the next president will have to seek more unpopular spending cuts and tax increases."[44]

Similarly, the St. Louis *Post-Dispatch* noted Mondale's "political courage to tell the people that tough measures in the form of higher taxes are needed to treat the deficit disease." It acknowledged that Mondale's approach "may well be susceptible to improvement" but, nevertheless, that "it is a serious attempt to deal with what by far is the most important problem confronting the nation's economy." As had others, it challenged President Reagan "to show the voters if he has a better hand to play – or if he is merely bluffing."[45] The Washington *Post* applauded Mondale's attempt to be specific, although it noted that "as a campaign tactic, the wisdom of declaration will depend on the voters' capacity to tolerate unpleasant truth." Reagan, it charged, "continues to use to the promise-them-anything approach that served him well in the 1980 race, leaving his challenger to deal with harsher realities."[46]

The Baltimore *Sun*, the Chicago *Tribune*, and the Dallas *Morning News* were critical of Mondale's proposals. The *Sun* stated that the plan "projects a tooth-fairy future of high growth and low inflation, interest, and unemployment rates." This, it maintained, "is the stuff of daydreams, especially coming from Jimmy Carter's vice president." It preferred a "bolder, more forward-looking tax reform and a greater emphasis on cuts in government spending."[47] The Dallas *Morning News* called Mondale's plan "a stupefying stew of wishful projections from flawed promises" and believed that the suggested tax increases "could cripple economic growth"[48] and have been "almost as attractive to the citizenry as a free root canal."[49] The Chicago *Tribune* said Mondale's plan "is not a good one," describing it as "dependent on gimmickry, good luck and evasion as any other" and saying that Mondale had chosen "bad" taxes to increase. It stated that "there is considerable evidence that Mr. Reagan's tax cut, despite its flaws, has spurred both work and savings – the foundation of economic growth." It acknowledged, however, that Reagan "knows some action on the budget will be needed after the election, and the voters have a right to know what it is before the election.[50]

Because it criticized both candidates, the *Christian Science Monitor* was judged neutral on the economy issue. Although acknowledging that Mondale "is right in seeking additional revenues to reduce budget deficits," it was uncertain whether "his tax package is necessarily the right step." It suggested that "raising taxes at a time of economic uncertainty seems dubious," that "a balanced policy of budget cuts ... coupled with modest tax-increase measures ... might be workable."[51] It criticized both, however, for not "really getting at the crux of the nation's economic challenge, namely the massive budget deficits that are expected to continue." Reagan, it charged, "has all but ignored the deficit issue during the campaign," and therefore, "even if he wins ... it will be difficult to call such a victory a 'mandate.'" Neither candidate, it claimed, had provided "honest talk of deficits."[52]

Assessments of the performances in the televised encounters between President Reagan and Walter Mondale (October 7) and between George Bush and Geraldine Ferraro (October 11) took most of the editorial space devoted to how the debates dealt with domestic affairs. A few papers discussed the substantive issues that were dealt with in the debates, and several were critical of the fact that the candidates were able to screen and reject proposed panelists and were critical of the debate format, which minimized direct confrontation of the candidates. Typical of the latter were the comments of the Los Angeles *Times*, which asserted that "having reporters ask questions of the candidates for president and vice president prevents the encounters from being true debates and turns them into a glorified 'Meet the Press.'" It also stated that "having absolute control over selection of the questioners ... is beyond the pale even for politicians." It said the League of Women Voters, which sponsored the debates, "should not allow it" and that "if there have to be reporters asking questions, the league should select them."[53]

Regardless of this general feeling, several papers voiced approval of the concept of televised encounters. The Atlanta *Constitution*, for example, called them "the most substantial" events since the convention and "balancing wheels in the presidential elections," which "give challengers a chance to make up at least some distance against the long advantages of incumbency."[54] The *Christian Science Monitor* stated that "the U.S. election process was well served by the presidential debate."[55] The Miami *Herald* believed that the debate "was quite useful as a focal point for capturing the nation's attention,"[56] and the New York *Times* asserted that televised meetings of the candidates "offer a chance for the public to finally zero in on a campaign that so far has flashed past in disjointed moments."[57] Finally, the Washington *Post* said that in any format, debates "tend to jog voters into doing what they know they should: watching the candidates in action to see how they take the initiative and respond to a situation that they and their staffs cannot entirely control."[58]

All but two of the papers that assessed the performances of Reagan and Mondale in their first debate judged Mondale the clear winner. Most referred to some hesitancy and rambling on the part of the president and to the confident and assertive manner of the challenger. The Chicago *Tribune*, for example, stated that Mondale "probably did himself some good" because he had "the edge on President Reagan in style of delivery." It noted that the Democratic candidate "was polite and yet forceful," with "no trace of whine." It believed that Reagan "was apparently trying to show his mastery of the details of public policy, but sometimes seemed to be sinking in them."[59] Similarly, the *Christian Science Monitor* believed that Mondale "was more relaxed, the more in command of his game plan, the more aggressive." Reagan, it said, "was off his anticipated form" and "appeared hesitant."[60] The Dallas *Morning News* said Mondale "showed great poise and ease in the spotlight.[61] The Des Moines *Register* asserted that Mondale "was in command from the beginning" and that he "was confident, relaxed and well-prepared." It characterized Reagan as "confused and fidgety."[62] The Los Angeles *Times* agreed that Mondale "not only handled the substantive issues deftly but also managed to upstage President Reagan at what Reagan usually does best – making a good impression."[63]

The Louisville *Courier-Journal* stated that Mondale "clearly benefited from the president's hesitancy and occasional confusion," but "more importantly, the Democratic challenger was sharp, well-informed and aggressive" and "seemed to catch Mr. Reagan by surprise with a combination of humor and graciousness."[64] Although the Miami *Herald* believed that both candidates scored points and covered a lot of ground," it acknowledged that Mondale won, "incontestably," because he was "poised," "displayed humor, grace, and confidence" and "mounted coherent arguments well-buttressed with fact, and ably articulated." Reagan, it said, "seemed visibly nervous" and repeatedly "groped for words."[65] The Milwaukee *Journal* asserted that Mondale "generally was more in command of pertinent facts" and "often more coherent in expressing his views."[66] The Portland *Oregonian* agreed, calling Mondale "confident, polished, pointed and precise" compared to Reagan, whom it said appeared "hesitant, uneasy and unable to convey many of the accomplishments of his administration."[67] Similarly, the St. Louis *Post-Dispatch* said that Mondale "acquitted himself honorably." On matters such as "organization, presentation, appearance, and analysis," it said, "the former vice president had it over the surprisingly flat Mr. Reagan." It maintained, however, that Reagan "coasted through the evening relatively unscathed."[68]

Less certain of the outcome were the Atlanta *Constitution* and the *Wall Street Journal*. The former questioned whether either candidate had won the debate: "Mondale did well. Reagan did not self-destruct."[69] The *Wall Street Journal* suggested that the idea that Mondale had won the debate "is subject to challenge," because "presidential debates, like ice dancing, are scored subjectively."[70]

The vice-presidential debate was significant historically because it featured the first woman nominated by either major party. It took on added importance because President Reagan's debate performance four days earlier was perceived negatively by most observers. Response to the vice-presidential debate among the leading newspapers was mixed; most, however, saw no clear winner and no major effect of the debate on the outcome of the election. The Baltimore *Sun* suggested that Ferraro "was cool and in command of her subject matter," displayed "an ability to discuss the issues," and "conveyed the impression that she is a strong-minded person with an intuitive sense that she knows where she wants the country to go." Bush, it believed, avoided "major gaffes that would embarrass the White House," but at times "displayed some the shrillness that was supposed to be his opponent's weakness."[71] The Chicago *Tribune* declared that both candidates "appeared to be well briefed and well groomed." Bush, it suggested, "was unusually animated, which did little to dispel his golly-gee preppy image," but Ferraro "balanced that by her unnecessary scolding of Vice President Bush for alleged condescension when he understandably tried to show off his foreign policy expertise." Neither, it believed, "could claim a clear victory."[72] Similarly, the *Christian Science Monitor* noted that Bush at times showed "a startlingly hyperactive enthusiasm" and that Ferraro "with a lawyerly manner, and her characteristic feistiness mostly subdued ... succeeded."[73]

The Los Angeles *Times* and the Dallas *Morning News* called the debate a draw. The former noted that the vice president "was exuberant without being aggressive" and that Ferraro "was more subdued than her reputation as a free-swinging campaigner might have led viewers to expect."[74] The *Morning News* stated that neither "committed any major gaffes," although "Bush's enthusiasm seemed a little out of control at times" and Ferraro "was perhaps too low key."[75] Although it said Bush's "cheerleading" for President Reagan was conducted "with all the zest of a four-year letterman on the pom-pom squad," the Louisville *Courier-Journal* noted that Ferraro was not "intimidated" and "showed that her feistiness is backed by a quick mind." It found that "neither Mr. Bush nor Ms. Ferraro appeared 'presidential'" but that "both were intelligent, well-informed and competent."[76] The Miami *Herald* declared: "Each did just fine. ... Each won, neither won. Each seems to have heartened his or her own partisans, in short."[77] The Milwaukee *Journal* asserted that "even if Geraldine Ferraro did not win a conspicuous victory ... she achieved something almost as valuable. ... She held her own." Ferraro, it continued, "established herself as a serious candidate to be reckoned with," and noted that Bush "was expansive and sometimes exuberant" and "took pains not to be stuffy."[78]

The New York *Times* and the Portland *Oregonian* suggested that both sides could claim success. The latter stated that both Bush and Ferraro "showed themselves to be informed, smart, principled, tough and articulate," that "each candidate won some debating points," and that each "actually laid out themes of their respective campaigns more effectively" than Reagan or Mondale had done.[79] The New York *Times* noted that Bush was "so exuberant" in his support of President Reagan "that he often bubbled over into gush." On other occasions, however, it believed that he "performed with ease and authority" and that Ferraro "though sometimes lacking fire, made her party's case" on various issues "and praised her running mate with grace."[80] The St. Louis *Post-Dispatch* maintained that "in terms of presentation, analysis, forcefulness and so on, the debate came as close as possible to a dead heat." Bush "drove home his points with force, kept his sentences on track and handled most of his facts and figures in impressive fashion," the paper said. Ferraro, it suggested, had "to dispel doubt that she is a credible candidate" and did so with "her words and composure."[81] Finally, the Washington *Post* was most expansive. It stated that both candidates had "their good moments and bad." Ferraro, it maintained, "was somewhat stumbling in her presentation" and "had the disconcerting habit of looking down as if to consult notes she was making." On the other hand, it believed that she "was strong in many of her ripostes to Vice President Bush's attacks on the Mondale-Ferraro ticket's positions" and "extremely effective when she got angry at him and also in her closing statement." Bush, it noted, "had much more authority in the second (foreign policy) part of the debate ... and in this area he was much more masterful than she." He was at this worst, the *Post* thought, "when he got stagy and by turns seemed to be frantic and heavyhanded in his politics of over practiced jokes and highly imitative – down to the latest aw shucks gesture – of his mentor, Ronald Reagan."[82]

Foreign Affairs Issues and Election Editorial Discussion

Fourteen foreign affairs issues appeared in the editorials of leading newspapers during the 1984 presidential campaign. The discussion of United States-Soviet relations, however, drew most of the attention (21.6 percent of all foreign affairs and mixed editorials). Next came the discussion of debates – foreign affairs (13.5 percent), general foreign affairs (12.4 percent), and international trade (10.8 percent). When these percentages were compared with those based on the number of printed lines (Table 69), all categories remained essentially the same.

Most editorial comment on United States-Soviet relations related to the meetings of Soviet Foreign Minister Andrei Gromyko with President Reagan and Walter Mondale in late September. Much of it emphasized the fact that President Reagan had not met previously with any Soviet leader and suggested that he should take advantage of this opportunity to lesson tensions between the two countries. Some editorials also noted concern about Mondale's meeting with Gromyko, which took place the day before Reagan's session. Other

Table 69: Percentage of Editorial Lines about 12 Specific Foreign Affairs Issues in 17 Prestige Newspapers during the 1984 Presidential Campaign

	Arms Control	Central America	Debates	General	Genocide Treaty	Immigration	International Trade	Middle East	National Defense	Philippines	U.S.-Soviet Relations	Miscellaneous*	No. of Lines
Atlanta *Constitution*	7.3%	10.4%	0.0%	17.9%	9.3%	8.7%	10.5%	0.0%	13.2%	8.5%	14.2%	0.0%	**646**
Baltimore *Sun*	5.1	8.2	23.0	11.4	0.0	3.8	8.0	17.9	4.2	0.0	18.4	0.0	**1,382**
Chicago *Tribune*	0.0	7.6	6.9	3.5	13.3	0.0	8.5	5.7	13.2	9.4	31.9	0.0	**577**
Christian Science Monitor	0.0	9.7	27.6	1.3	0.0	0.0	15.7	0.0	17.4	0.0	28.3	0.0	**815**
Dallas *Morning News*	18.8	13.5	2.2	14.7	0.0	0.0	7.8	17.2	4.0	0.0	21.8	0.0	**1,374**
Des Moines *Register*	5.5	20.7	13.5	41.7	0.0	0.0	4.6	0.0	0.0	0.0	14.0	0.0	**1,047**
Kansas City *Star*	23.0	0.0	0.0	0.0	30.4	0.0	0.0	0.0	0.0	0.0	0.0	46.6	**283**
Los Angeles *Times*	11.6	6.5	5.8	0.0	0.0	0.0	22.9	5.6	1.6	5.8	40.2	0.0	**926**
Louisville *Courier-Journal*	0.0	0.0	8.5	19.0	6.4	14.0	17.7	6.5	0.0	0.0	27.9	0.0	**926**
Miami *Herald*	0.0	19.0	12.2	17.6	9.1	11.3	11.0	0.0	0.0	0.0	19.8	0.0	**768**
Milwaukee *Journal*	7.5	0.0	11.0	19.4	7.8	0.0	8.4	21.7	0.0	7.8	16.4	0.0	**743**
New York *Times*	8.4	15.9	11.7	6.5	0.0	0.0	17.7	0.0	0.0	8.2	25.2	6.4	**907**
Portland *Oregonian*	0.0	0.0	4.9	7.0	0.0	9.3	18.6	12.4	14.7	0.0	21.6	11.5	**719**
St. Louis *Post-Dispatch*	5.1	0.0	14.4	5.9	8.5	0.0	9.6	28.4	0.0	5.1	19.0	4.0	**1,338**
San Francisco *Chronicle*	0.0	0.0	3.0	0.0	8.4	11.4	18.5	9.6	0.0	0.0	49.1	0.0	**334**
Wall Street Journal	1.0	8.7	26.8	2.7	0.0	0.0	10.8	4.2	21.8	0.0	24.0	0.0	**1,761**
Washington *Post*	6.2	12.9	9.1	9.8	4.5	0.0	9.3	8.5	3.3	4.3	32.1	0.0	**1,253**
Total Lines	**901**	**1,372**	**1,992**	**1,758**	**608**	**430**	**1,823**	**1,471**	**964**	**417**	**3,736**	**327**	**15,799**
% of Total	**5.7**	**8.7**	**12.6**	**11.1**	**3.9**	**2.7**	**11.5**	**9.3**	**6.1**	**2.6**	**23.7**	**2.1**	

* The miscellaneous category combines three issues: Grenada invasion (Kansas City *Star*: 71 lines; 0.5% of the total); Human rights (Kansas City *Star*: 61; 0.4%); Nuclear war (New York *Times*, Portland *Oregonian*, and St. Louis *Post-Dispatch*: 195; 1.2%)

editorials on the issue discussed Reagan's speech to the United Nations on September 24 and an interview with Soviet leader Konstantin Chernenko, which was printed in the Washington *Post* a few days before the televised presidential debate on foreign policy.

Although the Atlanta *Constitution* criticized President Reagan for an apparent change of attitude toward the Soviet Union "just a month before an election in which lapsed U.S.-Soviet relationships are something of a campaign issue,"[83] it also cited Soviet intransigence and stated that Reagan "can't bear the burden for the superpower impasse all by himself." The Post said "nothing substantive" came from the talks, "but not much was expected – not really."[84] The Baltimore *Sun* also believed that all of the responsibility for strained United States-Soviet relations "does not fall on the president's shoulders," but noted that "since this election year began, the president has softened his words and seized the initiative in seeking contacts." It called the session with Gromyko a "political gift" from the Soviet Union and stated that Mondale "is right in saying it is 'pathetic' that almost an entire presidential term has gone by without high-level conversations." The *Sun* added, "If it took the approach of this election to bring him to realize that 'peace' is good politics, so be it."[85] As to the meetings of both candidates with Gromyko, it suggested that "some marvelous role reversals" occurred: "Mr. Reagan played the peacenik and Mr. Mondale a self-proclaimed tough guy. It was all great political theater."[86] The Chicago *Tribune* granted that "the timing certainly is suspect – six weeks before the election" but allowed that Gromyko's visit "could provide the President with a rare chance to set right a major flaw in his foreign policy."[87] The *Tribune* said the meeting had worked to Reagan's advantage and that "even the Soviet's gestures in Mr. Mondale's direction only seem to emphasize ... his inclination to be too accommodating top international adversaries."[88]

The *Christian Science Monitor* noted that the White House "may well want to get as much political mileage from a Gromyko visit as possible to display the president as a seeker of peace" but suggested that "dealing with the Soviets is no tailgate picnic, even without the stadium roar of a presidential election in the background."[89] The Dallas *Morning News* acknowledged that Reagan's meeting with Gromyko as a minimum "will blunt Walter Mondale's accusations that Reagan threatens world peace through his alleged unwillingness to talk with the Soviets."[90] But it suggested that Mondale's meeting with Gromyko coming so close to the election "can't help making it seem a bit strained and foolish."[91] The Des Moines *Register* approved, however, saying that "as long as there is any chance of communication between Reagan and Gromyko, the meeting is worth having, whatever its political motivations."[92] The Los Angeles *Times* asserted that the Soviet Union "must know that a Gromyko-Reagan meeting will bolster the political position of the president." It added that one possibility is that Soviet leaders "have decided that Reagan will be reelected whether they like it or not and that it is against their interests to go on sticking their finger in the eye of the man who they believe will be president for another four years."[93] The *Times* thought that Mondale, by meeting with Gromyko a day before Reagan did, "is taking a calculated risk," since the Soviets "may be trying to meddle in the presidential election" but that his "stated purpose is laudable."[94] The Louisville *Courier-Journal* suggested that the "potential dividends to Mr. Reagan's campaign should be obvious to everyone, including those rascals in the Kremlin"; therefore, "they evidently have decided that a Reagan victory in November is inevitable."[95] The paper acknowledged, however, that Gromyko "could make a desperate attempt to influence the campaign by commenting publicly after chatting with the president and the Democratic challenger." Mondale, it noted "had best keep that risk in mind" when he meets with the Soviet foreign minister.[96]

Although it believed that no one "should expect Earth-shaking results," the Miami *Herald* stated that "direct talks between leaders, even if they achieve nothing more substantive than a civil tone, are more preferable to a dangerous hostility." It acknowledged that "only the willfully blind could fail to see presidential campaign politics in this meeting" and "that Mr. Reagan can only benefit politically by improving his 'peace' profile"; however, it suggested that political advantage to the president "should not be begrudged when it is won by meritorious initiatives, which the meeting with Mr. Gromyko assuredly is."[97] The Milwaukee *Journal* agreed, maintaining that "the most important thing to say about the scheduled meeting ... is that it could lead to improvement of the dismal and dangerous state of relations between the two countries." It emphasized, however, that "the meeting could make things worse." It criticized the president for the strained relations between the two countries and suggested that "this is an election year, and political constraints have required Reagan to set aside his central strategy for dealing with the Soviets."[98] The New York *Times* thought it "pathetic" that there was "any fuss being made about this meeting." The *Times* was critical of Mondale for letting "the vast issue of Soviet relations degenerate into the silly symbolism of who meets whom when." The critical question, it said, "is which man will better manage relations with Moscow."[99]

The St. Louis *Post-Dispatch* acknowledged that it "is self-evident that both men have significant political stakes in the conversations with the Soviet foreign minister." It believed that even though the meeting afforded Mondale "the unusual opportunity of seeming presidential as well as appearing informed, firm and reasonable," the Democratic candidate "starts at a disadvantage" because he "can announce no new agreements or policies" and "cannot criticize Mr. Reagan without alienating voters who would resent his comments as disloyal." The possible payoff for Reagan, the *Post-Dispatch* concluded, "is much greater." The paper suggested that the meetings "underscore the heavy responsibility that he must share with the Soviets for having allowed the superpower relationship to deteriorate so dangerously," but acknowledged that any easing of tensions would work to the president's advantage.[100] The San Francisco *Chronicle* noted the "political opportunism on the part of the president," but believed that "that does not lessen the propriety of the decision" to meet with Gromyko.[101] The *Wall Street Journal* suggested that Reagan took the Soviets "seriously enough to know that in an election campaign it doesn't hurt to demonstrate that you're trying to get on with the Russians, and more important, that you don't fear their bombasts." Regarding the meetings, it noted that "none of this tactical maneuvering alters much in the U.S.-Soviet relationship" but maintained that if Gromyko "tries to stir up election trouble for Mr. Reagan with provocative talk, he will probably find what that modern American expression 'laid back' means."[102] Finally, the Washington *Post* judged the Gromyko visit as a Soviet decision "to forget about defeating Ronald Reagan and to hop on his reelection bandwagon."[103] It blamed the president for not doing his part to reduce great-power tensions previously but noted that in this election year, he had to show "wondering citizens ... that he is in fact a reasonable peace-seeking man and ... the Russians that, in a second term, they will find him a serious negotiating partner." It suggested that the Soviets "made Mr. Mondale an offer which, for consideration of policy and politics alike, he could not refuse." Mondale's task, it believed, was "less complicated" than the president's, because he "has simply to show voters and Russians that he won't give away the store."[104]

Typical comments on President Reagan's speech to the United Nations came from the Chicago *Tribune* and the Milwaukee *Journal*.

The former called the speech "the most conciliatory speech on U.S.-Soviet relations he has made," The *Tribune* felt that if Reagan were reelected, "this speech ought to set the tone for his second term." It concluded that "good politics and sound foreign policy must correspond."[105] The Milwaukee *Journal* called the speech "belated and welcome," but expressed concern that "it may not be permanent." It maintained that the "absence of specific proposals encourages speculation that Reagan's speech was largely rhetorical, not substantive, designed more to curry favor with the U.S. electorate than to advance superpower diplomacy."[106]

The Des Moines *Register* and the Los Angeles *Times* summed up majority opinion on the Chernenko interview published in the Washington *Post.* The *Times* suggested that the interview "was seemingly timed to influence the debate Sunday night. ... But the tone of the Soviet leader's remarks and the absence of the usual vituperative language about U.S. policy in general and Reagan in particular, is encouraging."[107] The Des Moines *Register* stated that the timing of the interview "shortly before the presidential foreign policy debate, in the heat of the campaign – shows that he wants the state of superpower relations to be an issue in the election." It also believed that it "is probably an indication of just how badly he wants to see movement in stopping the arms race in space – movement he may think more likely in these pre-election days than later."[108]

The editorial discussion of the debates – foreign affairs editorials dealt primarily with the second presidential debate, which took place on October 21, and, secondarily, with foreign policy references in the vice-presidential debate. Almost all of the editorials dealing with the second presidential debate were neutral; that is, they supported neither candidate, supported both, or made negative comments about both. Only the Louisville *Courier-Journal* noted that President Reagan "was much more his normal self" but that he used "clumsy" language at times and was "unclear." Although it said Mondale "didn't make anything clear either," the *Courier-Journal* asserted that the debate showed that he "clearly is not a wimp many voters had concluded he must be" and that "he's obviously tough-minded, a leader."[109] The Milwaukee *Journal* stated that "in outlining solutions to the problems that beset the nation in areas of foreign policy and national security, Walter Mondale made the better case." Although it judged Reagan's performance as "genial, relaxed, and unflustered," the *Journal* thought "he was not sharp," especially in his "rambling and seemingly pointless" summation.[110] The St. Louis *Post-Dispatch* claimed that Reagan "played fast and loose with the facts" and that "time and time again, the president made claims that either bear no resemblance to reality or that flatly contradict previous statements of his." It noted that there "is no evidence that Mr. Reagan deliberately seeks to deceive the public" and that he "genuinely appears to believe what he is saying at the moment." Yet, it asserted, "a president who deludes himself cannot be trusted to make decisions based on facts as they are and events as they were – as opposed to facts as he wants them and a history that he wishes had taken place."[111]

The Baltimore *Sun* concluded that both candidates "did what they intended to do in their second debate ... and because of the logistics of the campaign, that adds up to a plus for Mr. Reagan." It noted that the president "displayed humor, portrayed himself as a man seeking peace and, above all, deflated questions about his age that represent the gravest threat to his reelection." It suggested that "while the president was off-balance at times, he was also quite human and therefore less menacing a figure than his opponents portray." Mondale, the *Sun* said, "once again skillfully carried the attack to his opponent" and "proved himself as a relentless, skillful debater – a politician more than able to hold his own in a medium considered Mr. Reagan's forte." It acknowledged, however, that "if the debate was the fairly even encounter we suspect it was, it may have been enough to protect the president's formidable lead."[112] The Chicago *Tribune* judged the debate as "pretty much ... an even contest" and suggested that "on matters of substance the two candidates tended to rise to a level of abstraction that obscured their differences rather than highlighted them."[113] The *Christian Science Monitor* concluded that "GOP supporters can feel reassured their campaign is again on track," because "Mr. Reagan came through the Kansas City event with a show of the familiar ease with an audience, humor, and composure for counterattacking missing from his first debate performance." It suggested that "Mr. Mondale's backers can likewise claim that their candidate again showed a conceptual grasp of the issues that contrasts with his opponent's more instinctual approach" and that he "continued to assure independents and nominal Democrats of his competence as a leader." The *Christian Science Monitor* expressed regret that the debate "focused more on the pursuit of national strength than on achieving an equal and parallel exercise of moral and diplomatic energy in pursuit of international peace."[114] The Dallas *Morning News* said that although Mondale's performance was "strong," voters perceive him as "someone who stands for policies and attitudes that lead to weakness."[115]

The Los Angeles *Times* stated that "based on the conventional if somewhat curious terms by which these things are judged, President Reagan can be said to have won this debate with Walter Mondale the other night if for no other reason than he didn't demonstrably lose it." The *Times* said that, on the substantive side, "and allowing for the usual misstatements and fuzziness of thought, that side of things yielded few surprises." It noted that "Mondale's theme that Reagan is a poorly informed and out-of-touch leader and Reagan's response that Mondale's record is one of weakness and indecisiveness only echoed what both men have been saying about each other for the better part of the campaign." Furthermore, the *Times* "doubted whether this debate shed much light on what will be the guiding principals and tactical thrusts of the nation's foreign policy over the next four years."[116] The Miami *Herald* stated that Reagan's "challenge was to convince voters that he is in fact a man of peace" and that Mondale "set out to prove that he is not the County Coward derided by President Reagan's macho supporters, but a hard-headed strategist who knows sometimes you gotta fight when you're a man." It suggested, in this regard, that "those familiar with the candidates' records might be forgiven for concluding that Mr. Reagan and Mr. Mondale each had walked out of Kansas City International Airport with each other's baggage." Both candidates, the *Herald* maintained, "evoked doubts about their capacity for leadership."[117]

In referring to the foreign policy debate, the New York *Times* said: "Call it, at that low level, a draw. Both succeeded in evading hard questions. It was the public that lost." It added that "their mutual name-calling not only replaced serious debate but prevented it," and asserted that "what the public lost in all this was a precious opportunity to be instructed in the risks and promises of different approaches." The candidates, the *Times* charged, "come to the debates obsessed with the knowledge that millions of voters are more concerned with personality than policy," and "thus intimidated into striking poses, they never even tried persuasion." It concluded: "On that most crucial test of leadership, both men failed."[118] The Portland *Oregonian* agreed, stating that although the debate demonstrated Mondale's "grasp of the issues and his presence under fire," it also "overlooked" all of the "sensitive" foreign policy issues and left voters "with less material at hand with which to make their decisions than they should have.[119] The *Wall Street Journal* criticized both candidates: "Opinions, names, ideas, catch phrases and insults were winging around the stage ... in an extraordinary fog of jumbled syntax and incomplete sentences." It stated that Reagan "has his record as president, and what he said Sunday night didn't depart significantly from that record," and suggested that "in some respects, Walter Mondale was the more intriguing figure" because of the lines he took on various issues that were harder than his previous stands.[120] Finally, the Washington *Post* made favorable comments about both candidates. It thought that Mondale "put on a presidential performance" by "deftly" illustrating his foreign policy theme, a "requirement for alert, knowledgeable and responsible leadership," and by rebutting the notion "that he would be soft in standing up to the Russians." It noted that President Reagan has "tried hard to reach out to those who have been unnerved by some of his policies and doubt his devotion to peace" and that he "was right when he said that all human rights are lost when a country goes totalitarian." It maintained that Reagan "did much better than he had done in the last debate" and "was easy and avuncular, and scored well in response to a question about his age."[121]

The foreign affairs comment on the vice-presidential debate was mixed. Several papers noted the greater experience of the Republican candidate. The Los Angeles *Times*, for example, stated that whereas Ferraro "faltered on foreign policy," Bush, "with his experience as head of the Central Intelligence Agency and as a vice president, sailed right into it."[122] The Louisville *Courier-Journal* wrote that "this is an area where Mr. Bush, a former Central Intelligence Agency director and ambassador to the United Nations and to China, had an obvious advantage in experience and expertise" and that "Representative Ferraro, on the other hand, was on generally unfamiliar ground."[123] The Washington *Post* also claimed that "Rep. Ferraro was weaker than Vice President Bush on foreign policy and national security material."[124]

The Baltimore *Sun* and the Milwaukee *Journal* wrote essentially neutral editorials, whereas the St. Louis *Post-Dispatch* favored Ferraro's performance. The *Sun* suggested that Bush used his advantage of experience in foreign policy matters "in a spirited way that gave him the edge in opinion polls," but that Ferraro, by choosing a more subdued, statesmanlike role, "may have increased her credibility," although it "cost her points in the debate sweepstakes."[125] The Milwaukee *Journal* described Ferraro as "formidable" and as "poised and forthright – especially when she chided Bush for having patronized her in presuming to instruct her on matters of foreign policy." It noted, however, that Bush "was at his best in his discussion of foreign affairs, an issue the Democrats have tried to exploit during the campaign."[126] The St. Louis *Post-Dispatch* believed the Democratic candidate "has a knack for conveying genuine feeling" and that when she "told off Mr. Bush for his patronizing lecture to her on the difference between Iran and Lebanon, Ms. Ferraro produced one of those rare political moments – full of tension and righteous emotion – that can have profound effects on a campaign." It believed that Bush "was often shrill and overdone in style" and suggested that "his disparaging crack at Mr. Mondale ('Whine on, harvest moon') was the low point" in the debates thus far.[127]

The issue of international trade developed early in the campaign after the United States International Trade Commission recommended to President Reagan that he establish tariffs and quotas on steel imports. The president was in a delicate political position on this issue, because much of the steel industry was located in key electoral states and because he had promoted the concept of free trade throughout his political career. Walter Mondale had gone on record in favor of a 17 percent quota for a five-year period, conditional on certain changes being made in the American steel industry. Reagan's decision on September 18 walked a line somewhere between the concept of free trade and specific tariffs and quotas. He established a limit of 18.5 percent on foreign steel penetration of the United States market but announced that steel-producing states would be asked to limit their exports voluntarily. The response of the leading newspapers to the president's decision was essentially positive, although most wanted no protective measures, and several which approved of his action did so only in the context of its being more appropriate than what his opponent had suggested.

The Atlanta *Constitution* called the announced policy "masterful politics" and noted that "with one stroke, Reagan had muted criticism of perceived administration inaction on unfair trade practices while appearing to stand fast upon his free-trade principles" and that "the beauty of it, from the White House standpoint, is that the program's implementation won't be truly tested until after November." It added: "It's a shame that the president felt compelled to indulge even these half-measures – or that Walter Mondale would go further yet – to redress the admittedly sorry plight of America's steelmakers." It declared: "Even couched as temporary remedies for transient imbalances, they throw the troubled world system further out of whack and invite painful retaliation against other sectors of the U.S. economy that count on exports to keep them in the black."[128] The Baltimore *Sun* called Reagan's action "an expedient solution to his thorny dilemma," one that "preserved the campaigning president's image as an ardent anti-protectionist, while allowing him to appear as though he is acting in the best interest of all those voters in the nation's steel mills and factories." It believed that "at worst, Mr. Reagan's plan purchases him additional campaigning time ... to appeal for votes in the nation's troubled steel belt states" and "at best it's a helpful salve to the deep and serious wounds afflicting the nation's steel industry." In any event, it preferred "the administration's choice of negotiated agreements to the prospect of foreign trade retaliation and domestic industrial fallout that would surely follow the 17 percent quota on steel imports suggested by Walter Mondale."[129] The Chicago *Tribune* stated that "Ronald Reagan, who before becoming president spent a quarter of a century evangelizing for the free market, has grown better at preaching government restraint than practicing it." It charged that the proposed voluntary agreements "will harm the U.S. economy and shelter the steel industry as surely as a quota while pretending to be something else."[130]

The *Christian Science Monitor* noted that "if trade is considered in this election, Mr. Reagan would seem to have the advantage," because "Mr. Mondale talks protectionism ... a proposal that could invite retaliation from abroad." It believed, however, that what was needed was "some clear talk" from both candidates about America's worldwide trade position generally.[131] The Des Moines *Register* maintained that President Reagan "had made the right decision ... in rejecting quotas and tariffs to protect American steelmakers from imports," because quotas and tariffs "would have made steel more costly for American users, threatened jobs in steel-using industries and invited retaliation by foreign countries against U.S. exports." Furthermore, it believed the decision was "politically courageous," since the president "risked angering many voters in key steelmaking states ... where import quotas are seen as job savers." It judged Mondale "wrong" in espousing a more protectionist stance.[132] The Los Angeles *Times* said that Reagan "showed both courage and wisdom in resisting pressure from the steelmaking states where steelmakers and steelworkers have made a habit of hiding poor management and unproductive operations behind restrictions of foreign competition." It called Mondale's suggestion "a sharply protectionist proposal with serious risks for consumers as well as American exporters." It noted, however, that there "is a danger that Reagan intends restrictions not much different from those proposed by Mondale but implemented through voluntary agreements."[133] The Louisville *Courier-Journal* wrote that President Reagan "passed a tough political test with flying colors" and that "by rejecting heavy-handed protectionism," he "should strengthen his support among advocates of free trade." It criticized Mondale for having "joined the protectionist chorus." Such measures, it stated, "are intended, of course, to protect jobs. But the cost to the rest of the economic world would be enormous."[134]

In discussing Reagan's voluntary-agreement approach, the Miami *Herald* asserted that he and his advisors "prudently recognized" that an unyielding free-trade approach "would be as damaging to the nation's long-term security as to the president's short-term re-election prospects." It believed that although Reagan "may test the limits of his conservative constituency's gullibility when he attempts to cloak his policy of 'voluntary' restraints in the rhetoric of free trade," his proposal "does chart a sensible middle course between the extremes of *laissez faire* and unbridled protectionism." It stated also that Reagan "not incidentally ... has outflanked his Democratic opponent, who had advocated strict import quotas."[135] The Milwaukee *Journal* acknowledged that there were "compelling human as well as political reasons" for President Reagan's decision but that, "nonetheless, his decision is a bad one because it threatens to worsen this country's economic problems." It was concerned about reprisals from "countries that have been itching to impose restraints on their agricultural imports from U.S. farmers" and asserted that, in any event, Reagan's help to the steel industry "should have been conditioned on an explicit agreement that, in return labor and industry would commit themselves to specific, permanent plans to restructure, reduce costs and in general become more competitive with foreign produces."[136] The New York *Times* called Reagan's proposal "a masterly solution to his political problem" because the reduction of imports he sought "should be enough to silence union and industry criticism of the Administration, undercutting Walter Mondale's appeal in the Rust Belt." It maintained, however, that "no matter how skillfully packaged ... these import restraints will aggravate the nation's economic problem," because they "will cost consumers billions and reduce the competitiveness of American manufacturers dependent on steel" and "will do little to halt the decline of America's big integrated steel makers."[137]

The St. Louis *Post-Dispatch* called Reagan's decision "a classic compromise on all counts." It gave the president "credit for resisting the pressure to adopt a more formal and drastic course of action." It noted that although the announcement of the policy "comes before the election, the deadline for negotiating the quotas is 90 days in the future, which conveniently puts it after the Nov. 6 election" and that, therefore, "Mr. Reagan is in a position to reap the political benefits from a move that has sufficient ambiguity to allow him to stand for free trade and for protecting steel at the same time."[138] The *Wall Street Journal* charged that Reagan's "big lead in the polls hasn't stopped him from acting like a normal politician, a little more normal than some of us would like." It noted that Reagan, in "making full use of his incumbency ... has just put a damper on whatever headway Walter Mondale might have been making with ... steelmakers." It asserted, however, that "this will not be free of charges to other voters, although "it could have been worse." In criticizing protectionism, it stated: "This may be good old-fashioned Republican politics, but it is not good economics, and hence not good politics for the longer pull."[139] Finally, the Washington *Post* called the president's plan "industrial policy in the worst and most corrupting sense – the sense in which the administration has always previously condemned it." It suggested that "in principle there's not much difference between Mr. Mondale's quota and Mr. Reagan's voluntary restraint agreements," but believed that, "in practice, Mr. Reagan's will be more harmful to the extent that they are more durable."[140]

Although a considerable amount of space on general foreign affairs was devoted to a variety of specific issues, primary concern was with the leadership characteristics of the candidates. Overwhelmingly, the emphasis was on President Reagan's record in foreign policy during his first term, and the comment, generally, was negative. Especially critical and lengthy in their remarks were the Des Moines *Register* and the Milwaukee *Journal*. The former initially noted that in this election year, the president was involved diplomatically more than ever around the world. It maintained: "Of course, there are reasons why all this is going on; many of those are spelled V-O-T-E-S." It acknowledged that "all this positive talk is immeasurably better than an intransigence that preceded it" and stated that perhaps "with all this pre-election negotiated solution activity, even this administration might just get the knack of it."[141] It charged that instead of a "clear-eyed, responsible and principled foreign policy, well-rooted in history," the Reagan approach was characterized by "the high stake and impassioned speech, the test of manhood and the show of strength." It maintained that "anticommunism is not enough to sustain an intelligent foreign policy. Yet that – and the American response of standing tall, meeting the test, matching wits – is the only discernible theme in this administration's foreign and national security policies.[142] It charged that Reagan's "faith in militarism and distrust of diplomacy risk the future life of this planet" and were "alone sufficient grounds for dismissal." It believed that "the realistic, if plodding approach advocated by Mondale – a recognition that the superpowers must always actually seek peace – would make the world safer."[143] The Milwaukee *Journal* stated that "in the field of foreign and national security, the four years of the Reagan administration often have brought drift and mismanagement, ringing claims unmatched by solid performance," and that it "is a record both dangerous and unnecessary." It believed that a nation as rich and powerful as the United States ... needs a president willing to work hard, with a concentrated and humane intelligence, to master the facts essential to meeting the world's extraordinary challenged." It noted that Reagan "has dismally failed to provide" that quality of leadership.[144] Concerning foreign policy matters, it suggested that "the challenger is distinctly more moderate, thoughtful, and knowledgeable than the president, despite Reagan's incumbency and easier access to data."[145]

The Atlanta *Constitution* also was critical of the president, but spent an equal amount of space on Mondale's behalf. It called the Democratic challenger "a 'philosophical heir' ... to such foreign policy stalwarts as John Kennedy, Henry Jackson, and his Minnesota mentor, Hubert Humphrey." and suggested he was "just as firm, just as skeptical about the intentions of Moscow or Havana or Managua," as they had been. It felt that the "'strength issue' has been a nagging debit for Mondale ever since the campaign began in earnest" but that he had dispelled this notion along the campaign trail. It noted that "Reagan may be a standup guy, but then so is Mondale." Furthermore, the *Constitution* believed that the "essential question before voters is which candidate is more thoughtful, which pays more attention to crucial details, which places greater stress on the arts of diplomacy than the science of war."[146] Referring to Reagan, it stated that "'standing tall' is no substitute for wisdom in the conduct of foreign policy." The presidency, it believed, demanded "a feeling for the complexities of international power," which Reagan did not have. Mondale, it asserted, "offers ... strong but posed international leadership."[147]

Other comments on this issue were similar but briefer. The

Chicago *Tribune*, for example, charged that "Mr. Reagan's ignorance about the Soviet Union and his air-headed rhetoric on the issues of foreign policy ... have reached the limit of tolerance and have become an embarrassment to the U.S. and a danger to world peace."[148] The Louisville *Courier-Journal* maintained that "while the Reagan campaign boasts of an America 'standing tall,' it can point to no foreign policy achievement comparable to the Camp David accords."[149] The New York *Times* called the president's diplomacy "mostly ineffective" and "dangerous."[150] The St. Louis *Post-Dispatch* declared that "in the final analysis, the question is, which man can more safely be trusted with the future of the Earth?" It preferred Mondale.[151] The Washington *Post* asked: "In what sense is America 'standing tall?'" It went on to criticize several specific policy initiatives of the president and to denounce "the level of infighting over ... national security issues "within the administration "as a reflection of policy disagreement and impasse."[152]

Only the Dallas *Morning News*, the Miami *Herald*, and the *Wall Street Journal* were supportive of President Reagan on general foreign affairs. The *Wall Street Journal* maintained that Reagan "has presided over ... the budding but nonetheless real reassertion of American will abroad"[153] and that there "is no reason for Mr. Reagan to be defensive about seeking peace through strength." Furthermore, it is claimed that there "is certainly no need to appease the foreign policy views of the Democratic left, which have been repeatedly rejected at the polls." It believed that the voters "are looking not for moral solace but for realistic leadership, and they are quite capable of recognizing it when they see it."[154] It decided that "on foreign policy, Ronald Reagan represents strength, and the national Democrats represent weakness."[155] The *Herald* stated that "with some exceptions, Mr. Reagan has responded decisively and appropriately to situations abroad." It believed that he "has proven to be an extraordinary leader" who "has taken stands on tough issues" of foreign policy on which "Mr. Mondale has yielded to pressure groups."[156] And the Dallas *Morning News* asserted that, under Reagan, "a generally firmer line in foreign affairs has won back some of the respect a vacillating America lost during the post-Vietnam era."[157]

Concluding Comments

One of the more obvious conclusions of this study is that the editorial endorsements of the leading newspapers did not reflect the majority sentiment of the voters in the 1984 presidential election. Although President Reagan received a large popular majority and an even greater electoral vote victory over Walter Mondale, the leading newspapers, by a small margin, supported Mondale (41.2 percent to 35.3 percent, with 23.5 percent uncommitted). Also, the partisan direction of editorial comments was overwhelmingly anti-Reagan.

Another comparison between the editorials of the leading newspapers and voters can be made regarding issues. Earlier, the seven major issues that were discussed on the editorial pages were considered within their respective contexts of domestic affairs and foreign affairs (Tables 68 and 69). For a more accurate assessment of the relative amount of space devoted to these issues, it was important to consider them together (Table 70). The three domestic issues ranked first, second, and third, and United States-Soviet relations ranked a close fourth. This result is not surprising, because, as Table 65 showed, 61.7 percent of all editorial lines were classified as domestic affairs. Interestingly, on the two major specific issues, the economy and United States-Soviet relations, President Reagan scored higher than Walter Mondale in mid-election Gallup Polls.[158] This distinguishes the leading newspapers from voters views, since editorials, generally, were very critical of the president on these issues. It should be noted, however, that the public's response to Gallup Polls was on general questions, whereas the editorials were considerably more specific, dealing with various aspects of these issues. Also, support for the president on these issues was influenced considerably by the public's assessment of his leadership abilities.[159] Nevertheless, the leading newspapers did not reflect closely the voters' views on the important issues.

Finally, the leading newspapers' post-election assessments should be noted. The papers essentially agreed that Reagan's victory over Mondale was a highly personal one, especially since no major shift toward the Republicans occurred in the congressional elections as might have been expected with a presidential landslide. Typical of the comments in this regard are those of the St. Louis *Post-Dispatch:* "His stunning triumph is a tribute above all else to his own personal appeal. The simple message of this election is that an overwhelming number of Americans wanted Ronald Reagan for another four years."[160]

The lack of a significant change in the partisan composition of Congress, however, raised the question of whether or not the presi-

Table 70: Percentage of Editorial Lines about Seven Principal Domestic and Foreign Affairs Issues in 17 Prestige Newspapers during the 1984 Presidential Campaign

	Debates: Domestic	Debates: Foreign	Economy	General: Domestic Affairs	General: Foreign Affairs	International Trade	U.S.-Soviet Relations	Number of Lines
Atlanta *Constitution*	13.0%	0.0%	11.4%	40.8%	14.6%	8.6%	11.6%	792
Baltimore *Sun*	13.7	17.3	3.5	37.1	8.6	6.0	13.8	1,838
Chicago *Tribune*	12.0	5.3	13.3	35.5	2.7	6.6	24.6	747
Christian Science Monitor	18.5	11.5	21.1	29.9	0.6	6.6	11.8	1,953
Dallas *Morning News*	22.7	0.9	24.1	33.5	6.3	3.3	9.2	3,235
Des Moines *Register*	6.6	7.8	24.9	25.7	24.2	2.7	8.1	1,806
Kansas City *Star*	22.8	0.0	20.1	57.1	0.0	0.0	0.0	364
Los Angeles *Times*	5.3	3.7	21.9	29.3	0.0	14.4	25.4	1,466
Louisville *Courier-Journal*	16.4	4.3	16.8	29.9	9.6	8.9	14.1	1,837
Miami *Herald*	16.1	8.0	6.9	37.3	11.5	7.2	13.0	1,169
Milwaukee *Journal*	14.1	5.3	20.1	39.4	9.3	4.0	7.8	1,555
New York *Times*	19.0	6.4	23.3	24.0	3.6	9.8	13.9	1,646
Portland *Oregonian*	17.1	2.6	5.1	50.4	3.7	9.8	11.3	1,367
St. Louis *Post-Dispatch*	14.0	10.3	15.7	35.3	4.2	6.9	13.6	1,865
San Francisco *Chronicle*	18.8	2.2	0.0	42.4	0.0	0.0	36.6	448
Wall Street Journal	5.9	18.1	14.8	35.9	1.8	7.3	16.2	2,605
Washington *Post*	16.6	3.8	14.2	43.7	4.2	3.9	13.6	2,964
Total Lines	**4,069**	**1,992**	**4,540**	**9,801**	**1,758**	**1,761**	**3,736**	**27,657**
% of Total	**14.7**	**7.2**	**16.4**	**35.4**	**6.4**	**6.4**	**13.5**	

dent received a mandate from the electorate, and if so, how it should be interpreted. The majority of papers described Reagan's victory as an indication of strong voter support of the programs he had initiated during his first term. The New York *Times* stated it best: "Voters resoundingly approved the president's performance so far .... He has won exactly what his partisans chanted for – Four More Years of the same. With a vengeance, the voters ratified the status quo."[161] Some of the papers that agreed added more specific comments, citing especially voter approval of his economic policies and of the good health of the economy in general.[162]

Although they basically agreed with these assessments of voters, a few papers perceived no mandate for the future either because they believed the president had given no specific indication during the campaign what his second-term policies would be[163] or because the election had produced no important shifts in the composition of Congress.[164] The Atlanta *Constitution*[165] agreed essentially with the *Wall Street Journal*' statement that "the public's election verdict was unambiguous," giving Reagan "every right to push his own agenda on taxes, spending, defense, and foreign affairs."[166] The Washington *Post* did not mention domestic issues, but noted that "the president can fairly claim to have renewed the mandate for the foreign policy of his past four years," which emphasized "the idea of building strength and conveying American will."[167]

This study of leading newspapers cannot account explicitly for the presidential outcome of 1984. Editorial emphasis during the campaign, however, suggests that presidential leadership style and the favorable performance of the economy were ultimately the deciding factors in Ronald Reagan's victory over Walter Mondale.

Notes

1. Interestingly, the high percentage of anti-Republican editorials contrasts sharply with six Gallup surveys taken between September and early November 1984, which show public support for the Republican ticket varying between 55 and 58 percent. "Gallup '84 Vote Analysis Shows Dramatic Shifts in Voting Patterns," *Gallup Report*, no. 230 (November 1984), p. 6.
2. Atlanta *Constitution*, Sept. 12, 1984.
3. *Ibid*, Oct. 4, 1984.
4. *Ibid*.

5. Des Moines *Register*, Nov. 4, 1984.
6. Milwaukee *Journal*, Oct. 28, 1984.
7. Ibid., Oct. 23, 1984.
8. Ibid., Oct. 28, 1984.
9. New York *Times*, Oct. 28, 1984.
10. St. Louis *Post-Dispatch*, Oct. 14, 1984.
11. Ibid., Sept. 27, 1984.
12. Ibid., Oct. 14, 1984.
13. Washington *Post*, Oct. 29, 1984
14. Louisville *Courier-Journal*, Oct. 21, 1984.
15. *Wall Street Journal*, Sept. 20, 1984.
16. Miami *Herald*, Oct. 28, 1984.
17. Dallas *Morning News*, Oct. 14, 1984.
18. Chicago *Tribune*, Oct. 28, 1984.
19. *Christian Science Monitor*, Sept. 14, 1984.
20. Ibid., Sept. 29, 1984.
21. Chicago *Tribune*, Oct. 28, 1984.
22. Dallas *Morning News*, Sept. 24, 1984.
23. Miami *Herald*, Oct. 28, 1984.
24. Milwaukee *Journal*, Oct. 26, 1984.
25. New York *Times*, Oct. 28, 1984.
26. St. Louis *Post-Dispatch*, Oct. 13, 1984.
27. *Wall Street Journal*, Sept. 20, 1984.
28. Washington *Post*, Oct. 29, 1984.
29. Ibid., Oct. 20, 1984.
30. Ibid, Oct. 29, 1984.
31. Des Moines *Register*, Nov. 4, 1984.
32. Mondale made his budget proposal public on September 10. His plan included a combination of tax increases and spending reductions that was estimated to trim $177 billion from a deficit that was expected to be $263 billion in 1989. Generally, he called for an increase in tax rates, but within the existing structure, and for the establishment of a trust fund for additional federal income to be used only to reduce the national debt. Also, the plan would have required Congress to raise taxes every time it expanded old programs or proposed new ones. Los Angeles *Times*, Sept. 11, 1984.
33. Atlanta *Constitution*, Sept. 13, 1984.
34. Des Moines *Register*, Sept. 12, 1984.
35. Los Angeles *Times*, Sept. 11, 1984.
36. Ibid., Oct. 26, 1984.
37. Louisville *Courier-Journal*, Sept. 12, 1984.

38. Ibid., Oct. 31, 1984.
39. Miami *Herald*, Sept. 12, 1984. In its editorial that endorsed President Reagan, the *Herald* continued to criticize the president for "refusing to acknowledge" the deficit problem but now judged Mondale's plan as offering "no real alternative," especially since his scheme "does not take into account the increased spending that his political promises would require elsewhere." Ibid., Oct. 28, 1984.
40. Milwaukee *Journal*, Sept. 8, 1984.
41. Ibid., Oct. 21, 1984.
42. Ibid., Oct. 12, 1984.
43. Portland *Oregonian*, Sept. 11, 1984.
44. New York *Times*, Sept. 11, 1984.
45. St. Louis *Post-Dispatch,* Sept. 12, 1984.
46. Washington *Post*, Sept. 11, 1984.
47. Baltimore *Sun*, Sept. 12, 1984.
48. Dallas *Morning News*, Sept. 13, 1984.
49. Ibid., Oct. 4, 1984.
50. Chicago *Tribune*, Sept. 12, 1984.
51. *Christian Science Monitor*, Oct. 12, 1984.
52. Ibid., Oct. 30, 1984.
53. Los Angeles *Times*, Oct. 18, 1984. Also, see Baltimore *Sun*, Oct. 11, 1984.; Kansas City *Star*, Sept. 19, 1984; Louisville *Courier-Journal*, Oct. 7, 1984; Miami *Herald*, Oct. 9, 1984; Milwaukee *Journal*, Sept. 19, 1984; New York *Times*, Sept. 23 and Oct. 9, 1984; St. Louis *Post-Dispatch*, Oct. 3, 1984; *Wall Street Journal*, Sept. 20, 1984; Washington *Post*, Sept. 20, 1984.
54. Atlanta *Constitution*, Oct. 9, 1984.
55. *Christian Science Monitor*, Oct. 9, 1984.
56. Miami *Herald*, Oct. 9, 1984.
57. New York *Times*, Oct. 7, 1984.
58. Washington *Post*, Sept. 20, 1984. The *Wall Street Journal* and the Baltimore *Sun* were critical of the debates. The former claimed (Oct. 9, 1984) that television debates "are, on the whole, one of the worst ways available to voters for examining issues and policies, and the latter maintained (Oct. 7, 1984) that the shortcoming of debates is the "emphasis on showmanship, on glibness, on appearance, on the memorable phrase rather than the profound thought or the careful policy position."
59. Chicago *Tribune*, Oct. 9, 1984.
60. *Christian Science Monitor,* Oct. 9, 1984.
61. Dallas *Morning News*, Oct. 9, 1984.

62. Des Moines *Register*, Oct. 9, 1984.
63. Los Angeles *Times*, Oct. 9, 1984.
64. Louisville *Courier-Journal*, Oct. 9, 1984.
65. Miami *Herald*, Oct 9. 1984.
66. Milwaukee *Journal*, Oct. 8, 1984.
67. Portland *Oregonian*, Oct. 9, 1984.
68. St. Louis *Post-Dispatch*, Oct. 9, 1984.
69. Atlanta *Constitution*, Oct. 9, 1984.
70. *Wall Street Journal*, Oct. 9, 1984. Because of President Reagan's lackluster performance in the first debate, the issue of age was considered briefly by several papers. Only the Milwaukee *Journal* (Oct. 11, 1984) suggested that the age factor should be scrutinized more carefully.
71. Baltimore *Sun*, Oct. 12, 1984.
72. Chicago *Tribune*, Oct. 13, 12984.
73. *Christian Science Monitor*, Oct. 15, 1984.
74. Los Angeles *Times*, Oct. 14, 1984.
75. Dallas *Morning News*, Oct. 13, 1984.
76. Louisville *Courier-Journal,* Oct. 13, 1984.
77. Miami *Herald*, Oct. 13, 1984.
78. Milwaukee *Journal*, Oct. 12, 1984.
79. Portland *Oregonian*, Oct. 13, 1984.
80. New York *Times*, Oct. 13, 1984.
81. St. Louis *Post-Dispatch*, Oct. 13, 1984.
82. Washington *Post*, Oct. 12, 1984.
83. Atlanta *Constitution*, Sept. 18, 1984.
84. Ibid., Oct. 2, 1984.
85. Baltimore *Sun*, Sept. 14, 1984.
86. Ibid., Sept. 30, 1984.
87. Chicago *Tribune*, Sept. 13, 1984.
88. Ibid., Oct. 2, 1984.
89. *Christian Science Monitor*, Sept. 12, 1984.
90. Dallas *Morning News*, Sept. 14, 1984.
91. Ibid., Sept. 25, 1984.
92. Des Moines *Register*, Sept. 15, 1984.
93. Los Angeles *Times*, Sept. 12, 1984.
94. Ibid., Sept. 18, 1984.
95. Louisville *Courier-Journal*, Sept. 13, 1984.
96. Ibid., Sept. 18, 1984.
97. Miami *Herald*, Sept. 13, 1984.
98. Milwaukee *Journal*, Sept. 13, 1984.

99. New York *Times*, Sept. 16, 1984.
100. St. Louis *Post-Dispatch*, Sept. 19, 1984.
101. San Francisco *Chronicle*, Sept. 12, 1984.
102. *Wall Street Journal*, Sept. 17, 1984.
103. Washington *Post*, Sept. 14, 1984.
104. *Ibid.*, Sept. 18, 1984.
105. Chicago *Tribune*, Sept. 26, 1984.
106. Milwaukee *Journal*, Sept. 25, 1984. See also, Baltimore *Sun*, Sept. 25, 1984; *Christian Science Monitor*, Sept. 27, 1984; Los Angeles *Times*, Sept. 25, 1984; Louisville *Courier-Journal*, Sept, 25, 1984; Portland *Oregonian*, Sept. 26, 1984; St. Louis *Post-Dispatch*, Sept. 25, 1984; San Francisco *Chronicle*, Sept., 26, 1984; *Wall Street Journal*, Oct. 4, 1984.
107. Los Angeles *Times*, Oct. 19, 1984.
108. Des Moines *Register*, Oct. 13, 1984. See also, Miami *Herald*, Oct. 19, 1984; New York *Times*, Oct. 19, 1984; Portland *Oregonian*, Oct. 20, 1984; St. Louis *Post-Dispatch,* Oct. 19, 1984; San Francisco *Chronicle*, Oct. 18, 1984; Washington *Post*, Oct. 18, 1984.
109. Louisville *Courier-Journal*, Oct. 23, 1984.
110. Milwaukee *Journal*, Oct. 22, 1984.
111. St. Louis *Post-Dispatch*, Oct. 24, 1984. The *Post-Dispatch*'s neutral article spoke briefly about the candidates' television performances and concluded that both had been successful – Reagan by concentrating on "atmospherics" and betting that "Americans will vote their emotions," and Mondale, by showing "a superior grasp of the issues" and that he "is a more serious student of policy." *Ibid.*, Oct. 23, 1984.
112. Baltimore *Sun*, Oct. 22, 1984.
113. Chicago *Tribune*, Oct. 23, 1984.
114. *Christian Science Monitor*, Oct. 23, 1984.
115. Dallas *Morning News*, Oct. 23, 1984.
116. Los Angeles *Times*, Oct. 23, 1984.
117. Miami *Herald*, Oct. 23, 1984.
118. New York *Times*, Oct. 23, 1984.
119. Portland *Oregonian*, Oct. 23, 1984.
120. *Wall Street Journal*, Oct. 23, 1984.
121. Washington *Post*, Oct. 22, 1984.
122. Los Angeles *Times*, Oct. 14, 1984.
123. Louisville *Courier-Journal*, Oct. 13, 1984.
124. Washington *Post*, Oct. 15, 1984.
125. Baltimore *Sun*, Oct. 14, 1984.

126. Milwaukee *Journal*, Oct. 12, 1984.
127. St. Louis *Post-Dispatch*, Oct. 13, 1984.
128. Atlanta *Constitution*, Sept. 20, 1984.
129. Baltimore *Sun*, Sept. 20, 1984.
130. Chicago *Tribune*, Sept. 23, 1984. The Portland *Oregonian* (Sept. 29, 1984) and the San Francisco *Chronicle* (Sept. 19, 1984) also noted that Reagan's decision went against his previous support of free trade.
131. *Christian Science Monitor*, Oct. 4, 1984.
132. Des Moines *Register*, Sept. 20, 1984.
133. Los Angeles *Times*, Sept. 13, 1984.
134. Louisville *Courier-Journal*, Sept. 20, 1984.
135. Miami *Herald*, Sept. 21, 1984.
136. Milwaukee *Journal*, Sept. 21, 1984.
137. New York *Times*, Sept. 17, 1984.
138. St. Louis *Post-Dispatch*, Sept. 20, 1984.
139. *Wall Street Journal*, Sept. 20, 1984.
140. Washington *Post*, Sept. 20, 1984.
141. Des Moines *Register*, Sept. 27, 1984.
142. Ibid., Oct. 21, 1984.
143. *Ibid.*, Nov. 4, 1984.
144. Milwaukee *Journal*, Oct. 24, 1984.
145. Ibid., Oct. 28, 1984.
146. Atlanta *Constitution*, Sept. 21, 1984.
147. Ibid., Oct. 19, 1984.
148. Chicago *Tribune*, Oct. 28, 1984.
149. Louisville *Courier-Journal*, Oct. 21, 1984.
150. New York *Times*, Oct. 28, 1984.
151. St. Louis *Post-Dispatch*, Nov. 4, 1984.
152. Washington *Post*, Oct. 29, 1984.
153. *Wall Street Journal*, Sept. 13, 1984.
154. Ibid., Oct. 19, 1984.
155. Ibid., Oct. 31, 1984.
156. Miami *Herald*, Oct. 28, 1984.
157. Dallas *Morning News*, Oct. 14, 1984.
158. On the question of who would do a better job of keeping the country prosperous, President Reagan was favored over Mondale, 54 percent to 30 percent. As to who would be better able to work with the leaders of the soviet Union to achieve world peace, Reagan's margin was 45 percent to 38 percent. "Reagan Seen as Better Able to Keep Nation Prosperous, Voters Split on Who Can Keep Peace,"

Gallup Report, no. 229, (Oct. 1984), p. 14.

159. For a brief analysis of the reasons why voters chose Reagan and Mondale, see "Character of Reagan Support Markedly Different Than in '80," *Gallup Report*, no. 230 (Nov. 1984), pp. 10-11.

160. The St. Louis *Post-Dispatch*, Nov. 7, 1984. Similar assessments of the presidential election as a personal victory for Reagan are found in the Baltimore *Sun*, the Los Angeles *Times*, and the New York *Times* on Nov. 7 and in the Atlanta *Constitution*, the Chicago *Tribune*, the Des Moines *Register*, the Louisville *Courier-Journal*, the Miami *Herald*, the Milwaukee *Journal*, the San Francisco *Chronicle*, and the *Wall Street Journal* on Nov. 8.

161. New York *Times*, Nov. 8, 1984. Similar assessments of the presidential election as evidence of voters support for President Reagan's first-term policies are found in the Atlanta *Constitution*, Nov. 8, 1984; Miami *Herald*, Nov. 9, 1984; *Wall Street Journal*, Nov. 8, 1984 and Nov. 14, 1984; Washington *Post*, Nov. 15, 1984.

162. See Des Moines *Register*, Nov. 8, 1984; Los Angeles *Times*, Nov. 7, 1984; St. Louis *Post-Dispatch*, Nov. 7, 1984; *Wall Street Journal*, Nov. 8, 1984.

163. See Baltimore *Sun*, Nov. 7, 1984; Milwaukee *Journal*, Nov. 8, 1984; Portland *Oregonian*, Nov. 7, 1984; St. Louis *Post-Dispatch*, Nov. ,7, 1984.

164. See Des Moines *Register*, Nov. 8, 1984, and St. Louis *Post-Dispatch*, Nov. 11, 1984.

165. Atlanta *Constitution*, Nov. 8, 1984.

166. *Wall Street Journal*, Nov. 8, 1984.

167. Washington Post, Nov. 8, 1984.

6

The Editorial Pages of Leading Newspapers in 1988

David S. Myers

The 1988 study of the editorials of leading newspapers covered the sixty-four day period from the editions of September 5, Labor Day, to November 7, the last full day of the campaign. Analysis procedures used in the 1984 study were repeated for 1988.

Again, the leading newspapers varied in their editorial endorsements. Those supporting Michael Dukakis were the Atlanta *Constitution*, the Des Moines *Register*, the Kansas City *Star*, the Louisville *Courier-Journal*, the Milwaukee *Journal*, the New York *Times*, and the St. Louis *Post-Dispatch*. Those endorsing George Bush were the Chicago *Tribune*, the Dallas *Morning News*, the Miami *Herald*, the Portland *Oregonian*, and the San Francisco *Chronicle*. The Baltimore *Sun*, the *Christian Science Monitor*, the Los Angeles *Times*, the *Wall Street Journal*, and the Washington *Post* were uncommitted, although partisan editorial comment in the Baltimore *Sun* was essentially anti-Republican, whereas that of the *Wall Street Journal* was noticeably anti-Democrat. Changes in endorsement between 1984 and 1988 occurred with two newspapers. In 1984 the Kansas City *Star* had endorsed Reagan, and the Washington *Post* had endorsed Mondale.

Number and Partisan Direction of Election Editorials

The number of election editorials on the 1988 presidential campaign and election by the leading newspapers varied between six (San Francisco *Chronicle*) and fifty-two (Des Moines *Register*). Of the total of 528 election editorials, 5.9 percent were pro-Democratic,

Table 71: Percentage of Election Editorial Lines about Two General Subject Areas in 17 Prestige Newspapers during the 1988 Presidential Campaign

	Domestic Affairs	*Foreign Affairs*	*Total No. of Lines*
Atlanta *Constitution*	81.9	18.1	1,058
Baltimore *Sun*	79.2	20.8	2,536
Chicago *Tribune*	92.7	7.3	1,403
Christian Science Monitor	78.7	21.3	1,550
Dallas *Morning News*	90.2	9.8	1,636
Des Moines *Register*	94.7	5.3	2,897
Kansas City *Star*	94.4	5.6	1,354
Los Angels *Times*	84.0	16.0	1,628
Louisville *Courier-Journal*	87.6	12.4	2,460
Miami *Herald*	81.4	18.6	1,145
Milwaukee *Journal*	83.7	16.3	1,982
New York *Times*	74.6	25.4	3,087
Portland *Oregonian*	94.3	5.7	1,346
St. Louis *Post-Dispatch*	76.4	23.6	3,149
San Francisco *Chronicle*	97.3	2.7	292
Wall Street Journal	67.6	32.4	5,136
Washington *Post*	86.5	13.5	2,760
Average	**82.2%**	**17.8%**	**Total 35,419**

27.3 percent were anti-Republican, 5.3 percent were pro-Republican, 7.7 percent were anti-Democratic, and 53.8 percent were neutral. The percentage of neutral editorials is high. This was expected, since the endorsements were split almost evenly, and a number of the papers were uncommitted. Of the partisan editorials, 71.1 percent were in the Democratic column (pro-Democratic plus anti-Republican editorials), and 28.3 percent were Republican (pro-Republican plus anti-Democratic editorials.). This was almost exactly the same as the partisan split in 1984. Also as in 1984, the significance of this is the fact that the overwhelming partisan comments, 71.7 percent of editorials that expressed a direction, were anti-Republican.[1] The anti-Republican emphasis was primarily a criticism of the tactics of George Bush, who was accused of running a negative campaign, and to a lesser extent a general concern about his attitude toward the economy.

Regarding the general categories of domestic affairs, foreign affairs, and mixed (i.e., those editorials addressing both domestic and

Table 72: Percentage of Partisan Editorial Lines about Domestic Affairs in 17 Prestige Newspapers during the 1988 Presidential Campaign

	Democratic		*Republican*		*Neutral*
	pD	*aR*	*pR*	*aD*	
Atlanta *Constitution*	7.8%	57.4%	8.0%	0.0%	26.8%
Baltimore *Sun*	0.0	24.7	2.4	0.6	72.3
Chicago *Tribune*	0.0	14.3	14.9	5.7	65.1
Christian Science Monitor	13.1	13.0	0.0	6.2	67.7
Dallas *Morning News*	4.1	2.4	36.3	2.4	54.8
Des Moines *Register*	13.2	48.5	0.0	0.0	38.3
Kansas City *Star*	1.7	62.0	0.0	0.0	36.3
Los Angels *Times*	0.0	10.1	0.0	0.0	89.9
Louisville *Courier-Journal*	16.5	24.5	0.0	1.5	57.5
Miami *Herald*	0.0	26.3	18.3	0.0	55.4
Milwaukee *Journal*	17.1	50.8	2.1	0.0	30.0
New York *Times*	15.2	21.5	3.7	1.8	57.8
Portland *Oregonian*	0.0	7.6	21.0	3.4	68.0
St. Louis *Post-Dispatch*	27.2	53.0	0.0	0.0	19.8
San Francisco *Chronicle*	0.0	0.0	61.3	0.0	38.7
Wall Street Journal	0.0	6.8	6.7	51.5	35.0
Washington *Post*	4.9	9.8	5.0	9.6	70.7
Number of Lines	**2,429**	**7,584**	**1,931**	**2,332**	**14,847**
	8.3%	**26.1%**	**6.6%**	**8.0%**	**51.0%**
Total Lines	**10,332**		**4,263**		
	34.4%		**14.6%**		

* pD = pro-Democratic; aR = anti-Republican; pR = pro-Republican; aD = anti-Democratic

foreign affairs), the percentage patterns generally were similar among the papers. The significant fact is that more than three-quarters of the editorials dealt with domestic issues. Although papers usually devote more editorial space to domestic matters, in no presidential election since the 1930s has so little editorial space been devoted to foreign affairs issues. It is as if the papers believed that the voters' decisions would not be affected at all by international concerns. (See Table 71.)

With one exception, the percentages of partisan direction of both domestic affairs and foreign affairs editorials followed that of the total number of election editorials. The exception was a considerable increase in anti-Democratic sentiment in foreign affairs. This is relatively insignificant, however, since the total number of editorials on foreign policy was small. Regarding domestic affairs editorials,

Table 73: Percentage of Partisan Editorial Lines in 17 Prestige Newspapers Devoted to Foreign Affairs during the 1988 Presidential Campaign

	Democratic		*Republican*		*Neutral*
	pD	*aR*	*pR*	*aD*	
Atlanta *Constitution*	0.0	53.6	0.0	41.7	4.7
Baltimore *Sun*	0.0	0.0	13.1	20.8	66.1
Chicago *Tribune*	0.0	0.0	19.6	0.0	80.4
Christian Science Monitor	0.0	24.2	0.0	0.0	75.8
Dallas *Morning News*	0.0	0.0	56.9	2.5	40.6
Des Moines *Register*	56.9	26.1	0.0	0.0	17.0
Kansas City *Star*	0.0	100.0	0.0	0.0	0.0
Los Angeles *Times*	0.0	28.5	0.0	0.0	71.5
Louisville *Courier-Journal*	18.0	0.0	0.0	19.6	62.4
Miami *Herald*	0.0	0.0	39.0	0.0	61.0
Milwaukee *Journal*	12.7	22.8	0.0	0.0	64.5
New York *Times*	2.7	19.1	6.8	0.0	71.4
Portland *Oregonian*	0.0	0.0	10.4	0.0	89.6
St. Louis *Post-Dispatch*	20.7	54.3	100.0	0.0	0.0
San Francisco *Chronicle*	0.0	0.0	100.0	0.0	0.0
Wall Street Journal	0.0	0.0	9.6	74.4	16.0
Washington *Post*	0.0	0.0	0.0	15.5	84.5
Number of Lines	**358**	**1,001**	**492**	**1,551**	**2,894**
	5.7%	**15.9%**	**7.8%**	**24.6%**	**46.0%**
Total Lines	**1,359**		**2,043**		
	21.6%		**32.4%**		

* pD = pro-Democratic; aR = anti-Republican; pR = pro-Republican; aD = anti-Democratic

the neutral category was highest, with 55.1 percent, whereas the anti-Republican sentiment (31.1 percent) easily surpassed the other partisan categories (5.4 percent pro-Democratic, 3.5 percent pro-Republican, 4.9 percent anti-Democratic).

A similar pattern emerged within the partisan direction of domestic affairs editorials was based on the number of printed lines. (See Table 72.) The anti-Republican and neutral comments declined slightly, and each of the other partisan columns increased somewhat. As in 1984, anti-Republican sentiment was most noticeable in the papers that endorsed the Democratic candidate.

When the partisan direction of foreign affairs editorials was based on printed lines (Table 73), there was a noticeable drop in the anti-Republican column, slight drops in the anti-Democratic and neutral columns, and small increases in the other partisan categories.

Because the amount of editorial space devoted to foreign affairs issues was so small, these changes are not extremely important.

Domestic Affairs Issues and Election Editorial Discussion

As in 1984, a number of different domestic affairs issues appeared in the leading newspapers' editorials on the 1988 presidential campaign. Again, discussion of domestic affairs in general drew most of the attention (25.5 percent of all domestic affairs and mixed editorials). Next came the discussion of debates – domestic affairs (18.4 percent), campaign tactics (12.6 percent), and the economy (11.3 percent). When these percentages were compared with those based on the number of printed lines (see Table 74), there were slight increases in the total percentages of space devoted to general domestic affairs matters and to the economy and corresponding decreases in the debates – domestic affairs and campaign tactics issue areas.

As is the case in all presidential campaigns, editorials classified as general domestic affairs in 1988 dealt with a variety of matters, such as the importance of registering and voting, the effects of public opinion polls and advertisements, and accounts of presidential candidates' travel and other activities. A few combined several specific issues but with no pervasive pattern of emphasis. Eight papers, however, wrote about the general philosophy or general characteristics of the candidates. The Chicago *Tribune* stated that the "George Bush who has run for president has not been the kind, thoughtful, fair and candid man we believe and hope he really is." It acknowledged, however, that he "remains one of the best-qualified people ever to seek the presidency" and that his character "is impeccable." It continued: "His record of hard and honest work in public service is unmatched. And his preparations for running the most important job on Earth are extraordinary." The *Tribune* criticized Dukakis for "letting his opponent set the tone and the agenda for the campaign" and maintained that a man "so easily forced off balance, pushed into running for president by backing up and explaining just might turn out to be a president forced to govern the same way."[2]

The Dallas *Morning News,* the Miami *Herald*, and the Portland *Oregonian* also were favorable toward Bush. The *Morning News* noted that Bush "has demonstrated great courage, high achievement and honorable service" in his public life and that he "has the edge in experience ... and best understands what government can and cannot

Table 74: Percentage of Election Editorial Lines in 17 Prestige Newspapers about 12 Specific Domestic Affairs Issues during the 1988 Presidential Campaign

	Campaign Finance	Campaign Tactics	Child Care	Debates: Domestic Issues	Economy	Education	Environment	Ethics	General	Health Care	Vice-Presidential Candidates	Miscellaneous*	Number of Lines
Atlanta *Constitution*	0.0%	12.0%	0.0%	14.4%	6.1%	0.0%	5.5%	0.0%	17.6%	7.9%	0.0%	36.5%	866
Baltimore *Sun*	2.5	17.3	0.0	19.8	7.5	3.0	0.0	2.5	30.3	2.6	1.0	13.5	2,008
Chicago *Tribune*	0.0	21.0	0.0	19.6	23.3	8.1	0.0	2.8	22.7	0.0	2.5	0.0	1,301
Christian Science Monitor	0.0	8.7	6.6	21.9	10.5	4.1	0.0	0.0	35.4	6.6	0.0	6.2	1,220
Dallas *Morning News*	0.0	11.4	0.0	20.3	12.1	0.0	0.0	2.7	44.6	0.0	0.0	8.9	1,476
Des Moines *Register*	2.5	10.1	0.0	24.5	7.1	2.3	0.0	2.7	22.8	0.0	7.2	20.8	2,744
Kansas City *Star*	0.0	21.7	9.8	7.4	16.7	0.0	7.9	12.6	12.6	0.0	0.0	11.3	1,278
Los Angeles *Times*	0.0	11.0	5.5	26.5	15.2	5.4	5.74	0.0	12.6	12.4	0.0	5.7	1,368
Louisville *Courier-Journal*	4.4	11.8	0.0	13.0	4.5	0.0	6.6	2.8	26.2	3.8	0.0	26.9	2,154
Miami *Herald*	0.0	0.0	6.8	24.7	6.7	0.0	5.8	13.1	18.2	0.0	0.0	24.7	932
Milwaukee *Journal*	0.0	21.8	4.7	14.7	16.6	3.1	6.8	0.0	18.9	2.4	0.0	11.0	1,658
New York *Times*	5.5	1.8	18.0	12.2	13.6	3.0	9.6	2.1	19.3	0.0	2.6	12.3	2,303
Portland *Oregonian*	5.0	0.0	0.0	19.6	15.5	0.0	0.0	13.6	46.3	0.0	0.0	0.0	1,269
St. Louis *Post-Dispatch*	3.1	12.3	2.9	10.6	5.0	0.4	3.2	0.0	39.1	2.8	10.0	10.6	2,405
San Francisco *Chronicle*	0.0	10.9	0.0	39.5	23.9	0.0	0.0	0.0	25.7	0.0	0.0	0.0	284
Wall Street Journal	0.0	4.0	0.0	9.6	18.3	3.7	0.0	9.1	32.3	5.1	0.0	17.9	3,470
Washington *Post*	2.8	9.0	5.1	15.4	11.6	7.7	0.0	2.5	26.4	4.9	0.0	14.6	2,387
Total Lines	**544**	**3,042**	**1,030**	**4,821**	**3,474**	**796**	**833**	**1,139**	**7,953**	**856**	**551**	**4,084**	**29,123**
% of Total	**1.9**	**10.5**	**3.5**	**16.6**	**11.9**	**2.7**	**2.9**	**3.9**	**27.3**	**2.9**	**1.9**	**14.0**	

* The miscellaneous category combines twelve lesser issues: Abortion (Baltimore *Sun*, Des Moines *Register*, Kansas City *Star*, Louisville *Courier-Journal*, New York *Times*, and Washington *Post*: 346 lines; 1.2 percent of the total); Agriculture (Des Moines *Register* and *Wall Street Journal*: 138; 0.5%); (*Continued on page 161*)

do." It believed that Dukakis "is the candidate of 'government,'" whereas Bush "is the candidate who best understands the limitations of government."[3] The Miami *Herald* stated that Bush "has the broader experience, nationally and internationally, where Mr. Dukakis has none" and that he "is a moderate with whom most Americans can feel comfortable." It asserted that in a comparison between the candidates, Bush "emerges as a seasoned leader with growth potential where Mr. Dukakis is ever the earnest technocrat." It described the Democratic candidate as "an ill-defined iceman."[4] The Portland *Oregonian* characterized Bush as "intelligent, non-ideological, open-minded." It admired his "capacity to reach to survive and to operate effectively in the stratospheres of party politics, international diplomacy, national security operations and governance" and noted that he "is exceptionally practiced at bringing people of different outlooks under one umbrella." It believed that his "leadership style would incline to cooperation, reasoned discourse and high ethical tone."[5]

Several papers' assessments were more favorable to Dukakis. The Des Moines *Register*, for example, stated that the Democratic candidate was better suited "in background and temperment" and that a governor "has direct experience in the nitty gritty of ... the very things that must move to the front burner of national attention." It acknowledged that Dukakis's "aloof, superior demeanor is not endearing, although it is well to remember that the nation is electing a chief executive, not a favorite uncle."[6] The Louisville *Courier-Journal* described Dukakis as "a high achiever" and "smart enough – and intellectually honest enough – to discard positions that are untenable and to grow in the job he seeks." It also suggested that he "deserved to be elected on his own merits" and that what he "may lack in warmth and humor he more that makes up in intelligence, integrity and compassion."[7] The Milwaukee *Journal* characterized Dukakis as "bright, hard working and resourceful," "pragmatic," and "courageous." It believed that although the Democratic candidate lacked Bush's national and international experience, he "seems free of the

---

(*Continued from page 160*) Civil rights (Baltimore *Sun*, Kansas City *Star*, St. Louis *Post-Dispatch*, and *Wall Street Journal*: 495; 1.7%); Crime (Atlanta *Constitution*, Baltimore *Sun*, Miami *Herald*, and New York *Times*: 270; 0.9%); Drug problem (Atlanta *Constitution*, Des Moines *Register*, Louisville *Courier-Journal*, Miami *Herald*, New York *Times*, and St. louis *Post-Dispatch*: 437; 1.5%); Energy (Dallas *Morning News* and Louisville *Courier-Journal*: 246; 0.8%); Housing (Des Moines *Register*, Louisville *Courier-Journal*, Milwaukee *Journal*, New York *Times*, *Wall Street Journal*, and Washington *Post*: 483; 1.7%); Labor (Des Moines *Register*, Louisville *Courier-Journal*, Milwaukee *Journal*, St. Louis *Post-Dispatch*, and Washington *Post*: 367; 1.3%); Supreme Court Appointments (Atlanta *Constitution*, Baltimore *Sun*, Dallas *Morning News*, Des Moines *Register*, Miami *Herald*, and *Wall Street Journal*: 435; 1.5%); Women's Vote (Baltimore *Sun*, *Christian Science Monitor*, and Washington *Post*: 184; 0.6%); Youth Volunteer Program (Atlanta *Constitution*, Los Angeles *Times*, Milwaukee *Journal*, New York *Times*, and Washington *Post*: 270; 0.9%)

mental rigidity that can limit a president's ability" to respond to important events.[8] The St. Louis *Post-Dispatch* noted that "in matters of vision, values and judgment, Michael Dukakis stands well above George Bush" and that "what he may lack in emotional appeal, he more than makes up for in common sense, compassion, and commitment."[9] It suggested that Bush, on the other hand, "entertains no firm convictions and thus is able to adopt the code of whoever is sponsoring him at the moment" and charged that "the common denominator of all the jobs he has held is that he left no personal stamp."[10]

The major specific domestic issue discussed by editorialists was debates on domestic affairs. The presidential candidates held formal, televised debates on September 25 and October 13. Senators Lloyd Bentsen and J. Danforth Quayle, the Democratic and Republic vice-presidential candidates, respectively, debated on October 5. Primarily, the editorial comments assessed the debate performance of each of the candidates; however, considerable space was also given to criticism of the debate format. Regarding the latter, for example, the Baltimore *Sun* believed that the "ground rules make it difficult for reporters to pin down candidates."[11] The Chicago *Tribune* said that both candidates "must share the blame for saddling the American people with another series of those made-for-television nondebates that are guaranteed to induce sleep or send viewers flipping through their channels for an old movie."[12] The Des Moines *Register* called the debates "just one more photo opportunity managed by campaign media advisers, a 'charade.'"[13] And the Kansas City *Star* concluded that the debates "have degenerated into nothing more than another campaign event, arranged by the candidates and under rules they impose" and that they "are more akin to joint frauds than debates."[14] The Los Angeles *Times* stated that "the chief aim of the participants was to sound profound and to avoid a major mistake" and that evasion "is another goal: trying to come across as knowledgeable and reasonable on the subject, but not answering the question directly."[15] The Louisville *Courier-Journal* thought that "the question-and-answer format and the short attention span fostered by television, will bar serious explanation of complex issues."[16] The Milwaukee *Journal* charged that the debates are staged affairs where candidates concentrate "on presenting prepackaged pictures and quotes" and maintained that "the public is not served by these tactics."[17] Finally, the Washington *Post* was "disappointed that the formats don't give candidates a chance to question one another, as they did tellingly in some primary debates."[18]

Comments on the first presidential debate stressed the candidates' debate style and substantive remarks. Editorialists sought to characterize the debate within the context of the campaign and relative to their judgment of each candidate's campaign goals and requirements for victory. Several papers judged Dukakis the winner. The Milwaukee *Journal*, for example, stated that the Democratic candidate deserves to be somewhat more satisfied" with the encounter than Bush. It believed that in matters of style, he "conveyed more poise, warmth and self-confidence" and "avoided the smugness that was a problem for him in the past," whereas Bush "often lapsed into the whiny irritability that his coaches had tried hard to eliminate." Regarding substance, it asserted that "both candidates did an adequate job of protecting their political philosophies and priorities."[19] The St. Louis *Post-Dispatch* said that Dukakis had "enhanced his chance of being elected president with a forceful performance" and "established himself more firmly than before as mature, knowledgeable and competent, with a vision far exceeding that of his rival." Although it described Dukakis as "somewhat wooden in his presentation, he emerged nonetheless as a candidate possessing both humane impulses and common sense."[20]

The Atlanta *Constitution* and the *Christian Science Monitor* also suggested that Dukakis had gotten the better of Bush in the debate but were more balanced in their comments. The latter noted that Dukakis "was the more focused, the more collected." Although the *Monitor* stated that Bush "did well, too," it believed that "neither candidate has yet been forced to say" what his specific economic and foreign policies would be.[21] The *Constitution* claimed that "Mr. Dukakis can be said to have done better for himself than Mr. Bush did" but that "both candidates missed some opportunities" to score debate points.[22]

Other papers approved of each candidate's performance and of the debate process, although a few felt that policy issues were not dealt with specifically enough. The Baltimore *Sun* characterized Bush as "relaxed and thoughtful – a more mature politician than he was four years ago" and said that in defending the Reagan administration "he did so by conveying the image of a man sailing his own course." It noted that Dukakis "had to show the country that he was presidential in dealing with an opponent already cloaked in the majesty of national office" and that "he achieved his aim." It wanted more details, however, "on what the candidates propose to safeguard the world's environment, trade and economic well-being."[23] The Chicago *Tribune* stated that both candidates were "agile and capable debaters, not timid about defending their positions," and that "most Americans probably came away a bit more comfortable that, no matter who wins in November, the republic isn't likely to dissolve into ashes."[24] The Dallas *Morning News* found that, "on a personal level, Vice President Bush appeared more human, Massachusetts Gov. Dukakis more dour." It added that "on the issues, each candidate needed to motivate a base constituency" and that "both succeeded."[25] The Des Moines *Register* wrote: "It was such a good debate, so evenly matched, that it undoubtedly bolstered each candidate's already-committed supporters, while still leaving large numbers of undecided voters scratching their heads." Although "both candidates deftly sidestepped questions on occasion and managed to stay fuzzy on some issues," it believed that "one could not watch the debate without getting a clear impression of the very real differences between George Bush and Michael Dukakis."[26]

The Los Angeles *Times* noted that the debate "served the nation's voters well, along with the fact that neither candidate made any serious errors." It maintained that Dukakis "was more specific on many issues – but perhaps he needed to be, since he still is not a familiar figure to most Americans." It stated that Bush "seemed uncertain at times, and was vague on many questions and inaccurate in several statements," and that Dukakis "still comes across as stiff and humorless, even when presented the opportunity in a specific question to demonstrate that he can be passionate."[27] The New York *Times* said that there "was a staged quality to the affair" and that the candidates were "coached to the tonsils." It asked for specifics: "What is it, Mr. Bush, that makes 'liberals' so downright dangerous? Beyond laundry lists, what is it, Mr. Dukakis, that you genuinely care about, and why?"[28] The *Wall Street Journal* asserted that "the voters came out winners" and that both debaters "finished Sunday evening as credible candidates." It added: "At the level of political personality, both men accomplished goals necessary to the successful completion of their campaigns." It believed that Dukakis "established himself as a legitimate Democratic candidate for the presidency" and that Bush "carried forward the politically unconventional theme he created around himself in his New Orleans acceptance speech – that of a decent, personable, and humane candidate."[29]

The second presidential debate occurred when Vice President Bush held a significant lead in national public opinion polls. Many presumed, therefore, that Governor Dukakis needed a major victory to give him any chance to close the gap by Election Day, whereas

Bush needed only to break even. The papers commented on this point and again criticized the lack of detailed discussion of specific issues. The Baltimore *Sun* stated that Dukakis "needed a big hit, and he did not get it," and that although he "tried hard to smile and lighten things up," he "was too intent on finding the breakthrough that didn't come." It noted that Bush, given a chance to say something nice about his opponent, "lavished praise on Michael Dukakis's pride in his family and his heritage." it described the response as "a softball answer to a softball question, but in terms of the Republican frontrunner's strategy, it was a hardball home run."[30] The *Christian Science Monitor* asserted that Dukakis "had some good lines, but he also lost some opportunities." It believed that Bush, on the other hand, "was more clearly at ease, relaxed," and that "his subjects and verbs agreed; his syntax hung together as never before." It continued: "The debates echo those of four years ago, when Walter Mondale knocked Mr. Reagan off stride in the first - only to have him come back strong in the second."[31] The Dallas *Morning News* maintained that Dukakis "needed to look like a winner ... to move ahead in the polls" but that he "did not score the knockout that would give his campaign a needed boost." In contrast, it wrote that Bush appeared "self-assured and affable" and was more successful than Dukakis in projecting himself "as a person that Americans could warm up to." It suggested that the Democratic candidate "needed to make a convincing case for change" but that Bush "made a more convincing case for staying the course of economic growth and peace through strength."[32]

The Des Moines *Register* described Bush's debate performance as "relaxed, confident, reassuring – and contemptuous of the intelligence of the American people." It wrote that Dukakis "put on a sickly frozen smile and became a caricature of someone trying to pretend they're (*sic*) someone else" and that he "looked almost pathetic" trying to be "Mr. Warmth." It also was critical of the fact that "neither candidate chose to break any new ground on the issues" or "is yet willing to level with the people" on specific policies.[33] The Los Angeles *Times* asserted that "even when they try to be relaxed and human, ... it seems rehearsed and calculated." It did not believe that voters got from either candidate "a coherent vision of a changing America and its needs in a changing world."[34] The Milwaukee *Journal* characterized the Republican candidate as "more relaxed and seemingly natural" and Dukakis as "warm at times" but still exhibiting "some of the edginess and brittleness that have handicapped his candidacy." It concluded that it was "hard to say at this point whether the debate had any bearing on the dynamics of the campaign" but guessed that "Dukakis didn't get the lift that he needed."[35]

The St. Louis *Post-Dispatch* suggested that the second debate brought the candidates' differences and values into sharper focus, especially on the issues of the death penalty and abortion. It described Dukakis's positions as "thoughtful, consistent and compassionate" and Bush as "inconsistent and insensitive and authoritarian." It believed that these differences "are important to voters because they reveal the value system each man would bring to the presidency." It continued: "Mr. Bush is a man without deeply rooted convictions who could not be counted on to make fine moral distinctions .... Mr. Dukakis possesses a coherent credo that would inform his decision-making at all levels of public policy."[36] The San Francisco *Chronicle* noted that both men "seemed more confident, more adept at discussing the issues and more knowledgeable about affairs of state – in short, more presidential." It maintained, however, that Bush "was the dominant figure" and that he "managed both to project calm capability, and also to come across as warm and caring." In contrast, it asserted that Dukakis "retreated into his carapace of serious, but dull, government executive."[37] Finally, the Washington *Post* described the second debate as a "rout," with Bush the clear winner. It wrote that Dukakis's debate problems proceeded from a basic strategic failing of his campaign, which it called "a misplaced insularity and smugness that appear to have caused him and his top aides to think that all you needed to do was say 'George Bush' and everyone in the country would start laughing and hissing, but mainly laughing." It stated, however, that the Republican candidate "got his revenge" and "has profited" from that miscalculation. It claimed that Bush "was able to upstage Mr. Dukakis personally ... and evidently take him by surprise." It believed that Dukakis "seemed so programmed, even strangled and subdued" that he "let himself be trapped by his opponent."[38]

Virtually all of the leading newspapers were critical of Bush's choice of Senator Dan Quayle as his running mate. Because the criticism continued throughout the campaign, there was considerable pressure on him to give a poised performance in the vice-presidential debate with no major gaffes and to display understanding of the principal issues facing the country. Most of the editorials on the vice-presidential debate stressed Quayle's responses to three similar questions that asked what he would do if he were suddenly thrust into the office of the presidency and to Quayle's comparison of his legislative record to that of John Kennedy before he had become president. Regarding the latter, the papers emphasized Bentsen's retort, which noted that he had served with and had been a friend of Kennedy and ended with the statement: "Senator, you're no Jack Kennedy."

Several papers were highly critical of Quayle's debate performance and judged Bentsen favorably. The Atlanta *Constitution* asserted that "nothing in Mr. Quayle's performance provided reassurance that he is ready to stand on the verge of the presidency." It found his answers "oblique and sometimes unresponsive." It believed that Bentsen "was the cooler, cannier head, in part simply because of his greater experience."[39] The Baltimore *Sun* maintained that Quayle "showed not only that he is no Jack Kennedy, he's hardly a Ted Agnew," and that "three times he ducked the question of how he would handle sudden ascent to the presidency." It noted that each time he responded "his visage du jour – squinty blue-eyed patriotism, clenched jaw determination – gave way to a frantic look as he reverted to a rote answer."[40] The Des Moines *Register* said that if the debate confirmed anything, it is that Bush "made a terrible misjudgment in selecting Quayle as his running mate." It called Quayle a senator "with an undistinguished record, a narrow range of experience and a shallow intellect," and referred to Bentsen's Jack Kennedy remarks as "so devastating because they were so true."[41] The Los Angeles *Times* criticized Quayle for "stumbling" over the question of what he would do if he suddenly became president and called him "over-programmed."[42] The Milwaukee *Journal* suggested that Bentsen "gave the nation substantial reason to feel confident about having him 'a heartbeat away from the presidency.'" It called the reference to Kennedy "Bentsen's biggest coup" and cited as Quayle's "biggest failure" his "inability to say anything coherent when asked three times what he would do if he were suddenly thrust into the presidency."[43] Finally, the Portland *Oregonian* wrote that Quayle was "thumped" by Bentsen and that the Democratic candidate gave "a performance that might have taken him from being of real help to Michael Dukakis only in Texas to a point where he is a national asset to the campaign."[44]

Several papers gave more balanced views. The Chicago *Tribune*, for example, noted that "neither candidate was above a little demagoguing and bobbing and weaving to answer the question he was programmed to respond to rather than those that were asked." It believed that Quayle "scored well on occasion" but that Bentsen's "relaxed manner and easy knowledge of his subject matter made him the more commanding presence."[45] Although the *Christian Science Monitor* stated that Bentsen "outclassed" Quayle, it "doesn't mean a clear victory" for him, because "the basic dynamic," which was that "the election is still George Bush's to lose," remained unchanged.[46] The Louisville *Courier-Journal* claimed that many debate viewers "will hope ... that neither guy ever advances to the starting lineup." Although it said that Bentsen "was more polished and occasionally showed signs of spontaneity," it called his Kennedy reference an "ugly put-down" that "sank to the level of personal insult." It continued: "While Mr. Kennedy had many other virtues, his legislative record wasn't much more impressive that Sen. Quayle's." On the succession question, however, it believed that Quayle "struck out every time."[47]

The Miami *Herald* stated that Quayle's performance "certainly met the minimal test" but that he "looked and sounded very young and showed no remarkable depth, wisdom, or wit to dispel that impression."[48] The New York *Times* believed that Quayle "met his handlers' modest goals," because he "did not stumble or fall." It suggested that he "appeared, at least in the early going, to grasp the subject matter" but that "he failed to convey depth and vision." It characterized Bentsen as "no ball of fire, but rather a paradigm of what Governor Dukakis offered in Atlanta: 'competence.'"[49] The Washington *Post* wrote that "both senators did what they had to do." It noted also that Quayle "was certainly in a more hostile journalistic environment that his opponent," especially since Bentsen had not been asked to respond to the succession question.[50]

Finally, the Dallas *Morning News* and the *Wall Street Journal* were somewhat favorable toward Quayle. The former noted that Bentsen "was both a more relaxed and forceful figure" but also that Quayle "gave a reasonable accounting of himself," "appeared dignified and provided measured responses," and "presented a good grasp of Republican positions and a passable defense of Reagan administration policies." It believed that although "the public's perception of Sen. Bentsen may have been strengthened, ... the public's fears of Sen. Quayle were at least somewhat dispelled."[51] The *Wall Street Journal* suggested that Quayle "is probably a few years away from being as composed and self-confident as one would ideally wish a president to be" and, therefore, that Bentsen, "at this point in his career, is better groomed to serve as caretaker." Yet, it continued: "Toward the end of the next presidential term, with Senator Quayle more experienced and Senator Bentsen in his 70s, the situation might be reversed."[52]

Another important domestic issue discussed by editorial writers concerned campaign tactics. Most of the comment was critical of the candidates for running negative campaigns. George Bush received the brunt of this criticism, because of his portrayal of Dukakis as a liberal out of the political and popular mainstream. Specifically, Bush hinted that Dukakis was unpatriotic for not supporting a required pledge of allegiance in the Massachusetts public schools, stressed his membership in the American Civil Liberties Union (ACLU), and accused him of being soft on crime for supporting a weekend furlough program for hardened criminals in Massachusetts. The furlough program was emphasized because Willie Horton, a black man who had been convicted of first-degree murder, had escaped to Maryland on a weekend pass, where he brutalized a white man and raped his fiance. In general, the editorials decried the lack of a meaningful debate on the issues and wove these specific emphases into their discussions. The Atlanta *Constitution*, for example, stated that Bush "seeks to narrow political discourse ... and to panic voters away from cooly examining the problem-solving potential of both parties." It called his "campaign to beat liberalism to death" an "act of intellectual thuggery"[53] and ridiculed his "crude attempts to impugn" Dukakis's patriotism.[54] It believed that the Republican candidate was "misleading voters wildly" when he charged that the Massachusetts furlough program was evidence that Dukakis was soft on crime.[55]

The Baltimore *Sun* asked: "Are we having a presidential election campaign ... or a tryout for a title role in a movie called 'The Demagogue'?" It suggested that both candidates "de-escalate the rhetoric," because "irresponsible talk demeans the speakers and the process."[56] It called Bush's criticism of the ACLU "a clever way to paint Mr. Dukakis into a liberal corner" but added that it "is misleading the public."[57] It characterized Bush's references to Willie Horton as "clearly calculated to appeal to racial if not racist sentiments."[58] Also, it criticized Dukakis because he ran "away from the L-word term until he realized it fit with the little-guy populism that belatedly energized his campaign."[59] Early in the campaign, the Chicago *Tribune* said, there was "a persistently troubling question" about Bush's campaign. Why he was "firing off charges, slurs, and innuendoes at his opponent," the paper wondered, since he had always been perceived as "nice" and "decent."[60] Later, it noted that "civility, truth, and honor were the first casualties of this unsavory contest" and that it was "probably too late to hope the nominees will display any redeeming social qualities between now and the election." It continued: "So, the negative has become the positive. If it works, it must be right. Nobody loses but the voter and the presidency."[61]

The *Christian Science Monitor* called the campaign "disappointing" and added: "If either were elected, would he sling such primordial political mud, such silly exaggeration, at leaders of other nations?"[62] It also noted that membership in the ACLU "shouldn't be a negative, especially if a candidate says where he differs with the organization's official positions."[63] The Dallas *Morning News* believed that the campaign was neither candidate's "finest hour." It stated that "both campaigns have collapsed into the morass of cliches, innuendo, guilt by association, and symbol manipulation"[64] and that "the jeers and sneers of the current campaign are enough to make voters want to put their fingers in their ears."[65] Similarly, the Des Moines *Register* suggested that "when they look for someone to blame for the ugliness of this campaign, the presidential candidates should try a mirror." It referred to "overblown language" that "may trigger passions not easily releashed" and asserted: "It doesn't make any difference who started the irresponsibility. Its continuance discredits both. Worse it threatens the political legitimacy of the winner. The spewing of irrelevant slurs may win an election but it can leave the right to govern in doubt."[66] The *Register* also characterized Bush's attacks on the ACLU as "cheap-shot" and charged that he "has borrowed McCarthy's tactic of implying guilt by association to discredit the American Civil Liberties Union and anyone who supports it."[67]

The Kansas City *Star* referred to the "nastiness of the campaign" and to the fact that the candidates "want to win so badly they will wink at the debasement of the process."[68] Specifically, it accused Bush of "pandering" to racists by bringing up the Horton furlough[69] and of "distortion of a widely used rehabilitation effort at a time when authorities are trying to cope with overcrowded prisons."[70] The Los Angeles *Times* characterized the campaign as "deplorable" and "contemptible" and as "without doubt the nastiest and most cynical contest for the White House in memory, and – worse – the most devoid of substance as well."[71] The Louisville *Courier-Journal* called the campaign "deploring." It charged that Bush "has dwelled on bogus issues and used cheap shots" and that Dukakis sounded "like a clone of George Bush." It stated that Bush "slides past bona fide issues" and that Dukakis "is doing the same."[72] It believed that Bush "has the lead when it comes to distortions, innuendos and personal attacks" but that the Democratic candidate "has shown that he, too, can tell an occasional whopper."[73] Specifically, it called Bush "crass" for making patriotism and the pledge of allegiance an issue and added: "It's plainly hypocritical for ... Mr. Bush – and others who speak out so often in favor of less government – to support so brazen an attempt to force the heavy hand of orthodoxy on the nation's classroom."[74]

The Milwaukee *Journal* suggested that "negative campaigning seems to sway voters" often enough "to make the practice profitable." It was disturbed by "misrepresentation, either by outright misstatement of facts or by using an isolated fact to make a false point."[75] Specifically, it referred to Bush's "cheap shots about the pledge of allegiance, the American Civil Liberties Union and a prison furlough program" as tactics that "may have polluted the political atmosphere."[76] The New York *Times* believed that "even in a negative campaign for President, one topic that ought to be off-limits is questioning an opponents loyalty to country." It asserted that Bush was "operating close to the borderline of decency" by "carping about the flag and the American Civil Liberties Union" and that "in time, innuendoes about loyalty and civil liberties are likely to backfire, as likely to annoy and alienate voters as to attract them."[77] Referring to the use of the pledge of allegiance and the ACLU as campaign issues, the St. Louis *Post-Dispatch* charged that Bush had run a "smear" campaign, which "debased the electoral process of the United States, introducing a new lot of cynicism." Also, it wrote that "it is not as though Mr. Bush occasionally stepped off the high road; he left the Republican National Convention on the low road and has clung to it." It continued: "There are no gradations between honorable and dishonorable. The latter described Mr. Bush's campaign conduct in a single word."[78] Finally, it believed that Bush's tactics in attacking the ACLU "smack of demagoguery and are especially unbecoming in a candidate who says he wants a kinder, gentler nation."[79] The San Francisco *Chronicle* suggested that both candidates were "throwing too much mud and generating too little light." It stated that although "negative campaigning is tempting to a politician," that "kind of thing does not last," because the voters "get suspicious – and tired – of the negative stuff."[80]

Essentially, the *Wall Street Journal* was supportive of the specific references Bush made on the campaign tactics issue, saying that voters found the pledge of allegiance, the ACLU, and the furlough "compelling issues." It continued: "The common thread is that the vast majority of Americans reject the strain of moral relativism that runs so strongly through the nation's cultural and intellectual elite." It suggested that there is "this sense of community that ordinary people seek in the Pledge and other rituals of life" and that people who oppose the pledge requirement and who believe criticism of their position is a smear of their patriotism just "do not understand this country." The same editorial used the moral relativism argument to discuss similarly the ACLU and the Horton furlough. It asserted that these "symbolic issues ring with so many voters; what ever their narrow interests, they want to vote against relativism and for the values they share."[81] Furthermore, the Journal believed that these issues "pumped some genuine voter concerns into the election."[82] The Washington *Post* called the campaign "terrible" and a "national disappointment." It also believed that Bush "was really the major source and cause of the tawdriness of the campaign" and that much of what he said "was divisive, unworthy and unfair."[83] It maintained that his "assault on Gov. Dukakis's Americanism ... and his ACLU-bashing are particularly cheap and repulsive" but balanced those thoughts by reminding readers that "the late spring and summer air were filled with vicious and unjustified Democratic tee-hees about Mr. Bush's supposed lack of manhood." It characterized voters as "desperate" for both candidates to deal with substantive issues.[84]

The final specific domestic policy issue discussed on the editorial pages of the leading newspapers was the economy. Specific references differ among presidential election campaigns, but economic matters traditionally are a primary concern; 1988 was no exception. Although several papers criticized the candidates for not offering proposals to deal with the failures in the savings and loan industry, including alleged government mismanagement,[85] all but three of the papers[86] devoted virtually all of their editorial comments to the budget deficit and to the national debt generally and to specific suggestions made by Vice President Bush and Governor Dukakis to alleviate the problems. Bush had suggested a flexible freeze on budget increases at no more than the rate of inflation, no new taxes, a modest-tax-deferred savings program to encourage saving among families earning less that $50,000,[87] and a decrease in the capital gains tax. Dukakis called for a tax increase only as a last resort and proposed the hiring of more Internal Revenue Service staff to generate new revenue through stricter enforcement of tax laws.

The Atlanta *Constitution* charged that "both presidential candidates have dodged the problems posed by the Reagan administration budget deficits" but supported Dukakis's suggestion "of chasing down deadbeats" who "get away with ducking their taxes."[88] The Baltimore *Sun* noted that "neither presidential candidate will commit himself to a rebuilding of the revenue base by the only realistic means available – new taxes." It wrote that Bush "keeps prattling about 'growing out' of the red," and Dukakis "is so paralyzed by the devastating political results of Walter Mondale's 1984 promise to boost taxes that he forfeits any chance of making the deficit a real issue."[89] The Chicago *Tribune* stated that neither candidate "has had anything solid to say about whacking the deficit." It asked if Bush's pledge of no new taxes means "he'll go along with increases in the old ones"[90] and asserted that his flexible freeze proposal "will not do enough to stem the flow of red ink."[91] It called Bush's tax-deferred savings plan "modest" but "a step in the right direction."[92] The *Christian Science Monitor* wrote that although "it's not clear that Bush's tax pledge can hold up," he "has repeated this message so often that he has his Democratic opponent, ... painted into a corner" where he "dares not say flatly that taxes must be increased to close the federal budget gap."[93] It believed also that Dukakis "is fighting an uphill battle if he tries to say that these are not good times for most Americans."[94]

The Dallas *Morning News* called the federal deficit a "lurking danger," which "neither candidate is talking much about." It was concerned that "both candidates, especially Michael Dukakis, are busy touting programs to widen the deficit."[95] It described Bush's tax-deferred saving plan as "a modest proposal at best" but acknowledged that he "has raised an important issue that needs to be explored further."[96] The Des Moines *Register* stated that whichever candidate is elected, "the new president's options will be severely limited by one gargantuan reality – the budget deficit." It blamed the Reagan administration for the fiscal problems and noted that Bush "incredibly" wants "more of the same." It continued: "Bush pounds his fist and says, 'No new taxes!' That's another way of saying, 'America will not pay its own way; we'll go hat in hand to foreigners for more loans!'" It believed that Dukakis "has experience in innovative approaches in Massachusetts, and he is the kind of person to squeeze the most out of every nickel – an essential quality in what must be several years of austerity ahead."[97] Noting that "politicians like to tell us pleasant things" because "they can often win elections by doing so," the Kansas City *Star* suggested that the Republican candidate "forgives those who adopt a wait-and-see attitude when he offers assurances that he has an easy plan to balance the budget without raising taxes."[98] It stated that Bush's tax-deferred saving plan "sounds good" but that if he really believes that lowering taxes "will actually raise revenues by stimulating the economy," why stop "at the paltry amount that his proposed savings plan offers."[99] Finally, it called Bush's proposal to cut capital gains taxes "another tax bonanza for wealthy people."[100]

The Los Angeles *Times* asserted that both Bush and Dukakis "talk tough about federal budget deficits" but that "their proposed solutions are squishy, if not starry-eyed." It added: "Both candidates have programs that would require more money, and neither has produced a revenue plan to cover the full cost while cutting the deficit." Specifically, it charged that by pledging no new taxes, "the vice president restricts his ability as president to meet national needs."[101] It referred to his "so-called savings plan" as proof that he "doesn't have any real ideas – at least that he cares to talk about – for encouraging the big boost in the personal savings rate that the country needs."[102] The Louisville *Courier-Journal* acknowledged that both candidates had plans to bring down the deficit but reminded readers that "so did Ronald Reagan in 1980 when the deficit and the debt was about one-third what they are now."[103] The Milwaukee *Journal* stated that "one of the strongest arguments against entrusting the presidency to George Bush is his irresponsible approach to budget deficits." It charged that he "has become a virtual prisoner of the voodoo economics that he deplored in 1980."[104] Furthermore, it believed that he "complicates matters with his unconditional opposition to any tax increase" and that "a balanced budget predicated on Bush's 'flexible freeze' is simply not credible." Although Dukakis also was not willing to advocate new taxes, the *Journal* said, he "at least is too responsible to pretend that circumstances requiring new taxes could never arise." Finally, it called Dukakis's demand for greater efforts to make tax evaders pay "courageous"[105] and Bush's criticism of the suggestion "shoddy."[106]

The New York *Times* wrote that "neither George Bush nor Michael Dukakis seems to see political advantage in advancing a realistic proposal for deficit reduction" and that Bush "has even taken a step backward" with his no-tax pledge. It was critical of the candidates' other proposals also. It called Dukakis's plan to crack down on tax evaders "frustratingly vague"[107] and asserted that Bush's tax-deferred saving plan "wouldn't deliver much help either"[108] and that his proposal to reduce the capital gains tax was a "new supply-side fantasy."[109] The St. Louis *Post-Dispatch* declared that whichever candidate was elected, "the transcending reality of his presidency will be staggering budget deficits." It noted that "neither presidential candidate has addressed the dominating fact of the deficits as forthrightly as it deserves to be, but Mr. Dukakis has been more realistic than Mr. Bush," because he "has conceded the possibility of a tax increase.[110]

The *Wall Street Journal* acknowledged that Dukakis "is of course right that it's not realistic to promise no new taxes under any circumstances ever" but asserted that a new tax increase "would merely open the spending floodgates, reducing the deficit temporarily if at all."[111] Also, it charged that the Democratic candidate "refuses to admit the possibility ... that a lower capital-gains rate would actually produce more revenues." It added: "Yet misunderstanding the revenue effects of changes in the capital-gains tax is the immediate cause of Governor Dukakis's budget problems back home in Massachusetts."[112] Finally the Washington *Post* wrote that Bush's tax-deferred savings plan "points in the right direction, although its dimensions are too small to make much difference."[113] It said that "notoriously, neither candidate has a plausible approach" to the budget deficit. Further, the *Post* called Dukakis's suggestion to balance the budget through better tax enforcement a "foredoomed experiment" that "would take a couple of years" and criticized Bush's "adamant refusal to raise taxes." It believed that in principle, Dukakis's "position is less disingenuous that Mr. Bush's, but as a practical matter they both come out at about the same place."[114]

Foreign Affairs Issues and Election Editorial Discussion

Seventeen foreign affairs issues appeared in the editorials of the leading newspapers on the 1988 presidential campaign. The discussion of foreign affairs in general drew most of the attention (34.4 percent of all foreign affairs and mixed editorials). Next came discussion of national defense (15.6 percent) and debates on foreign affairs (13.9 percent). When these percentages were compared with those based on the number of printed lines (Table 75), there was a slight decrease in general foreign affairs matters, a substantial de-

Table 75: Editorial Lines in 17 Prestige Newspapers about 11 Specific Foreign Affairs Issues during the 1988 Presidential Campaign, in Percents

	Central America	Debates: Foreign Affairs	Foreign Investments in U.S.	General	International Finance	International Trade	Middle East	National Defense	Nuclear Weapons	United Nations	Miscellaneous*	Number of Lines
Atlanta *Constitution*	0.0	4.7	41.7	0.0	0.0	22.4	0.0	31.2	0.0	0.0	0.0	192
Baltimore *Sun*	21.2	11.4	0.0	31.0	0.0	3.4	11.4	11.4	0.0	10.2	0.0	528
Chicago *Tribune*	0.0	0.0	0.0	58.8	0.0	0.0	0.0	0.0	0.0	0.0	41.2	102
Christian Science Monitor	0.0	3.9	0.0	14.5	0.0	0.0	0.0	56.7	0.0	24.9	0.0	330
Dallas *Morning News*	0.0	16.9	0.0	9.4	0.0	73.7	0.0	0.0	0.0	0.0	0.0	160
Des Moines *Register*	0.0	14.4	0.0	85.6	0.0	0.0	0.0	0.0	0.0	0.0	0.0	153
Kansas City *Star*	100.0	0.0	0.0	0.0	0.0	0.0	0.0	0.0	0.0	0.0	0.0	76
Los Angeles *Times*	28.4	5.8	0.0	7.3	25.4	33.1	0.00	0.0	0.0	0.0	0.0	260
Louisville *Courier-Journal*	0.0	10.8	19.6	69.6	0.0	0.0	0.0	0.0	0.0	0.0	0.0	306
Miami *Herald*	27.2	7.0	0.0	39.0	0.0	0.0	26.8	0.0	0.0	0.0	0.0	213
Milwaukee *Journal*	0.0	0.0	0.0	6.5	0.0	0.0	14.5	42.0	9.2	0.0	27.8	324
New York *Times*	5.6	3.3	0.0	20.6	0.0	5.1	0.0	46.4	8.3	0.0	10.7	784
Portland *Oregonian*	89.6	0.0	0.0	10.4	0.0	0.0	0.0	0.0	0.0	0.0	0.0	77
St. Louis *Post-Dispatch*	11.3	2.3	0.0	15.2	9.9	5.6	0.0	25.0	10.5	20.2	0.0	744
San Francisco *Chronicle*	0.0	0.0	0.0	100.0	0.0	0.0	0.0	0.0	0.0	0.0	0.0	8
Wall Street Journal	8.7	4.9	1.1	38.2	6.7	14.3	0.0	20.2	0.0	0.0	5.9	1,666
Washington *Post*	0.0	0.0	17.2	55.0	0.0	0.0	12.3	15.5	0.0	0.0	0.0	373
Total Lines	**661**	**318**	**222**	**1,886**	**254**	**585**	**210**	**1,387**	**173**	**286**	**314**	**6,296**
% of Total	**10.5**	**5.1**	**3.5**	**30.0**	**4.0**	**9.3**	**3.3**	**22.0**	**2.7**	**4.5**	**5.1**	

* The miscellaneous category combines five lesser issues: Angola (*Wall Street Journal*: 98 lines; 1.6% of the total); Space Policy (New York *Times*: 84; 1.3%); South Africa (Milwaukee *Journal*: 55; 0.9%); United States-Soviet Relations (Chicago *Tribune*: 42; 0.7%); World Population (Milwaukee *Journal*: 35; 0.6%).

crease in debates–foreign affairs, and a substantial increase in the national defense issue area. Interestingly, Central America and international trade were issues that surpassed debates–foreign affairs in terms of the number of lines. The primary reason for these unusual statistics is that the leading papers simply did not write many editorials that dealt entirely with foreign affairs (65 out of 528).[115] For this reason, the following account of editorial page comment on foreign affairs in 1988 is limited to a summary of the general attitudes toward the two candidates of those leading newspapers that expressed opinions.

A number of papers cited Bush's superior experience in foreign affairs and supported him over Dukakis on the issue of foreign policy leadership. The Baltimore *Sun*, for example, noted that Bush "continues to hold the edge in international diplomacy," because he "has fewer illusions that his opponent about what goads the Soviet Union toward a less expansionist path, even in the Gorbachev era."[116] The Chicago *Tribune* maintained that Dukakis "has not made a convincing case that he would be as adept as Bush in setting defense and diplomatic policies."[117] Similarly, the Dallas *Morning News* stated that Bush "is the best choice to deal with both the nation's enemies and friends" and the he "has proved he understands the judicious use of power, and how to maintain the fine balance between force and diplomacy."[118] The Louisville *Courier-Journal* asserted that the Democratic candidate "hasn't spelled out ... a convincing plan for maintaining America's security and protecting America's interests in an often hostile world." It believed that on these matters, Bush "is not only more experienced but also more likely to be realistic."[119]

The Miami *Herald* maintained that whereas Dukakis "represents a blank slate in foreign affairs" and "has failed to articulate persuasively how he would make the transition from parochial state issues to being the nominal leader of the Free World," Bush promises "continuity," which "is why most of America's allies hope" that he is elected.[120] The San Francisco *Chronicle* noted that Bush "has more experience, as well as a tougher attitude."[121] The *Wall Street Journal* criticized Dukakis's positions on Nicaragua, Angola, weapons modernization, the War Powers Act, and the use of force to further United States interest. It charged that he "is as far to the left as ... any major presidential nominee since George McGovern, and maybe since Henry Wallace left the Democratic Party in 1948" to run as the candidate of the Progressives.[122] Finally, the Washington *Post* stated that Dukakis's views and inclinations on foreign policy "come across as academic, insular, unschooled, risky" and that this "is ... the one truly disabling feature of his candidacy." It added that although Bush "is not without his defects in this area," he "is much more conversant with both defense and foreign policy, and he speaks on both with more authority, understanding, and sense than Gov. Dukakis does."[123]

The Des Moines *Register*, the Milwaukee *Journal*, and the St. Louis *Post-Dispatch* were supportive of Governor Dukakis and very critical of Vice President Bush. The *Register* referred to Bush's "shaky record" in foreign policy, especially that he "has become a part of an administration that turned its back on the rule of law" and condoned the creation of a secret government-within-a-government accountable to no one, a betrayal of democratic traditions." It continued: "If he is so adept at foreign relations, why did Bush not spot the folly of the illegal and amateurish Iran-contra scandal?" It noted that Dukakis's "lack of experience in foreign affairs is a shortcoming, but he recognizes a fundamental that Bush does not: A nation is only as strong as its economy."[124] The Milwaukee *Journal* asserted that "for a person who has spent years in government, Bush's national security views are a bit of a muddle." It believed that Dukakis "seems free of the mental rigidity that can limit a president's ability to respond to international events."[125] The St. Louis *Post-Dispatch* charged that Bush's "over-emphasis on military spending "reveals a vision so conditioned by the Cold War that he cannot see that national security is defined by far more than armed might" but that Dukakis "possesses a broader perspective" and "recognizes the differences in world affairs between peace and armed truce and between stability and enforced order."[126]

Finally, the *Christian Science Monitor*, the Los Angeles *Times*, and the New York *Times* wrote balanced editorials. The *Christian Science Monitor* suggested that the present international environment calls for "temperate leadership" and that "either candidate would be more moderate than the other makes out."[127] The Los Angeles *Times* noted that Bush "needs to rationalize" his thoughts concerning new weapons and improved relations with the Soviets and to "show the electorate where they will lead in the 1990s." Similarly, it believed that the challenge for Dukakis was "to demonstrate how his proposals will lead to a nation in which more people share in the economic prosperity while maintaining a strong defense with a real prospect for achieving arms reductions with the Soviets."[128] And the New York *Times* stated that "on foreign relations, both men have had remarkably little to say" and that neither "shows much appreciation of the opportunities and risks" associated with changes in the Soviet Union. It called Bush "more confident and conversant" with foreign policy questions but noted that Dukakis "at least recognizes that national security depends on economic strength."[129]

Concluding Comments

As in 1984, the editorial endorsements of the leading newspapers did not reflect the majority sentiment of the voters in the 1988 presidential election. Although Vice President Bush won a solid popular majority and an even greater electoral vote victory over Governor Michael Dukakis, the leading newspapers, by a small margin, supported the Democratic candidate (41.2 percent to 29.4 percent, with 29.4 percent uncommitted). Also, as noted above, the partisan direction of editorial comment was overwhelmingly anti-Republican.

Another comparison between the editorials of the leading newspapers and voters can be made regarding issues. Earlier, the four major domestic affairs issues and the principal foreign affairs issue that were discussed on the editorial pages were considered within their respective contexts (see Tables 74 and 75). For a more accurate assessment of the relative amount of space devoted to these issues and to emphasize again how little was written on foreign affairs issues generally, it was important to consider them together (see Table 76). The four domestic issues ranked substantially above the primary foreign affairs issue. This result was expected, because, as Table 71 showed, 82.2 percent of all editorial lines were classified as domestic affairs. This emphasis coincides with the results of a Gallup Poll taken early in the campaign, which showed that domestic issues were overwhelmingly of greater concern to the electorate than were foreign policy issues.[130]

Finally, the leading newspapers' post-election assessments should be noted briefly. The principal division among them was on the question of whether the election served as a mandate for George Bush. A number of the papers believed that it did. The Atlanta *Constitution* and the San Francisco *Chronicle* serve as examples. The former stated that "if the election contains any discernible message, ... it is that the American people want a continuation of the

Table 76: Editorial Lines in 17 Prestige Newspapers about Principal Domestic Affairs and Foreign Affairs Issues in the 1988 Presidential Campaign, in Percents

	Campaign Tactics	Debates: Domestic Affairs	Economy	General Domestic Affairs	General Foreign Affairs	Number of Lines
Atlanta *Constitution*	24.0%	28.8%	12.2%	35.0%	0.0%	434
Baltimore *Sun*	20.8	23.9	9.0	36.5	9.8	1,668
Chicago *Tribune*	23.1	21.5	25.5	24.8	5.1	1,187
Christian Science Monitor	10.8	27.2	13.0	44.1	4.9	982
Dallas *Morning News*	12.7	22.7	13.6	49.9	1.1	1,320
Des Moines *Register*	14.5	35.4	10.3	32.9	6.9	1,901
Kansas City *Star*	37.3	12.6	28.5	21.6	0.0	746
Los Angeles *Times*	16.5	39.7	22.8	18.9	2.1	911
Louisville *Courier-Journal*	18.1	19.8	6.8	40.2	15.1	1,407
Miami *Herald*	0.0	42.1	11.4	31.3	15.2	546
Milwaukee *Journal*	29.8	20.0	22.6	25.9	1.7	1,215
New York *Times*	3.4	22.7	25.3	35.7	12.9	1,243
Portland *Oregonian*	0.0	23.8	18.9	56.5	0.8	1,041
St. Louis *Post-Dispatch*	17.2	14.8	7.0	54.5	6.5	1,725
San Francisco *Chronicle*	10.6	38.4	23.3	25.0	2.7	292
Wall Street Journal	4.8	11.6	22.2	39.1	22.3	2,864
Washington *Post*	12.8	21.6	16.3	37.2	12.1	1,694
Total Lines	**3,042**	**4,821**	**3,474**	**7,953**	**1,886**	**21,176**
% of Total	**14.4**	**22.8**	**16.4**	**37.5**	**8.9**	

relative moderation of the last two years of the Reagan administration."[131] The *Chronicle* asserted that "the American people have left no doubt about their desire to continue on the general course set eight years ago by Ronald Reagan of California."[132]

Several papers believed that no mandate could be read into the election result. The Baltimore *Sun*, for example, claimed that Bush "does not bring a mandate" to office, because he "kept his plans vague, except for some no-tax-boost promises that will have to be broken or stepped around."[133] Noting the return of a Democratic majority in Congress, the Des Moines *Register* wrote that "a president with an electoral mandate usually can steamroll Congress, ... but Bush has no mandate."[134] The Los Angeles *Times* agreed, saying, "there was no mandate beyond his campaign-driven pledge not to raise taxes."[135]

As before, a study of the editorials of leading newspapers cannot account explicitly for the outcome of a presidential election. Editorial emphasis during the campaign, however, was on domestic issues, which coincided with the interests of the public. Although some of the information above suggests some differences of opinion between the papers and the electorate, it appears that voters assessed economic conditions favorably, approved of the fact that the United States was at relative peace in the world, and chose to place in office the candidate most closely associated with present conditions.

Notes

1. Interestingly, the high percentage of anti-Republican editorials contrasts sharply with the final Gallup Poll taken November 3-6, 1988, which showed the Bush-Quayle ticket leading Dukakis-Bentsen 53 percent to 42 percent. "Bush Maintains 11-Point Lead in Final Gallup Poll," *Gallup Report*, no. 278 (Nov. 1988), p. 2.
2. Chicago *Tribune*, Oct. 23, 1988.
3. Dallas *Morning News*, Oct. 16, 1988.
4. Miami *Herald*, Oct. 30, 1988.
5. Portland *Oregonian*, Oct. 30, 1988.
6. Des Moines *Register*, Oct. 30, 1988.
7. Louisville *Courier-Journal*, Oct. 30, 1988.
8. Milwaukee *Journal*, Oct. 23, 1988.
9. St. Louis *Post-Dispatch*, Oct. 23, 1988.
10. Ibid., Oct. 30, 1988.

11. Baltimore *Sun*, , Oct. 5, 1988.
12. Chicago *Tribune*, Sept. 23, 1988.
13. Des Moines *Register*, Oct. 10, 1988.
14. Kansas City *Star*, Oct. 7, 1988.
15. Los Angeles *Times*, Sept. 24, 1988.
16. Louisville *Courier-Journal*, Sept. 25, 1988.
17. Milwaukee *Journal*, Sept. 25, 1988.
18. Washington *Post*, Sept. 14, 1988. See also, Atlanta *Constitution*, Sept. 27, 1988; Dallas *Morning News*, Sept. 26, 1988; Miami *Herald*, Sept. 25 and Oct. 15, 1988; New York *Times*, Sept. 7 and Oct. 15, 1988; Portland *Oregonian*, Oct. 8, 1988.
19. Milwaukee *Journal*, Sept. 26, 1988.
20. St. Louis *Post-Dispatch*, Sept. 27, 1988.
21. *Christian Science Monitor*, Sept. 27, 1988.
22. Atlanta *Constitution*, Sept. 27, 1988.
23. Baltimore *Sun*, Sept. 26, 1988.
24. Chicago *Tribune*, Sept. 27, 1988.
25. Dallas *Morning News*, Sept. 26, 1988.
26. Des Moines *Register*, Sept. 27, 1988.
27. Los Angeles *Times*, Sept. 27, 1988.
28. New York *Times*, Sept. 27, 1988
29. *Wall Street Journal*, Sept. 27, 1988. The Louisville *Courier-Journal*, the Portland *Oregonian*, and the San Francisco *Chronicle* on the same date all acknowledged the candidates had done well and termed the debate a successful campaign event.
30. Baltimore *Sun*, Oct. 14, 1990
31. *Christian Science Monitor*, Oct. 17, 1990
32. Dallas Morning *News*, Oct. 14, 1988.
33. Des Moines *Register*, Oct. 15, 1988. The Miami *Herald* made similar criticisms on the same date.
34. Los Angeles *Times*, Oct. 15, 1988.
35. Milwaukee *Journal* Oct. 14, 1990
36. St. Louis *Post-Dispatch*, Oct. 15, 1988.
37. San Francisco *Chronicle*, Oct. 15, 1988.
38. Washington *Post*, Oct. 16, 1988.
39. Atlanta *Constitution*, Oct. 7, 1988.
40. Baltimore *Sun*, Oct. 7, 1988.
41. Des Moines *Register*, Oct. 7, 1988.
42. Los Angeles *Times*, Oct. 7, 1988
43. Milwaukee *Journal*, Oct. 6, 1988.
44. Portland *Oregonian*, Oct. 7, 1988.

45. Chicago *Tribune*, Oct. 7, 1988.
46. *Christian Science Monitor*, Oct. 7, 1988.
47. Louisville *Courier-Journal*, Oct. 7, 1988.
48. Miami *Herald*, Oct. 7, 1988.
49. New York *Times*, Oct. 7, 1988.
50. Washington *Post*, Oct. 7, 1988.
51. Dallas *Morning News*, Oct. ,6, 1988.
52. *Wall Street Journal*, Oct. 7, 1988.
53. Atlanta *Constitution*, Nov. 1, 1988. Similar criticisms of Bush's use of the word liberal are found in the Miami *Herald* (Oct. 30, 1988) and the Milwaukee *Journal* (Nov. 1, 1988).
54. Atlanta *Constitution*, Sept. 14, 1988.
55. Ibid., Oct. 13, 1988.
56. Baltimore *Sun*, Sept. ,11, 1988.
57. Ibid., Oct. 11, 1988.
58. Ibid., Oct. 25, 1988.
59. Ibid., Nov. 1, 1988.
60. Chicago *Tribune*, Sept. 28, 1988.
61. Ibid., Oct. 11, 1988.
62. *Christian Science Monitor*, Sept. 14, 1988.
63. Ibid., Sept. 29, 1988.
64. Dallas *Morning News*, Oct. 16, 1988.
65. Ibid., Oct. 22, 1988.
66. Des Moines *Register*, Sept. 8, 1988.
67. Ibid., Sept. 28, 1988. Similar criticism of Bush's attacks on the ACLU were in the Los Angeles *Times* (Sept. 28, 1988), the Louisville *Courier-Journal* (Sept. 26 and Oct. 2, 1988), the Milwaukee *Journal* (Sept. 28, 1988) and the St. Louis *Post-Dispatch* (Oct. 2, 1988).
68. Kansas City *Star*, Oct. 11, 1988.
69. Ibid., Oct. 11, 1988.
70. Ibid., Nov. 4, 1988.
71. Los Angeles *Times*, Oct. 25, 1988.
72. Louisville *Courier-Journal*, Sept. 16, 1988.
73. Ibid., Oct. 3, 1988.
74. Ibid., Sept. 23, 1988. Similar criticism of Bush's use of patriotism and the pledge of allegiance in the campaign were in the Milwaukee *Journal* (Sept. 19 and Sept. 23, 1988), the New York *Times* (Oct. 30, 1988), and the St. Louis *Post-Dispatch* (Oct. 2, 1988).
75. Milwaukee *Journal*, Oct. 11, 1988.
76. Ibid., Oct. 19, 1988. Similar criticisms of Bush's use of furlough issue are found in ibid. (Oct. 30, 1988), the New York *Times* (Nov.

4, 1988), the St. Louis *Post-Dispatch* (Oct. 21, 1988), and the Washington *Post* (Oct. 25, 1988).
77. New York *Times*, Sept. 18, 1988.
78. St. Louis *Post-Dispatch*, Nov. 6, 1988.
79. Ibid., Sept. 18, 1988.
80. San Francisco *Chronicle*, Oct. 12, 1988.
81. *Wall Street Journal*, Oct. 3, 1988.
82. Ibid., Oct. 28, 1988.
83. Washington *Post*, Nov. 2, 1988.
84. Ibid., Oct. 3, 1988.
85. See Chicago *Tribune* (Oct. 2, 1988), the Dallas *Morning News* (Sept. 23, 1988), and the Miami *Herald* (Sept. 28, 1988).
86. The San Francisco *Chronicle* (Nov. 1, 1988) wrote favorably about the economy in general. It praised the policies of the past eight years and asserted that Bush "will carry forward the great benefits of Ronald Reagan's economic revolution." The Miami *Herald* (Oct. 30, 1988) mentioned that "the economy is enjoying the longest sustained expansion ever" and criticized Dukakis for talking as if "collapse of prosperity is imminent." It also believed that Bush's program "would build upon and refine the successful economic policies of the Reagan years." The Portland *Oregonian* (Sept. 5, 1988) encouraged the candidates to discuss the economy in the campaign and wrote an article that was an informative, nonpartisan account of the budget situation (Oct. 20, 1988).
87. The tax-deferred savings plan would have enabled each family to deposit up to $1,000 in a special savings account, where it would be required to leave the money for a minimum of five years. The interest would have been tax exempt until the money was withdrawn.
88. Atlanta *Constitution*, Oct. 24, 1988.
89. Baltimore *Sun*, Sept. 19, 1988.
90. Chicago *Tribune*, Oct. 14, 1988.
91. Ibid., Sept. 14, 1988.
92. Ibid., Oct. 1, 1988.
93. *Christian Science Monitor*, Oct. 20, 1988.
94. Ibid., Sept. 15, 1988.
95. Dallas *Morning News*, Sept. 15, 1988.
96. Ibid., Sept. 29, 1988.
97. Des Moines *Register*, Oct. 30, 1988.
98. Kansas City *Star*, Oct. 18, 1988.
99. Ibid., Oct. 2, 1988.
100. Ibid., Oct. 27, 1988.

101. Los Angeles *Times*, Sept. 18, 1988.
102. Ibid., Sept. 29, 1988.
103. Louisville *Courier-Journal*, Oct. 13, 1988.
104. Milwaukee *Journal*, Nov. 6, 1988.
105. Ibid., Oct. 23, 1988, and Sept. 17, 1988.
106. Ibid., Oct. 5, 1988.
107. New York *Times*, Sept. 6, 1988.
108. Ibid., Oct. 6, 1988.
109. Ibid., Oct. 30, 1988. See also, ibid., Oct. 6, 1988.
110. St. Louis *Post-Dispatch*, Oct. 23, 1988. An argument for new taxes to deal with the budget situation is found in ibid., Oct. 16, 1988.
111. *Wall Street Journal*, Oct. 17, 1988.
112. Ibid., Nov. 1, 1988. The *Wall Street Journal* also wrote three negative editorials (Oct. 24, Oct. 26, and Nov. 3, 1988) on the tax and budget situation in Massachusetts.
113. Washington *Post*, Sept. 30, 1988.
114. Ibid., Oct. 30, 1988.
115. By comparison, in 1984, 210 of 605 editorials dealt entirely with foreign affairs issues.
116. Baltimore *Sun*, Nov. 6, 1988.
117. Chicago *Tribune*, Oct. 23, 1988. See also, ibid., Sept. 18, 1988.
118. Dallas *Morning News*, Oct. 16, 1988.
119. Louisville *Courier-Journal*, Oct. 30, 1988. See also, ibid., Sept. 11, 1988.
120. Miami *Herald*, Oct. 30, 1988.
121. San Francisco *Chronicle*, Nov. 1, 1988.
122. *Wall Street Journal*, Sept. 13, 1988. See also, ibid., Oct. 17, 1988.
123. Washington *Post*, Nov. 2, 1988.
124. Des Moines *Register*, Oct. 30, 1988.
125. Milwaukee *Journal*, Oct. 23, 1988.
126. St. Louis *Post-Dispatch*, Oct. 23, 1988. See also, ibid., Oct. 13, 1988.
127. *Christian Science Monitor*, Sept. 14, 1988.
128. Los Angeles *Times*, Oct. 15, 1988.
129. New York *Times*, Oct. 30, 1988.
130. A September 1988 Gallup Survey found that 45 percent of the voters considered that economic problems were the most urgent concerns facing the nation. The leading non-economic worries were drugs (11 percent), the fear of war and international tensions (9 percent) and poverty (7 percent). "Republicans Gain on Issue

Barometer," *Gallup Report*, no. 227 (Oct. 1988), p. 2.
131. Atlanta *Constitution*, Nov. 10, 1988.
132. San Francisco *Chronicle*, Nov. 10, 1988. See also, Chicago *Tribune*, *Christian Science Monitor*, Portland *Oregonian*, and *Wall Street Journal*, all on Nov. 10, 1988; Dallas *Morning News* (Nov. 9, 1988), and Washington *Post* (Nov. 14, 1988).
133. Baltimore *Sun*, Nov. 9, 1988. The Milwaukee *Journal* (Nov. 9, 1988) and the St. Louis *Post-Dispatch* (Nov. 13, 1988) also claimed that Bush did not make his policy plans clear in the campaign.
134. Des Moines *Register*, Nov. 10, 1988. The Los Angeles *Times* (Nov. 12, 1988) and the New York *Times* (Nov. 11, 1988) also noted that Bush was unable to influence voters top support a Republican majority in Congress.
135. Los Angeles *Times*, Nov. 9, 1988.

7

Public Attitudes about Coverage and Awareness of Editorial Endorsements

Hugh M. Culbertson and Guido H. Stempel III

Franklin D. Roosevelt won four sweeping presidential election victories despite the fact that, in total numbers, newspaper editorial endorsements went as high as 3-1 against him.[1] Such outcomes have led many observers to attribute little influence to editorial pages.

Recently, however, research has suggested that editorials can have significant impact, even in presidential races where partisan leanings affect voting and candidates receive massive news coverage.[2] This chapter addresses two questions not clearly studied in past research. First, how many readers actually become aware of editorial endorsements? (After all, an endorsement seemingly could have no direct impact on a reader unless he or she were aware of it!) Second, do readers who are aware of an endorsement attribute a partisan leaning to a paper's news coverage?

The study focused on two cities, each with a prestige newspaper. The Louisville *Courier-Journal* has endorsed Democratic presidential candidates consistently in recent years – up to and including the 1984 race. And the Chicago *Tribune*, whose publisher Joseph Medill helped Abraham Lincoln become the Republican Party's first candidate for president, has backed every Republican presidential candidate since.

Each city had a "second" paper, the *Times* in Louisville and the *Sun-Times* in Chicago, neither of which had provided consistent editorial endorsements during a period of twenty to thirty years, though both endorsed Democratic candidate Walter Mondale in 1984. Although content data were not studied on these papers, reader perceptions of them were compared with perceptions of the *Tribune* and *Courier-Journal* to shed some light on how readers view the prestige press.

In regard to this last issue, these hypotheses were tested.

Focus of the Study

Hypotheses

Hypothesis 1: Readers show higher awareness of editorial endorsements by the prestige papers studied than by "other" papers in the same communities.

Two arguments support this proposition. First, the prestige paper's overall reputation should be clearly defined and widely known by virtue of the paper's role as a leading community voice. Second, as noted earlier, both the *Courier-Journal* and the *Tribune* had consistently supported presidential candidates of the Democratic and Republican parties, respectively, over a long period, perhaps creating a reputation for party support that would carry over to the 1984 election. In contrast, the competing papers in the same towns had not been so consistent. The Louisville *Times* had endorsed Democratic candidates in 1948 and in the 1950s and 1960s, according to the *Editor &Publisher* survey of newspaper endorsements, but had made no endorsement in 1976 and had not reported endorsements in 1972 or 1980. Also, the Chicago *Sun-Times* had endorsed Jimmy Carter in 1976 and 1980, perhaps leading some younger voters to regard it as Democratic. Previously, however, the *Sun-Times* had swung back and forth, supporting a Democrat in 1948, the GOP in 1952, 1956, and 1960, a Democrat in 1964 and a Republican in 1968.

Hypothesis 2: Readers inclined to vote against the candidate endorsed by a prestige paper will tend more than supporters of that candidate to perceive the paper as biased in favor of its "endorsee" in news coverage. Furthermore, this will only or primarily among relatively less-educated readers and among those aware of editorial endorsements.

This hypothesis posits what social psychologists call a contrast effect, a tendency to perceive a paper's opposition to one's own position as having a clear-cut, marked opposing stance. At least three distinct bases exist for expecting such a result:

1. Work in psychophysics perception of physical quantities such as weight, volume, and light intensity. In such research, subjects judge quantities with reference to predetermined anchors or contextual stimuli. They typically assimilate an object of judgment toward

anchors similar to it but contrast the object (perceive it as very different) from anchors quite unlike it. Carolyn Sherif, Muzafer Sherif, and Robert Nebergall[3] and Melvin Manis[4] have obtained similar results in judgments of verbal messages on pro-con continua where respondents' own attitudes were viewed as perceptual anchors.

2. Psychological balance theory,[5] which implies a felt need to agree with a communication source whom we admire, but to discount – and perhaps denigrate as being on the "lunatic fringe" – sources with whom we disagree.

In studies of issue stands attributed to presidential candidates, Donald Granberg and colleagues have found a consistent tendency to assimilate one's preferred candidate to one's own positions on issues but a less consistent inclination to contrast non-preferred candidates.[6] These researchers note that the absence of clear contrast effects in candidate rating does not square neatly with balance theory. They believe such findings may stem from something like a "pollyanna effect" (a tendency to think positively and not denigrate even opposing political candidates).[7]

None of the above research asked respondents to rate media institutions' stands. However, theoretical and empirical support for Hypothesis 2 does emerge if one assumes that (a) editorial support for a candidate one opposes creates a felt need to denigrate the paper, and (b) such denigration might sensitize readers to deviations from normative expectations such as fairness or balance in news coverage.

In this connection, several studies suggest a tendency to attribute bias when an article departs from one's expectations or disagrees with one's own views. In a signal-stopping study, Robert Stevenson and Mark Greene[8] found a tendency to attribute bias to and question statements with which one disagrees when reading articles. Also, local business people have been shown to perceive newspaper business coverage unfavorably when raters' own businesses were mentioned in a paper less than expected.[9] And Douglas Kocher and Eugene Shaw[10] found a suggestive (but not statistically reliable) tendency to perceive a story as biased when that story, on the whole, opposed a reader's own point of view.

The role of education in Hypothesis 2 stems from the tenet in the Sherifs' social-judgment theory that perception hinges on a kind of "tug of war" among attitudinal, social, and cognitive anchors.[11] Presumably, more highly educated people have relatively high awareness of and a tendency to analyze content of news coverage.

This, in turn, should provide a basis other than the reader's own attitude for assessing message content, reducing assimilation to or contrast from that attitude in judgment.

Hypothesis 2 was not extended to nonprestige papers because, assuming they have somewhat less credibility than prestige publications, contrast effects could be mild or non-existent with them. In a related vein, Alexis Tan[12] found a tendency to assimilate messages attributed to highly credible sources, but not to those with low credibility. Melvin Manis[13] and Elliot Aronson and his associates,[14] among others, have reported supportive data.

3. People may simply assume that editorial-page endorsements reflect a viewpoint for the entire paper, including news columns. John Robinson[15] found in a study of the 1968 presidential election that almost 90 percent of those within a national sample who perceived newspaper leanings correctly identified local papers' editorial endorsements – even though data apparently came in response to a question on whether a paper's reporting took sides for or against one of the candidates. Apparently, then, few people differentiated clearly between news columns and editorials *vis-a-vis* the direction of partisan leanings.

Such results suggest an assumption by many news consumers that bias stems largely from partisan preferences and policies of news personnel. In analysis, if Explanation 2 or 3 above were correct, the hypothesized tendency of respondents who oppose a paper's endorsement to see the paper as favoring that candidate in news coverage should disappear when one focuses on those not aware of candidate endorsement. And if Explanation 1 has validity, the tendency should exist only or primarily among respondents with lesser educations.

Method

We conducted telephone surveys in Chicago and Louisville in late October and early November of 1984. Random-digit dialing was used. Interviews were completed with 456 adults in Louisville between October 23 and October 28 and with 364 adults in Chicago between October 31 and November 5.

Interviewing was done by graduate and advanced undergraduate journalism students from the E. W. Scripps School of Journalism at Ohio University. All had previous experience in telephone interviewing and were trained for this specific survey. Interviewers were instructed to make three attempts to reach a number. Completion rates, adjusted for proportion of business telephones, were 62 percent in Louisville and 56 percent in Chicago. One reason for the lower rate in Chicago was that we interviewed up to 10 p.m. the night before the election and did not have time to complete the third attempt in most cases in that city.

Findings

Some general descriptive information about the samples and their overall perceptions of media coverage follows.

First, both samples had some over-representation of females. Women accounted for 57 percent of the Louisville respondents for whom gender was recorded, and 58 percent of those in Chicago.

Second, eliminating "undecided" respondents, 64.5 percent of those in Chicago said they would vote "today" for Mondale, 35.2 percent for Reagan. That squared almost perfectly with election returns in the city, which ran 64.5 percent for Mondale and 35.5 percent for Reagan. In Louisville, however, the sample's margin for Reagan (62.6 percent to 37.4 percent, eliminating don't- knows and no-answers) exceeded the election margin in Jefferson County (57.8 percent to 42.2 percent) by almost 5 percentage points. Although the discrepancy between survey and election returns was less than two standard errors, it was larger than one might wish for. However, this discrepancy might stem in part from a tendency, shown across the nation, for undecided voters to move toward Mondale more often than toward Reagan late in the campaign.

Third, most respondents appeared to have made up their minds quite firmly by the time of the survey. In Chicago, 88 percent said they were very certain they would vote for the candidates they had indicated they would vote for "today." In Louisville, 75 percent indicated they were very certain. The number who admitted to being not very certain or not certain at all was small – 3 percent in Chicago and 7 percent in Louisville. Such widespread certainty (and probably fairly high attitude intensity or involvement) might enhance contrast effects of the type predicted in Hypothesis 2.[16]

Fourth, level of education was roughly equal in both samples and fairly close to census averages. Twenty-four percent of Chicago respondents reported having college degrees, compared with 21

Table 77: Respondents Saying Newspaper and Television News Favored Particular Presidential Candidates in News Coverage

1968*	Newspapers 50% Television 22%	
1984	Louisville *Courier-Journal* favored one side or the other (n = 210)	45%
	Louisville *Times* favored one side or the other (n = 139)	39%
	TV networks in Louisville favored one side or the other (n = 275)	17%
	Chicago *Tribune* favored one side or the other (n = 95)	52%
	Chicago *Sun-Times* favored one side or the other (n = 104)	49%
	TV networks in Chicago favored one side or the other (n = 172)	19%

* In response to question: "Would you say that the (newspaper, radio station, magazine, television station) reporting you (heard, read) took sides either for or against one of the candidates or parties, or that it did not take sides?" See John P. Robinson, "Perceived Media Bias and the 1968 Vote: Can the Media Affect Behavior After All?" *Journalism Quarterly* 49 (2): 239-246 (Summer 1972).
Note: Except for 1968 data, all data stemmed from 1984 study, with data collected in October and November 1984. The reported base figures exclude" don't know" and no-answer responses.

percent in Louisville.

Fifth, readership of hometown papers was higher in Louisville than in Chicago. In all, 80 percent of the Louisville respondents reported subscribing to the *Courier-Journal*, the *Times* or both. Fifty-two percent of the Chicago sample members subscribed to the *Tribune*, the *Sun-Times* or both.

Sixth, as in past studies, respondents tended to ascribe partisan leanings to press coverage more often when referring to newspapers than to television. In 1968, 50 percent of users within a national sample felt their newspapers had taken sides in reporting the campaign.[17] Percentages here, shown in Table 77 with don't-knows and no-answers excluded, were slightly lower in Louisville but very close to 50 percent with the Chicago sample. Furthermore, in 1968, only 22 percent of users had seen television as similarly partisan in coverage. Comparable figures from the current study were 17 percent in Louisville and 19 percent in Chicago. (Differences among viewers of the three commercial networks were minute and are not reported here.)

Table 78: Subscribers Correctly Identifying Presidential Candidate Endorsements by Prestige and "Other" Newspapers

	*Prestige Paper**	*"Other" Paper**
Chicago	46% (100)	27%[a] (125)
Louisville	31% (210)	19%[b] (230)

a $X^2 = 7.77; p < .01; df = 1$
b $X^2 = 7.65; p < .01; df = 1$
* Prestige papers studied were the *Courier-Journal* in Louisville and the *Tribune* in Chicago. The *Courier-Journal* endorsed Democrat Walter Mondale, while the *Tribune* endorsed Republican Ronald Reagan.
"Other" papers were the *Times* in Louisville and the *Sun-Times* in Chicago, both of which endorsed Mondale.

The data in Table 78 support Hypothesis 1. In Chicago, 46 percent of all *Tribune* readers correctly reported the paper's Reagan endorsement, compared with only 27 percent of all *Sun-Times* subscribers who correctly noted that paper's Mondale leaning. Furthermore, a surprising 17 percent of the *Sun-Times* subscribers thought it had endorsed Reagan.

In Louisville, only 31 percent of *Courier-Journal* readers demonstrated awareness of that paper's Mondale endorsement. While modest, that figure significantly exceeded the 19 percent among *Times* readers.

Overall, then, Table 78 indicates that less than one-half of all subscribers were aware of their papers' editorial stances in the presidential race. This figure stands in marked contrast to Robinson's 1968 study, which suggested 90 percent success in discerning directions of leanings by those who perceived the existence of a leaning. Unfortunately, the present study did not permit separation of those who saw a paper as endorsing the opponent of a candidate who was actually endorsed from respondents who perceived that no endorsement had occurred. Thus data here are not really comparable to Robinson's.

Many respondents thought news coverage by these papers in fact favored the candidates they had endorsed. In Chicago, 45 percent of the *Tribune* subscribers thought the paper favored Reagan in its coverage, whereas 20 percent of the *Sun-Times* subscribers thought their paper favored Mondale in its coverage. In Louisville, 35 percent of the *Courier-Journal* subscribers thought the paper had favored Mondale, compared to 17 percent of *Times* subscribers who thought their paper favored Mondale. But, as Table 79 shows, those respondents who perceived the *Tribune* as favoring Reagan in its coverage and those who perceived the *Courier-Journal* as favoring Mondale

Table 79: Percentage of Space or Time Devoted to Each Side in Coverage of the 1984 Presidential Campaign by the Chicago *Tribune*, the Louisville *Courier-Journal*, and the Network Television Early Evening Newscasts

	Democratic	*Republican*	*Totals*
Chicago *Tribune*	47.7%	52.3%	4,595 column inches
Louisville *Courier-Journal*	57.9%	42.1%	3,719 column inches
ABC	33.3%	66.7%	13,077 seconds
CBS	54.0%	46.0%	9,764 seconds
NBC	48.6%	51.4%	16,134 seconds

Note: Neutral space and time excluded

in its coverage happened to be correct.

These data may reflect a tendency to "merge" editorial-page and news-column coverage in readers' thinking, not a presumption of purposeful reporting bias. With all four papers, perceived editorial endorsement and perceived leaning in coverage correlated substantially and significantly. Phi coefficients between perceived endorsement and coverage leaning were 0.55 with the *Tribune*, 0.53 with the *Courier-Journal*, and 0.35 with the *Times*. The association was less marked (*tau* c = 0.12) with the Chicago *Sun-Times*, perhaps partly because the editorial-endorsement item there was not coded dichotomously (correct vs. incorrect response).

Hypothesis 2 specifies in part that readers disposed to vote against the candidate endorsed by a prestige paper tend more than supporters of that candidate to perceive the paper as favoring the "endorsee" in news coverage. Forty-five percent of *Courier-Journal* subscribers who said they would vote "today" for Reagan felt the paper favored Mondale in news coverage. Among the subscribers supporting Mondale, however, only 20 percent perceived a pro-Mondale leaning in news coverage. The difference between these two percentages was highly significant.

In Chicago, a comparable trend held. Fifty-four percent of all *Tribune* subscribers who favored Mondale saw that paper's news-column coverage as leaning toward Reagan, the candidate whom the newspaper supported. Only 32 percent of the Mondale supporters gave a like response. The difference narrowly missed statistical significance – probably because of the small number of *Tribune* subscribers in the sample.

Table 80: Respondent Preferences for Endorsed and Non-Endorsed 1984 Presidential Candidates

	Would Vote for for Endorsed Candidate "Today"	*Would Vote for Non-Endorsed Candidate "Today"*
Louisville		
Total	20% (64)	45% (114)[a]
Aware of *Courier-Journal* Endorsement of Mondale	44% (18)	92% (39)[b]
Not Aware of *Courier-Journal* Endorsement of Mondale	11% (46)	20% (75)[c]
Chicago		
Total	32% (34)	54% (41)[d]
Aware of *Tribune* Endorsement of Reagan	61% (13)	85% (20)[c]
Not Aware of *Tribune* Endorsement of Reagan	14% (21)	24% (21)[c]

a $X^2 = 9.58$; $p < 0.01$; df = 1; b $X^2 = 11.66$; $p < 0.01$; df = 1; c Not significant; d $X^2 = 3.42$; $p < 0.06$; df = 1

Hypothesis 2 specifies that the above-noted relationship holds only or primarily among readers aware of a paper's editorial endorsement. Small subgroup N's did not permit a conclusive test of this proposition. Table 80, however, provides tentative support. In Louisville, 92 percent of all pro-Reagan voters aware of the *Courier-Journal*'s Mondale endorsement, but only 44 percent of the "aware" Mondale supporters saw the paper's news coverage as leaning toward the Democrats. The phi coefficient here was a substantial 0.53. Turning to the "unaware" subscribers, however, the phi became a mild, non-significant 0.12.

In Chicago, small subgroup N's precluded significance in separate analyses for those aware and those not aware of the *Tribune*'s Reagan endorsement. As predicted, however, the relationship between personal voting intent and perceived news coverage stand proved stronger (phi = 0.27) among the "aware" respondents than among those who were not aware (phi = 0.03).

Overall, then, awareness of a prestige paper's endorsement appeared to mediate the impact of people's attitudes on assessment as to fairness of news coverage. Awareness of endorsement may have provided a kind of trigger for voter attitude to color perceptions

Table 81: Prestige Paper Subscribers Who Would Vote For or Against Candidates Endorsed by Those Papers and Who Saw Papers as Favoring the Parties of the Endorsed Candidates in News Columns

	*"Would Vote Today" For Candidate Endorsed by Paper**	*"Would Vote Today" Against Candidate Endorsed by Paper*
Perceived paper as favoring party of endorsed candidate (All respondents)	25% (98)	47%[a] (155)
Perceived paper as favoring party of endorsed candidate (Persons without college degrees)	17% (70)	44%[b] (111)
Perceived paper as favoring party of endorsed candidate (Persons with college degrees)	43% (28)	56%[c] (43)

* The Louisville *Courier-Journal* endorsed Walter Mondale; the Chicago *Tribune* endorsed Ronald Reagan.
a $X^2 = 12.04$; $p < .001$; df = 1; phi = .23
b $X^2 = 11.82$; $p < .001$; df = 1; phi = .28
c $X^2 = 0.68$; $p > .05$; df = 1; phi = .13

of coverage.

Another phrase within Hypothesis 2 specifies that the indicated association would hold among less-educated respondents but not clearly or markedly among those with higher educations. Table 81 provides general support. Combining data from both samples, 47 percent of all subscribers planning to vote against the papers' endorsed candidates saw news coverage as biased against those candidates. Among the supporters of endorsed candidates, however, the comparable figure was just 25 percent.

Controlling for education, the basic association just reported held significantly and moderately (with phi = 0.28) among those without college degrees, but non-significantly and very mildly (with phi = 0.13) among degree holders.

Although not conclusive, these results suggest that, as social judgment theory implies, subscriber attitude had a substantial and genuine association with assessment of news coverage primarily when a person has little education – and thus probably few information cues to go on in news assessment.

Interestingly, the relationship specified in Hypothesis 2 did not hold with "other papers," the Chicago *Sun-Times* and the Louisville *Times*. As noted and predicted earlier, awareness of editorial endorsements by these papers was fairly infrequent under any circumstances.

Also, although data are not reported here, subscribers' own attitudes did not correlate significantly with perceived direction of editorial endorsement by any paper. Presumably, an endorsement is usually clear-cut and verifiable. Within news coverage, however, partisan leanings are not spelled out explicitly. Such leanings, like beauty, thus reside largely in the eye of the beholder.

The coverage by the three television networks varied widely, as Table 79 shows. CBS gave the Democrats slightly better coverage, while NBC gave a smaller margin to the Republicans. ABC, however, gave the Republicans a 2-to-1 margin. Yet, respondents were not any more aware of ABC's favoritism than they were of that of the other networks, and nearly as many ABC viewers in both Chicago and Louisville thought ABC coverage favored the Democrats as thought it favored the Republicans. The percentage of respondents in either city who thought that television coverage favored one candidate or the other, however, was much smaller than the percentage who thought that newspaper coverage favored a particular candidate.

Conclusions

The major finding here about endorsements is simply that the great majority of respondents were unaware of which candidate the newspaper they read had endorsed. As hypothesized, however, readers of the two prestige papers were more likely to know which candidate their paper had endorsed than were readers of the other two papers. Of those who knew which candidate the paper they read had endorsed, the majority thought that paper favored that candidate in the news coverage. We hypothesized that this would be less likely to be the case for the two prestige papers, but that was not so. Our content analysis results do indicate the the Louisville *Courier-Journal* readers and Chicago *Tribune* readers who believed that those papers favored the candidate they had endorsed were right.

We did find, as expected, that respondents who supported the opponent of the endorsed candidate were more likely to perceive the paper as favoring that candidate than were those who supported the endorsed candidate. We also have a tentative finding that this was more likely to be the case for those who knew which candidate the paper endorsed.

Far fewer respondents perceived that network television news coverage favored one or the other of the candidates than perceived that newspaper coverage favored a candidate. Since ABC favored the Republicans by a far wider margin than either newspaper favored a candidate, one must wonder why there was so little awareness of this. It may be that one of the things that an endorsement does is to raise the question of whether or not a newspaper's coverage favors the candidate of its choice. Still, the much higher perception of favoritism in newspaper coverage than in television coverage is a matter deserving serious consideration by endorsing newspapers and researchers alike.

Notes

1. Verne E. Edwards Jr., *Journalism in a Free Society* (Dubuque, Iowa: William C. Brown Company, 1970), p. 169.
2. Robert E. Hurd and Michael W. Singletary, "Newspaper Endorsement Influence on the 1980 Presidential Election Vote," *Journalism Quarterly*, 61:332-338 (Summer 1984); John P. Robinson, "The Press as King Maker: What Surveys from Last Five Campaigns Show," *Journalism Quarterly*, 51:587-594, 606 (Winter 1974).
3. Carolyn W. Sherif, Muzafer Sherif and Robert E. Nebergall, *Attitude and Attitude Change* (Philadelphia: W. B. Saunders Company, 1965), pp. 8-11.
4. Melvin Manis, *An Introduction to Cognitive Psychology* (Belmont, Calif.: Brooks/Cole, 1976), pp. 263-278.
5. Leon Festinger, *A Theory of Cognitive Dissonance* (Stanford, Calif.: Stanford University Press, 1957); Charles Osgood and Percy Tannenbaum, "The Principle of Congruity in the Prediction of Attitude Change," *Psychological Review*, 62:42-55 (January 1955).
6. Donald Granberg, "Social Judgment Theory," in Michael Burgoon, ed., *Communication Yearbook 6* (Beverly Hills, Calif.: Sage Publications, 1982), pp. 304-329; Donald Granberg and Edward Brent, "Perceptions of Issue Positions of Presidential Candidates,"

American Scientist, 68:617-625 (November-December 1980); Donald Granberg, Wayne Harris and Michael King, "Assimilation but Little Contrast in the 1976 U.S. Presidential Election," *Journal of Psychology*, 108:241-247 (July 1981); Donald Granberg and John Seidel, "Social Judgments on the Urban and Vietnam Issues in 1968 and 1972," *Social Forces*, 55:1-15 (September 1976).

7. Granberg and Seidel, *Social Judgments*.

8. Robert L. Stevenson and Mark T. Greene, "A Reconsideration of Bias in the News," *Journalism Quarterly*, 57:115-121 (Spring 1980).

9. John N. Rippey, "Perceptions by Selected Executives of Local News Coverage," *Journalism Quarterly*, 58:382-387 (Autumn 1981).

10. Douglas J. Kocher and Eugene F. Shaw, "Newspaper Inaccuracies and Reader Perceptions of Bias," *Journalism Quarterly*, 58:471-474 (Autumn 1981).

11. Muzafer Sherif and Carolyn W. Sherif, *An Outline of Social Psychology* (New York: Harper and Brothers, 1956), pp. 37-74.

12. Alexis S. Tan, "Exposure to Discrepant Information and Effect of Three Coping Modes," *Journalism Quarterly*, 52:678-684 (Winter 1975).

13. Melvin Manis, "The Interpretation of Opinion Statements as a Function of Message Ambiguity and Recipient Attitude," *Journal of Abnormal and Social Psychology*, 63:76(1961); *Idem*., "The Interpretation of Opinion Statements as a Function of Recipient Attitude and Source Prestige," *Journal of Abnormal and Social Psychology*, 63:82 (1961).

14. Elliot Aronson, Judith Turner and J. Merril Carlsmith, "Communicator Credibility and Communication Discrepancy as Determinants of Opinion Change," *Journal of Abnormal and Social Psychology*, 67:31 (July 1963).

15. John P. Robinson, "Perceived Media Bias and the 1968 Vote: Can the Media Affect Behavior After All?" *Journalism Quarterly*, 49:239-246 (Summer 1972).

16. Sherif, Sherif and Nebergall, *Attitude and Attitude Change*, pp. 118-122.

17. Robinson, "Perceived Media Bias."

8

The Total Picture: Press, Politicians, and the Public

Guido H. Stempel III and John W. Windhauser

There were no complaints about coverage of the 1984 campaign, but in 1988 the media got caught in the backlash of a new complaint. It was, said the Republicans, the media's fault that there was too little coverage of issues. The Bush staff had issued more than a hundred position papers, but the media ignored them. It is not clear that either George Bush or Dan Quayle made much use of those papers either.

What is clear is that the game of criticizing media coverage of the presidential election, now forty years old, has entered a new stage. This complaint challenges the very way that the media have covered presidential campaigns. It has been event-oriented coverage, and position papers are not events. Speeches by candidates, on the other hand, are events, even when the candidate is saying the same thing for the fiftieth time. Furthermore, television has caused coverage to focus on the sound bites – the brief visual. Roger Ailes, media adviser to both Ronald Reagan and George Bush during their presidential campaigns, reported that sound bites, which used to average fourteen seconds in length, averaged only nine seconds in 1988.[1] Yet those nine-second images dominated not only television coverage but newspaper coverage as well. Any explanation of issues that took longer than nine seconds was likely to get lost in the shuffle.

The Republican response on issues, first articulated by George Bush in the second debate of the 1988 campaign, is easy to understand. The style of the Bush campaign is the style that has succeeded for the Republicans at the presidential level for twenty years. They were not interested in experimenting with having issues play a larger part in the campaign. The ball is thus in the media's court, and they must reevaluate the place of position papers in campaigns. They may conclude, however, that they are not newsworthy or at least not as newsworthy as speeches by candidates.

Our results leave no doubt that the coverage of issues was minimal. Two-thirds of the stories in newspapers and news magazines and on television newscasts dealt with politics and government, candidate strength, and poll results. A modern-day Rip Van Winkle who slept thorough the 1980s and then read about the campaign of 1988 would not suspect that we had federal deficits running in excess of $200 billion, that we had major problems in our education system, or that we had major problems with nuclear technology. Such problems were not the stuff of the 1988 campaign.

It should be noted, incidentally, that there really were no major differences between different types of media. It is obvious that the focus on sound bites would minimize issue coverage on television. Yet the print media followed the lead of television here and focused on the same things that television did through the use of sound bites.

Our results also indicate that there was no more coverage of issues in 1984 than there was in 1988. In 1984, however, the absence of issue coverage was not noticed as much and did not in itself become an issue as it did in 1988. A 1985 poll by the Los Angeles *Times* showed that the American public differed with President Reagan on ten of thirteen major issues.[2]

That suggested what our 1984 results also see, that the Reagan landslide was not basically related to issues. It could not have been the result of issues brought out in the campaign because not that many were brought out. It was, rather, the result of the personal popularity of an incumbent president.

The absence of complaints from both sides in 1984 is not too difficult to understand. Undoubtedly, it was partly due to the one-sidedness of the election result. Reagan got 59.1 percent of the vote. His popular vote total of 52,609,799 and his Electoral College total of 525 were both records. Also, he was as gracious in victory as Mondale was in defeat. There did not seem to be much to quibble about.

Our 1984 data indicate that neither side had a great deal to complain about. After looking at seventeen major newspapers, three news magazines, and the early evening newscasts of three television networks, we concluded that both sides got ample coverage.

That is not a new finding. As we already have indicated, many other studies have reported the same. What makes it noteworthy in this instance is that no other study has looked at such a large slice of the election coverage by American media. This is not to state that we looked at everything. That would have been impossible. We did, however, look at coverage by a major groups of daily newspapers, the three major television networks, and the three major news magazines. Also, we looked at the coverage for the entire presidential campaign from Labor Day to election eve. No other study has analyzed so much campaign coverage.

To be sure, there were differences between the various media. The St. Louis *Post-Dispatch* and Los Angeles *Times* had about three pro-Democratic stories for every two pro-Republican stories. The Louisville *Courier-Journal* and the Atlanta *Constitution* were not far behind. The *Christian Science Monitor* was nearly the opposite, with four pro-Republican stories for every three pro-Democratic stories. *Newsweek* had nearly twice as many pro-Republican stories as pro-Democratic stories, but *Time* gave the Democrats a 55-45 edge. The three television networks all learned slightly to the Republican side, but the ratios of Republican to Democratic stories were remarkably similar.

If there were these differences, they were hardly monumental. News judgment is at best an art, not an exact science, and competent, unbiased journalists will disagree on the relative merits of a given story.[3] What is meaningful in St. Louis may not be so in Boston, and what is happening in the country as a whole may appear different from different perspectives.

What stands out here, in the final analysis, is not how different these media were but how alike they were. There clearly was an effort by each of these media to present both sides of the story in the 1984 presidential campaign. Clearly, both sides had the opportunity to get their message to the American people.

Furthermore, when we looked at the differences to see whether they were related to editorial endorsements in the case of newspapers, we found little relation between endorsements and news coverage. True, the St. Louis *Post-Dispatch*, the most favorable to the Democrats in its coverage, did endorse Mondale. But the second most favorable to the Democrats was the Los Angeles *Times*, which endorsed neither candidate. Neither did the *Christian Science Monitor*, which was most favorable to the Republicans.

Nor was there any discernible pattern for either the television networks or the news magazines. What we found ran contrary to the conventional wisdom about the political leanings of thee media.

In short, we did not find any basis for suggesting bias on the part of any of these media individually or on the part of these twenty-three media as a whole in 1984.

Aside from the matter of issue coverage, there was not much for either party to complain about in 1988. All but one of the newspapers were less than 5 percent away from a 50-50 split, and eight of the seventeen were less than 2 percent away from a 50-50 split. The paper most favorable to the Republicans was the Louisville *Courier-Journal,* previously a long-time supporter of the Democrats. Although the Milwaukee *Journal*, which endorsed Dukakis, was most favorable to the Democrats, it was only slightly more so than the Portland *Oregonian*, which endorsed Bush. In short, endorsements clearly were not related to coverage, and these newspapers obviously were striving for balanced coverage.

The same can be said for the news magazines, although it manifested itself in a different way. About a third of the articles in the news magazines were neutral, that is, they presented both sides equally. As was the case in 1984, it was *Time*, normally considered Republican in leaning, that was most favorable to the Democrats, whereas *Newsweek*, considered liberal, was most favorable to the Republicans.

The three television networks all favored the Republicans in their coverage, but by a relatively slight amount, and it was CBS, usually considered Democratic in its leaning, that was most favorable to the Republicans.

Thus the overall impression we have of these twenty-three media is that they did let both sides be heard. What deviations there were from absolutely equal coverage seem to be the ones that inevitably occur in any kind of coverage simply because honest news people differ in their judgment of what is newsworthy.

Our analysis of the coverage of issues in both campaigns does raise a concern. The focus of the coverage in both years was on the strength of the candidates and the general area of politics and government. It was not, by and large, on campaign issues. There tends to be a reasonable amount of coverage of defense and economic activity. Yet in 1984 there were only six stories on the economy in both the Kansas City *Star* and the *Wall Street Journal* and only eight in the *Christian Science Monitor* and Baltimore *Sun* during the sixty-three days of the campaign. There were only eight altogether inn the three news magazines. Given the size of the deficit, the high rate of unemployment and the problem of the foreign trade deficit, this hardly seems sufficient.

There was more coverage of economic activity in 1988, with none of the newspapers having fewer than fifteen stories, and the news magazines and television networks both showing increases in this category.

Yet limited as the coverage of the economy was, it dwarfed coverage of education and science and technology by comparison. Only five newspapers had as many as ten stories dealing with education in the 1984 campaign, and only two did in 1988. There were no articles focusing primarily on education in either year in the news magazines, and few in the network television newscasts. The Washington *Post*, with twelve stories on science and invention in 1984, had more than the other sixteen newspapers combined. In 1988 there was somewhat more coverage of science and invention in the newspapers, but the Kansas City *Star*, with ten stories, had the highest number. Neither the news magazines nor television news provided significant coverage of science and invention either year.

We believe that the lack of coverage of the economy, education, and science largely reflects what the candidates did with these issues. They didn't get coverage because the candidates did not address them in any significant fashion. Yet this is surprising, given the concerns that there were about the economy in both 1984 and 1988 and given the emphasis on education and the claims of accomplishment in that area by the Republicans. With science and technology, there is a slightly different perspective. In an economy that is ostensibly moving toward high tech endeavors while heavy industry is fading out, federal policy in science and technology surely is important. Furthermore, by 1988 there were some problems with nuclear arms plants that clearly involved the federal government.

Although it is clear that the economy, education, and science got minimal coverage at best from the press because the candidates did not emphasize them, that does not excuse this failure to cover them. It still would have been possible for the press to take the initiative and take steps to develop coverage of these issues.

The question becomes one of who sets the agenda for the press coverage of a political campaign, the politicians or the press or the public. The evidence is that in these two presidential campaigns, it was the politicians, with the result that some important, but difficult, issues received little attention.

This pattern also is evident in the study of editorials reported in Chapters 5 and 6. A considerable portion on the editorial comment appearing in 17 prestige newspapers concerned the candidate debates. The quotes indicate, however, that those editorials tended to discuss how the candidates performed in the debates and whether they were right or wrong on positions, rather than exactly what their positions were. This also tended to be true of the discussion of other matters in editorials, and it does not seem that the editorials contributed greatly to discussion of the substance of issues.

What about the public? How did it view coverage of these campaigns? We are not aware of any national surveys that asked this specific question about either campaign, although there have been some that have asked about the press in general and political coverage overall.[4] Nor has there been a great deal of attention paid to this question in other years.

We have some indication at leat of public reaction from the study reported in Chapter 7, however; some broader inferences can be drawn from that study of Chicago and Louisville voters. We are not aware of any other studies that both gauge public attitudes about coverage by a particular newspaper and provide content analysis showing what the coverage actually was.

The most surprising finding of the Chicago-Louisville study was the lack of awareness of whom the local newspapers had endorsed. The Chicago result was doubly perplexing – 46 percent of the Chicago respondents knew the *Tribune* had endorsed Reagan, much higher than the comparable figure for other newspapers we asked about. on the other hand, we have to wonder how anyone in Chicago wouldn't know. After all, the *Tribune* has endorsed every Republican presidential candidate since Abraham Lincoln. The other half of the Chicago response was even more puzzling. Although 44 percent of Chicago respondents thought they knew whom the *Sun-Times* had endorsed in 1984, only 27 percent really did; the other 17 percent erroneously thought the *Sun-Times* had endorsed Reagan.

The Louisville results are no more encouraging. Thirty-one percent of those respondents knew that the *Courier-Journal* had endorsed Mondale, whereas only 19 percent were aware that the Louisville *Times* had endorsed Mondale. The *Courier-Journal* has not supported Democrats with either the regularity or the fervor that the Chicago *Tribune* has backed Republicans, but its Democratic leaning in recent years has been no secret.

The results in these two cities lead us to suggest that the public is probably a lot less aware of editorial endorsements than the press realizes. October of presidential campiagn years is always full of stories about whom the major papers have endorsed, and news people obviously consider those stories of some importance and interest. From our study, however, we have to wonder if readers do anything more than yawn politely at such disclosures.

A second issue addressed by the Louisville-Chicago study was whether readers thought the newspaper's coverage favored the endorsed candidate. Slightly less than half of the respondents indicated that this was what they perceived. In this instance, coverage by the *Tribune* and the *Courier-Journal* did, in fact, favor the candidates they endorsed, as the tables in Chapter 7 indicate.

Finally, this study looked at whether readers perceived coverage of the candidates they favored was favorable or unfavorable. The indication was that people tended to feel that coverage favored the other candidate – the one they opposed.

We suspect that both these findings about the perceived leaning of coverage would generally be true with the readers of most newspapers in this country. It would appear that the individual's own preference with regard to the candidates is the most important single factor in how he or she perceives coverage. The expectation seems to be that the coverage will be unfavorable to the candidate the voter prefers. What the paper actually does in its coverage may not overcome that predisposition.

So we have on the one hand a lack of awareness and probable lack of concern about whom the local newspaper endorses, and on the other hand some degree of dissatisfaction with coverage of the presidential campaign. Yet the public has not been vocal on this subject. It may be time, however, to pay more attention to the public on this question.

What, then, can we expect in future elections? The answer may lie in the answer to a question posed earlier in this chapter: Who will set the agenda for campaign coverage? Will it continue to be the candidates and their staffs, or will the press exercise greater initiative and thereby bring more attention to the issues?

It could be that the public will set the agenda, but it is difficult to imagine a spontaneous movement by the public to steer the political dialogue to the vital issues. Furthermore, it is not clear that the politicians or the press are eager to read the signs from the public. Two examples come up in this regard.

First, it is axiomatic that negative advertising is the only way to go. A lot of candidates have won using negative advertising, true; but some candidates have lost using negative advertising. There was a classic case in 1988 in Ohio in what some thought was the Senate race the Republican Party most wanted to win. It pitted George Voinovich, the mayor of Cleveland and the former lieutenant governor, against incumbent Howard Metzenbaum, one of the most liberal Democrats in the Senate. Voinovich used negative advertising, with the climax being an ad that charged Metzenbaum with being soft on child pornography. Metzenbaum's ads refuted those charges, pointing to his record, and he won by 16 percent.

Second, immediately after the 1988 election, the Stock Market fell for several days. The experts, agreeing more than usual, said it was because the financial community was not convinced that George Bush had an adequate answer to the deficit. In other words, "no new taxes" and "flexible freeze" did not add up to a position on this major issue. For all its successes, the Bush campaign did have this one notable failure.

Will political strategists get the message from these two incidents? It is hard to be optimistic. Might the press pick up the message and press politicians on the matter of issues? Perhaps.

If politicians keep pointing to position papers the way Bush did in 1988, the press will not be able to ignore them the way it has in the past. Position papers could become more important and of more interest than routine campaign events. If the press starts writing stories about candidates' position papers, the candidates are likely to start talking about them.

It could be the case, too, that the personalities of candidates make a difference in the extent to which certain issues are discussed. A John Kennedy, for instance, would not have let his opponent make "liberal" a negative epithet. Instead, he might have turned it into a discussion of what liberals stood for on major issues. His opponent would have been forced to respond in kind.

Yet there seems little basis to assume that a change is likely in the next presidential campaign. This study shows that neither candidates nor the press dealt adequately with issues in the 1984 or 1988 campaigns. The candidates differed considerably, but the campaigns did not. It would appear that the die has been cast.

Notes

1. Ailes, personal communication, June 9, 1990.
2. David Shaw, "Public and the Press – Two Viewpoints," Los Angeles *Times* , Aug. 11, 1985, pp. 1, 12-13.
3. See Guido H. Stempel III, "Gatekeeping: The Mix of Topics and the Selection of Stories," *Journalism Quarterly,* 62:791-796 (Winter 1985).
4. See American Society of Newspaper Editors, *Newspaper Credibility: Building Reader Trust* (Reston, Va.: ASNE, 1985), pp. 36, 39, 53, 68.

Bibliography

Books

American Society of Newspaper Editors. *Newspaper Credibility: Building Reader Trust.* Washington, D.C.: American Society of Newspaper Editors, 1985.

Blumberg, Nathan. *One Party Press?* Lincoln: University of Nebraska Press, 1954.

Edelman, Murray. *Constructing the Political Spectacle.* Chicago: University of Chicago Press, 1988.

Festinger, Leon. *A Theory of Cognitive Dissonance.* Stanford, Calif.: Stanford University Press, 1957.

Graber, Doris A. *Mass Media and American Politics.* Washington, D.C.: Congressional Quarterly, 1984.

Hofstetter, C. Richard. *Bias in the News.* Columbus: Ohio State University Press, 1976.

Jamieson, Kathleen Hall. *Packaging the Presidency: A History and Criticism of Presidential Campaign Advertising.* New York: Oxford University Press, 1984.

Keogh, James. *President Nixon and the Press.* New York: Funk and Wagnalls, 1972.

Kraus, Sidney. *Televised Political Debates and Public Policy.* Hillsdale, N.J.: Lawrence Erlbaum Associates, 1988.

Lang, Gladys E., and Kurt Lang. *Politics and Television.* Chicago: Quadrangle, 1968.

______ *Politics and Television Re-viewed.* Beverly Hills, Calif.: Sage, 1984.

Lichter, Robert S., Daniel Amundson, and Richard Noyes. *The Video Campaign: Network Coverage of the 1988 Primaries.* Washington, D.C.: American Enterprise Institute and Center for Public Affairs, 1988.

Neuman, W. Russell. *The Paradox of Mass Politics: Knowledge and Opinion in the American Electorate.* Cambridge: Harvard University Press, 1986.

Patterson, Thomas E. *The Mass Media Election.* New York: Praeger, 1980.

Patterson, Thomas E. *The Unseeing Eye: The Myth of Television Power in National Elections.* New York: G.P. Putnam's Sons, 1976.

Rowse, Arthur. *Slanted News.* Boston: Beacon Press, 1957.

Salinger, Pierre. *With Kennedy.* New York: Doubleday, 1968.

Sherif, Carolyn W., Muzafer Sherif, and Robert E. Nebergall. *Attitude and Attitude Change.* Philadelphia: W.B. Saunders Company, 1965.

White, Theodore H. *The Making of the President.* New York: Atheneum, 1961.

Monographs

Hofstetter, C. Richard. "News Bias in the 1972 Campaign." *Journalism Monographs*, no. 58, November 1978.

Markham, James W., and Guido H. Stempel III. "Pennsylvania Daily Press Coverage of the 1956 Campaign: A Measurement of Performance." University Park: Pennsylvania State University School of Journalism, 1957.

Articles

Altheide, David L. "Three-in-One News: Network Coverage of Iran." *Journalism Quarterly*, 59:481-486 (Autumn 1986).

Buss, Terry F.,, and C. Richard Hofstetter. "The Logic of Televised News Coverage of Political Campaign Information." *Journalism Quarterly*, 54:341-349 (Summer 1977).

Chaffee, Steven H., L. Scott Ward, and Leonard P. Tipton. "Mass Communication and Political Socialization." *Journalism Quarterly*, 47:647-659, 666 (Autumn 1970).

Foote, Joe S., and Michael E. Steele. "Degree of Conformity in Lead Stories in Early Evening Network Newscasts." *Journalism Quarterly*, 63: 19-23 (Spring 1986)

Granberg, Donald, Wayne Harris, and Michael King. "Assimilation but Little Contrast in the 1976 U.S. Presidential Election." *Journal of Psychology*, 108:241-247 (July 1981).

Granberg, Donald, and John Seidel. "Social Judgments on the Urban and Vietnam Issues in 1968 and 1972." *Social Forces*, 55:1-15 (Sept. 1976).

Higbie, Charles E. "1960 Election Studies Show Broad Approach, New Methods." *Journalism Quarterly*, 38:164-170 (Spring 1961).

_______ "Wisconsin Dailies in the 1952 Campaign: Space vs. Display." *Journalism Quarterly*, 31:56=60 (Winter 1954).

Hofstetter, C. Richard, and Terry F. Buss. "Bias in Television News Coverage of Political Events: A Methodological Analysis." *Journal of Broadcasting*, 22:517-530 (Fall 1978).

Hurd, Robert E., and Michael W. Singletary. "Newspaper Endorsement Influence on the 1980 Presidential Election Vote." *Journalism Quarterly*, 61:332-338 (Summer 1984.

Katz, Elihu. "Platforms and Windows: Broadcasting's Role in Election Campaign." *Journalism Quarterly*, 48:304-314 (Summer 1971).

Klein, Malcolm W., and Nathan Maccoby, "Newspaper Objectivity in the 1952 Campaign." *Journalism Quarterly*, 31:285-295 (Summer 1974).

Kobre, Sidney, "How Florida Dailies Handled the 1952 Presidential Campaign," *Journalism Quarterly*, 30:163-169 (Spring 1953).

Kocher, Douglas J., and Eugene F. Shaw. "Newspaper Inaccuracies and Reader Perception of Bias." *Journalism Quarterly*, 58:471-474 (Autumn 1981).

Latimer, Margaret K. "The Newspaper: How Significant for Black Voters in Presidential Elections?" *Journalism Quarterly*, 60:1-24 (Spring 1983).

Lowry, Dennis T. "Measures of Network Bias in the 1972 Presidential Campaign." *Journal of Broadcasting*, 18:387-402 (Fall 1974).

Lucas, William A., and William C. Adams. "Talking Television and Voter Indecision." Journal of Communication, Spring 1976, pp. 84-90.

Mulaney, Gary D., and Terry F. Buss. "AP Wire Reports vs. CBS TV News Coverage of a Presidential Campaign." *Journalism Quarterly*, 56:602-610 (Autumn 1979).

Markham James W., and Guido H. Stempel III, "Analysis of Techniques in Measuring Press Performance." *Journalism Quarterly*, 34:187-190 (Spring 1957).

Myers, David S. "Editorials and the Economy in the 1976 Presidential Campaign." *Journalism Quarterly*, 55:755-760 (Winter 1978).

______ "Editorials on the Economy in the 1980 Presidential Campaign." Journalism Quarterly, 59:414-419 (Autumn 1982).

______ "Editorials and Foreign Affairs in the 1972 Presidential Campaign." *Journalism Quarterly*, 51:251-257,296 (Summer 1974).

______ "Editorials and Foreign Affairs in the 1976 Presidential Campaign." *Journalism Quarterly*, 55:92-99 (Spring 1978).

______ "Editorials and Foreign Affairs in Recent Presidential Campaigns." *Journalism Quarterly*, 59:541-547 (Winter 1982).

O'Keefe, Garrett J. "Political Malaise and Reliance on Media." *Journalism Quarterly,* 57:122-128 (Spring 1980).

Robinson, John P. "Perceived Media Bias and the 1968 Vote: Can the Media Affect Behavior After All?" *Journalism Quarterly*, 49:239-246 (Summer 1972).

______ "The Press as King Maker: What Surveys from the Last Five Campaigns Show." *Journalism Quarterly,* 51:587-594 (Winter 1974).

Robinson, Michael J. "Television and American Politics: 1956-1976." *The Public Interest*, Summer 1977, pp. 3-9.

Rudd, Robert, and Marjorie J. Fish. "Depth of Issue Coverage in Television." *Journal of Broadcasting and Electronic Media*, 33:197-202 (Spring 1989).

Rutkus, Dennis S. "Presidential Television." *Journal of Communication*, 26:73-78 (Spring 1976).

Stempel, Guido H., III. "The Prestige Press Covers the 1960 Presidential Campaign." *Journalism Quarterly*, 38:157-163 (Spring 1961).

______ "The Prestige Press Meets the Third-Party Challenge." *Journalism Quarterly*, 46:699-706 (Winter 1969)

______ "The Prestige Press in Two Presidential Campaigns." *Journalism Quarterly*, 42:15-21 (Spring 1965).

Stempel, Guido H., III, and John W. Windhauser. "Coverage by the Prestige Press of the 1988 Presidential Campaign." *Journalism Quarterly*, 66:894-896 (Winter 1989).

______ "The Prestige Press Revisited: Coverage of the 1980 Presidential Campaign." *Journalism Quarterly,* 61:49-55 (Spring 1984).

Stevenson, Robert L., and Mark T. Greene. "A Reconsideration of

Bias in the News." *Journalism Quarterly*, 57:115-121 (Spring 1980).

Stovall, James Glen, "Coverage of the 1984 Presidential Campaign." *Journalism Quarterly*, 65:443-449 (Summer 1988).

______ "Foreign Policy Issue Coverage in the 1980 Presidential Campaign." *Journalism Quarterly,* 59:531-540 (Winter 1982).

______ "The Third-Party Challenge of 1980: News Coverage of the Presidential Candidates." *Journalism Quarterly*, 62:266-271 (Summer 1985).

Westley, Bruce H., Charles E. Higbie, Timothy Burke, David J. Lippert, Leonard Maurer, and Vernon A. Stone. "The News Magazines and the 1960 Conventions." *Journalism Quarterly*, 40:525-531, 647 (Autumn 1963).

Index

About the Contributors

Guido H. Stempel III is director of the Bush Research Center and a distinguished professor in the E.W. Scripps School of Journalism at Ohio University. He has made studies of coverage of eight presidential campaigns.

John W. Windhauser is an associate professor of journalism in the Manship School of Journalism at Louisiana State University. He has made studies of coverage of three presidential campaigns as well as of state and local elections.

Hugh M. Culbertson is a professor of journalism in the E.W. Scripps School of Journalism at Ohio University. He has made numerous studies of reporters, sources, and gatekeeping, as well as studies of two presidential campaigns.

Dru Riley Evarts is a professor of journalism in the E.W. Scripps School of Journalism. She has made studies of coverage of three presidential campaigns.

David S. Myers is professor of political science at the University of West Florida. His two studies in this volume continue the analysis of campaign editorials that he did in the 1972, 1976, and 1980 presidential elections.